GRAHAM SWIFT

MAKING
AN
ELEPHANT

WRITING FROM WITHIN

ALFRED A. KNOPF · NEW YORK
2009

THIS IS A BORZOI BOOK
PUBLISHED BY ALFRED A. KNOPF

www.aaknopf.com

Originally published in Great Britain by Picador,
an imprint of Pan Macmillan Ltd., London.

Library of Congress Cataloging-in-Publication Data

Swift, Graham, [date]
Making an elephant : writing from within / by Graham Swift.—1st American ed.
p.   cm.
Includes bibliographical references.
ISBN 978-0-307-27099-3 (alk. paper)
1. Swift, Graham, 1949–   2. Authors, English—20th century—Biography.   I. Title
PR6069W47 Z46 2009
823'.914—dc22   2009014052

Manufactured in the United States of America
First United States Edition

FOR CANDICE

You attempt to breathe life into these people and
if you're lucky they breathe life into you

Caryl Phillips: interview with Graham Swift

Heavens! Was I born for nothing but to write?

Alexander Pope: 'Epistle to Dr Arbuthnot'

Contents

Contents

Contents

Introduction

This book began as no more than the collection of pieces of occasional non-fiction, published or unpublished, that writers of fiction are sometimes tempted to put together, but in the course of assembling it I've tried to thread the pieces in a way that generally offers, to borrow a phrase of Kipling's, 'something of myself'.

I've often stated—one or two such statements are revisited in these pages—that in my fiction I avoid the autobiographical and don't base my work on my own direct experience. I've never been a butcher, a prison-visiting detective or a son of the Fens. Nor do I base my characters on people I know, let alone my friends. As an author who's favoured the intimacy of the first person over the 'authorial' third person, I'd regard it as a mark of achievement if in my work the author seems to vanish; and the occasional strange sensation of that actually happening as I write is, for me, one of the thrills of the act of writing. This book tries to show the other side of the coin. I haven't attempted to disappear in it. It even gives some emphasis to the personal touch.

It's true that in a fundamental sense all fiction writing is autobiographical, since where else does it come from but from within the author? Writing is also something, I've found, that constantly brings you up against yourself and surprises you with the discovery of what you have inside. But this often intensely personal process is very different from the notion that fiction is just a recycling of the contents of the writer's life. I find distasteful the idea that writers are on a permanent reconnaissance trip—one eye always on the lookout for what might fuel their work—as I find wearisome the surprisingly common assumption among readers and even some professional commentators that novels must surely be about what has actually happened to the author. I thoroughly believe that the novel isn't some separate area of specialized mental activity, but a thing that reflects and serves life—D. H. Lawrence went so far as to call it 'the one bright book of life'—but I also believe that there is writing and there is life.

This book may have several things to say about writing and writers, but I hope it offers a glimpse or two into my life—my writer's life or just my life. Looking through it, I find in fact that there's quite a lot in it about getting away from writing, or about not getting round to it.

It's very much a book about people, and in choosing its contents I've tried to share it with my friends. Sometimes this is literally the case—several interviews are included—but a main aim has been to offer portraits of and pay tribute to individuals I've been lucky enough to know, sometimes just briefly, sometimes over long periods of my life. I've tried to give some sense of their personal company. Some of them are gone now; others are very much present, and I've stretched the range of this aspect of the book to embrace at least two figures I could not possibly have met or known, though they've been for me like presences.

I apologize to the friends featured in these pages for any errors and misrepresentations, and simultaneously apologize to many friends who aren't mentioned. This book is in no way comprehensive and their exclusion isn't meant disloyally, but simply springs from the vagaries of how most of the pieces first came about. A number stem from previous publications. Some have been revised or added to extensively, some left as they were. One or two were written some while ago but never published, a few have been written expressly for this book or to provide links in its framework.

The framework is broadly chronological, but (as in my novels) some liberties are taken with time. The book starts, as it were, when I was six and ends with a man who lived in the sixteenth century. In between, there is some more modest hopping forward or back.

This is a collection of non-fiction, but included in it is some poetry. The arrangement isn't meant to suggest that the poetry is the filler in a sandwich. I'm not sure whether poetry falls into the category of fiction or non-fiction, or is a separate sphere altogether. The poems were produced in a between-novels interval when I didn't quite know what I wanted to do next, yet wanted to keep my engine running in an interesting, different way. I found myself just writing poems for a while, then it stopped. I've no idea if such a phase will come upon me again.

The author at work in the 1950s.

SANTA'S CLINIC

CROYDON, 1955

I have two memories of childhood which have become permanently entangled with each other. One is of being taken when I was very small to have my polio inoculation, an event anticipated with a mounting dread which the actual procedure did nothing to dispel. A special clinic had been set up in a local hospital, where small children passed through one door to the needle-plying doctors, then emerged through another where a grimly smiling nurse doled out sweets. There was a lot of screaming and blubbing, not only from those about to go in, but, rather more seriously, from those coming out, unconsoled by their sugary hand-outs. I can't remember if I cried myself. I've probably suppressed the trauma. But I do remember that the nurse with the sweets seemed as much a part of the ordeal as anything else.

I have the dimmest recollection of being prepared at my primary school for this event and of part of the dread being the realization that there was no route of exemption. As an infant, you could wriggle, almost by definition, out of most things, but this was brutal conscription aimed at the most tender. It was certainly beyond me to appreciate that the business of the two doors was my lucky birthright—the National Health Service in its own zealous infancy—and something for which I ought really to have been very glad. A whole generation, for the first time in history, was being spared at least one very nasty form of being crippled for life.

I must have had my polio jab around Christmas time, because the second memory is of being with my mother in a Croydon department store where a lavish, glittery Santa's grotto had been constructed. Here again there were the small children entering through one door then emerging through another, with, instead of sweets, little wrapped gifts in their hands. True, many of these children came out gleefully smiling, but not a few, I noticed, came out in tears. The similarities were too vivid, the throwback to that hospital room too overpowering. If I had any plans for calling on Santa, they stopped right there.

Whatever age I was, I knew more about Santa Claus than I did about polio. I didn't know why polio (a rather nice-sounding word) had to be avoided or how having a needle thrust in your arm could possibly ensure this. But I knew about reindeer and chimneys. If superstition consists of submitting to bizarre rituals in the cause of something you cannot rationalize, then that experience of the syringe and of the nurse sticking a sweet on my tongue like a communion wafer was superstition unqualified.

The Santa Claus business, though, isn't really about superstition. It's about that stuff—or that partner at least—of fiction, the suspension of disbelief.

I can't remember ever utterly believing in Santa Claus, but I do remember, even quite consciously, suspending my disbelief —playing along with the parental conspiracy—for the sake of the magic of the fiction. My instinct, seeing those tearful faces leaving the grotto, was that here was magic being destroyed.

Children aren't stupid or impercipient creatures, but they have a benign, if also vulnerable, capacity to enter wholeheartedly into the spirit of an invention. The average adult is embarrassed by things made up. He or she prefers the no-nonsense efficacy of vaccine and syringes: magic made scientifically transparent. If you want to destroy the power of fiction the best way to do it is to attempt to give it material form—to hire real-life Santas and stick them in papier-mâché grottoes. I think those children crying after visiting Santa had suffered something much worse than the puncturing of their arms: the shattering of their dreams. Watching them, I must have concluded that if you got up close to a real-life Santa he might not prove so wonderful after all. If I'd been older I might have embellished this apprehension with cynical details. He might have broken veins and insincere eyes. He might have alcohol on his breath and even, after a hard day's ho-ho-ing, do things with those little boys and girls he shouldn't. Worst of all, he might simply not *convince*. My answer to all this, my way of protecting the magic, was to stay away from the dubious old fellow. So far, I have never stepped into Santa's grotto.

But I still have a pale floret on my left arm which has protected me, like some talismanic tattoo, from a real and cruel disease.

Fiction is also a kind of inoculation, a vaccine, preserving us from such plagues as reality can breed. But, like all true vaccines, it will work only if it contains a measure of the plague itself, a tincture of the thing it confronts. There may be no sure inoculation or remedy against the sufferings of an infant whose dreams of Santa have been broken by actually paying him a visit. Yet perhaps there is: that is, precisely to tell the story of just such an upsetting visit; to construct from that a new, less comforting but no less involving adventure of the little boy or girl's encounter with the real adult world lurking within the enchanted grotto.

After well over three decades of being a writer of fiction, I still believe that fiction—storytelling—is a magical thing. Why else do we still talk about being under a story's 'spell'? However we may analyse or try to explain it, the power of a good story is a primitive, irreducible mystery that answers to some need deep in human nature. I think it's salutary for even the most modern writer to recognize this—that you are, as it were, dealing with something beyond you, with a force you can never outguess. Once you make a complete and exclusive equation between what you consciously put in and the effect that will emerge (and, time and time again, it's very hard to avoid doing this), you will have lost something. Your writing may be competent, but it will be diminished.

For writer and reader, fiction should always have that flicker of the magical, but it also does something that's completely the opposite. Repeatedly, fiction tries to embrace, to capture, to confront—often grimly and unflinchingly—the real. This is one of its supreme functions too: to bring us down to earth. No better vehicle for this descending journey has been found than the novel. Indeed, from *Don Quixote* to *Madame Bovary* and onwards, fiction has been centrally concerned with the demolition of magic and dreams; with the way in which our airy notions come up against the hard facts or downright banality of experience. This is entirely healthy: fiction as a corrective to our evasions of an uncompromisingly concrete world. But the remarkable thing about fiction is that it can perform the two apparently contradictory tasks at the same time. It can be both magical and realistic. When we read *Don Quixote* or *Madame Bovary* we don't feel coerced into bathos, we feel a thrill.

Back in the 1980s, when my first novels were published, a literary term had for some while been enjoying a vogue: 'magical realism'. I admit that when I wrote *Waterland* I even thought I was being a bit of a magical realist myself. The term has now long passed its sell-by date, and was fairly bogus in the first place. It seemed to encapsulate perfectly that twofold and paradoxical nature of fiction; but if that were so, it was really saying nothing new or revelatory and, in practice, it reeked of a rather programmatic specialism. It owed a lot to some then-popular Latin American writing in which surreal or supernatural events might be 'realistically' injected into the naturalistic tissue of a novel, or real events might acquire a magical flavour. Writers had been doing this sort of thing for centuries, but 'magical realism' implied that by the mixing in of such fantastical stuff, some much-needed magic could be put *back* into fiction. As if it had ever gone.

The real magic (if that expression is legitimate) of fiction goes much deeper than a few sprinklings of hocus-pocus, but we know when it's there and we feel its tingle in the spine. There can even be something magical about the perfectly judged and timed revelation on the page of an unanswerable truth we already inwardly acknowledge. In good fiction, without any trickery, truth and magic aren't incompatible at all.

To come back to Santa in his grotto—or rather to his real-life, historical originator. The actual Saint Nicholas was a much less cosy, if more saintly, figure than our Father Christmas, and well enough acquainted with the sordid realities of the world. One of his good deeds was to intervene to prevent a penniless father putting his three daughters on the streets. Posterity has turned him into a more magical yet more flimsy and sentimental creation—bound to come to grief in the form of a sobbing, disillusioned child in a modern department store.

Was it outside Santa's grotto that I had my first intimation of the dual nature of fiction? I doubt it very much. I just hadn't got over my polio jab. Our age believes implicitly in vaccines, in hard knowledge and clinical veracity, but it also makes an increasing commercial razzmatazz out of Christmas. Since the Fifties, in fact, Christmas has spread like some infection for which there is as yet no known vaccine. It stages its first outbreaks in early October, if not before. The razzmatazz may be manifestly grotesque and blatantly money-spinning, but within it is the neurotically spiralling symptom of our need for magic. If this were not the case, why not construct a consumer bonanza out of any old date? We have got our sense of magic wrong. It's gone far beyond the truth. Fiction can help to put the relationship right.

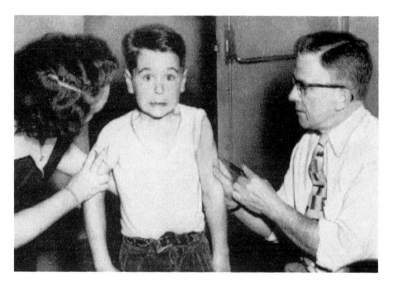

Early victim of the polio jab.

ISAAC BABEL

GREECE, 1967

'Which writers have influenced you?' is a complicated question. How writers affect other writers is as mysterious and misunderstood as how writers are made in the first place. The word 'influence' itself is misleading. It assumes that one writer's writing can directly shape and inform another's, as it can, but surely the most important influences aren't influences in this sense at all. They are those other writers who, though they may not leave on you any stylistic mark, yet ignite or reignite your simple desire to write.

In September 1967 I found myself in Thessaloniki, northern Greece, with two days or so to kill before catching a train, for which I had dated tickets, all the way back across Europe to London and home. Five months before, at the age of seventeen, I'd set off in the reverse direction with just a rucksack and no previous unshepherded experience of 'abroad', and I was now at the end of a long, looping journey that had taken me from mainland Greece island-hopping across the Aegean, zigzagging overland as far as eastern Turkey, back again to Istanbul and European Turkey, then across the newly opened borders of Bulgaria to Plovdiv and Sofia, finally winding through the Bulgarian mountains and forests southwards again to Greece.

Less than a year before, I'd taken an exam which had won me a place at Cambridge the following October, and, with that secured, my school had very leniently allowed me and a few others like me to 'disappear' without completing the remaining school year. One drizzly lunchtime in December 1966, without ceremony or formality, I and a couple of friends simply sauntered out of the school gates, knowing we would never walk through them again.

I had already decided by then that I wanted to spend a good part of the free months ahead of me travelling and that my first destination would be Greece and the eastern Mediterranean. I got a temporary job that winter and by the following April had saved up the critical sum of fifty pounds, which, in those days of exchange restrictions, was the maximum you could take on any trip abroad. Meanwhile, there'd been a military coup in Greece, tanks on the streets, and the country was being placed, with consequences yet unknown, under one of the worst dictatorships to afflict post-war Europe. This didn't deter me. With a rucksack and fifty pounds and a rail ticket to Athens—the return ticket yet to be finalized—I set off.

I certainly knew then, in a secretive, submerged way, that I wanted to be a writer. I knew it as a schoolboy, which is what I still essentially was. When people ask me when did I first want to write, I usually say it was in my teens, it happened with adolescence, but I think it may really have begun a lot earlier, and my first and perhaps most significant 'influences' would have been the first real books I read. I'm not thinking of great literature, just of regular kids' books, boys' adventure stories, with a leaning perhaps to anything historical. They were the books that first made me thrill to what writers could put between the covers, and first implanted the idea that I might do something similar myself.

By the time I left school I'd read a fair amount of serious classic literature, and I would be going to Cambridge to do more of the same. My own literary ambitions remained in tacit suspension, virtually unacted upon, and this was to remain the case for several years yet. It was one thing—not a difficult thing—to want to be a writer; another to become one, though I genuinely felt I was gripped by something more than a mere fancy.

Looking back, I think the truth was that I was *scared* of my ambition, scared of discovering that I didn't have what it took to fulfil it. It's very easy when you're young to place yourself in a postponing, self-deceiving cocoon. If you never put your possible delusion to the test, you'll never suffer the pain of knowing it was a delusion. On the other hand, I think the fact that I was scared of my ambition was a measure of its being real. I knew that eventually I'd have to confront it, and I knew, since it was an entirely solitary, unfostered ambition, that I might need some external catalyst to push me to the task.

But I don't think I set off with my rucksack in some Kerouacish way, looking for experience I might 'use'. I think I just wanted to have an interesting time and, in a general, unliterary way, to discover what initiative I had. The cliché would be that I wasn't being so independent: I was simply joining the hippy trail. This was true to the extent that, though I travelled mostly alone, I quite often bumped into others doing something similar, following an east-bound, vagabond urge. But if I ever actually thought of reaching Kathmandu, the reality was I scarcely penetrated the Middle East. I don't think I really had any distant goal in mind. The aim was to wander. I followed my nose, my instinct, my whim, but I kept a fairly shrewd eye on how far you could stretch fifty pounds.

I do remember, when I set off, wanting very much to turn my back on everything I'd known so far: school, the suburbs, the Home Counties, a pretty sheltered domestic family life, even some of the real attractions, if you were seventeen, of England in the Sixties. That turning-the-back principle—certainly more instinct than whim—was very strong.

At any rate, that five-month journey was a very unbookish affair. I hardly read a single thing all the time, and perhaps books and literature were among the things I wanted temporarily to ignore. By the time I reached Thessaloniki I was a fairly hardened traveller and a more educated person than I'd been when I'd walked out through those school gates. When you travel rough there are extraordinarily intense changes not just of scene but of mood and luck, and I'd learnt to relax into the unpredictability as you gradually learn to ride the swaying of a ship. I'd even become a little addicted to the ups and downs. If it was good, you made sure you moved on before it paled—the memory bright and safe in your rucksack. If it was bad, then there was always the next place. The turning-the-back principle worked in that local and immediate way too.

I'm still rather amazed I survived the journey at all. Fifty pounds was worth more then, but it was a paltry sum to spread over five months. I eked it out partly by sometimes 'working my way', partly through some astonishing hospitality, but partly also by occasionally half starving and by sleeping in the open: on beaches, in ditches, under forest trees, or, when I was in the Turkish interior, in 'dosshouse' conditions. But I never suffered any major mishap, any physical injury or act of violence—though I witnessed a few and I actually took (this now seems absurd but it felt like a good idea at the time) to sleeping with a knife under whatever formed my pillow at night. Everything I had was on my person or in my rucksack and, though I frequently left that rucksack in insecure places for whole days at a stretch, neither it nor anything it contained was ever stolen. Perhaps there was nothing in it, really, to attract a thief.

To cap it all, when I reached Thessaloniki and picked up my return rail ticket I even had some money left. I checked into a fleapit hotel in the rough part of town near the station, though it was luxury compared to some places I'd known. I then proposed to myself that for the remaining thirty-six hours or so I would lead a life of relative style, mooching round the more salubrious parts of the city, patronizing the ritzy waterfront cafes (complete scruff though I was) and pleasantly using up my cash.

I don't recall whether I saw this period as a conscious process of decompression, a return to 'civilization', or whether I'd suddenly become aware again of things that lay ahead of me, or inside me, but one thing I thought it would be good to do was read a book. I had the money to buy one. I went into a bookshop, something I hadn't done for five months, found the fairly small English-language section and picked out the Penguin translation of Isaac Babel's *Collected Stories*. It cost me twenty-five drachmas and I have it still.

When I'd left school I had barely heard of Isaac Babel. I didn't know that even then, in Russia, it was scarcely possible to read him. His work was only just emerging from its long official freeze following his death under Stalin, and a Russian reprint of his collected stories was yet to appear. The single volume of short fiction I held in my hand in Thessaloniki was really all that was left of a brutally short but courageous life—shortened, in a sense, by Babel's own remarkable self-curtailment.

In the 1930s, when Babel was not yet forty and the forces of repression had gathered round his still burgeoning career, he had opted for a virtual and defiant silence. In a barbed speech in 1932 he'd lamented that the writers of his time had been deprived of an essential right, the right to write badly—that is, to write well but not in a way deemed correct by the powers that be.

By becoming 'silent', Babel was not submitting, but choosing to preserve in suspension, and to advertise provocatively, his right to 'write well'.

This only made him subject to increasing menace. By the late Thirties Babel was not only 'silent', but had 'disappeared'. He died in circumstances that have never been fully clarified, though it was in one of Stalin's concentration camps in 1939 or 1940, and his literary reputation remained extinguished by the authorities for years to come.

Babel had already been brave in another way. He was a writer who always made much play of his intellectualism, his 'writerliness'. A photograph taken in his thirties shows a chubby-faced man with a high forehead, thin-rimmed glasses and a hesitant, humorous expression—an amiable schoolmaster. But this self-fostered image had not prevented him from serving between 1918 and 1920 in the post-revolutionary wars, in particular with General Budyonny's Cossack cavalry in Poland in 1920. And it was this experience that had produced the collection of short stories called *Red Cavalry* that I began to read, after reading Lionel Trilling's introduction, in the hot September sunshine in Thessaloniki.

That a bespectacled Jewish intellectual should have attached himself to a regiment of Cossack cavalry was extraordinary in itself. As an exercise in outsiderdom it could hardly have been more extreme; as an experiment in literary discovery it might have been doomed. But the stories I began to read are electric in their intensity and in their fearsome yet rapturous physicality. It was clear—though I hardly thought of such things on that first reading—that in his still forming 'writerliness' Babel had sought some raw and uncompromising collision of mind and matter, something rather different, as Lionel Trilling observes, from Hemingway's quest (it wasn't so long since I'd first read *In Our Time*), which can be more or less reduced to a moralizable seeking of courage or stoic virtue. Babel's desire seemed to be for an ego-obliterating connection with the very springs of action and emotion.

The *Red Cavalry* stories are at once lyrical and violent, ecstatic and amoral, affirmative and cruel: primitive stuff, yet great, exquisitely crafted literature. It's not difficult to see—though, again, I scarcely had these reflections on that first encounter —how, despite their declarative title and despite Babel's loyalty to Bolshevism, they would have fallen foul of any paranoid-authoritarian regime. They simply penetrate areas of human nature that lie beyond political programming, even revolutionary agendas. They sit uneasily with today's prim notions of political correctness; they certainly offended the political correctness of his time.

But Babel didn't just write about war and violence. He wrote in his painfully short writing life about many of life's joys: about his native Odessa, about France, where he travelled in the late 1920s. Along with his skill for compact and galvanized narrative, he has an incomparable gift for simultaneously condensing and celebrating all manner of physical sensation, which makes the regular term 'description' seem limp. He also wrote about literature, part of him remaining true to that essential writerly self which he could both mock and cast into the cauldron of human strife.

I can't really explain, beyond the obvious power of his words on the page, the instant rapport I felt for Babel. The very idea of a rapport is presumptuous and absurd. We were light years apart in experience and circumstance. My ancestry on my mother's side happens to include a Russian-Jewish or Polish-Jewish element and some of my forebears came from those margins of Poland

and Russia over which Budyonny's cavalry fought. But that connection is far-fetched.

And, needless to say, though I was eventually to become a writer, I've never written anything that's remotely like Babel.

Yet the fact remains that I wasn't just ignited by reading him. I've admired and been excited by many writers, but very few indeed have given me the feeling, which isn't really to do with literature at all but more like some strange personal intuition, that not only would I have liked to meet them, but, had we met, we would almost certainly have got on.

Later, when I'd found out more about Babel, I could go some way to analysing, if never fully explaining, the rapport. Babel, in his 'writerly' way, constantly stressed that he was not a 'natural'. Writing was a struggle for him; words had to be wrested out of him. He admired writers whom he believed were natural. Of Tolstoy he said that the world seems to 'write through him'. I wonder, now, if the notion of the natural writer isn't entirely mythical. The natural writers are just the ones who make it look natural—even Tolstoy didn't work in an oracular trance, he just worked. But when I was seventeen, turning eighteen, I certainly believed in natural writers. I thought they were the *real* writers. And this was perhaps the nub of my fear about my ambition: I knew I wasn't a natural writer. If I were, I'd already *be* a writer; there'd be no question of becoming one. The only way I could be a writer would be by making myself one, by squeezing the writer out of me. By work. And I was afraid of that work and of perhaps discovering there was no writer there.

Reading Babel didn't quicken the process. I wouldn't truly become a writer for another six or seven years; and, oddly enough, Greece would again be involved. But Babel certainly quickened *me*. And from then on I felt he was 'at my side': this wonderful, vanished storyteller whom I yet felt, very foolishly no doubt, I could have met, liked and talked with long into the night.

One of those natural writers Babel admired was Maupassant and there is a story by Babel called, itself, simply 'Guy de Maupassant'. It tells how the Russian narrator, a writer and a thinly disguised version of the younger Babel, comes under the spell of Maupassant's stories through an affair with a woman who is translating them (badly) into Russian. The Babel character improves her translations, thus becoming more entangled with her, but meanwhile becoming increasingly smitten by the French author. It's in this story that Babel penned his perhaps most quoted sentence, that 'no iron can pierce the heart with such force as a full stop in the right place'. A heart-piercing statement itself. The story ends with the Babel-narrator reading, late at night, a life of Maupassant, in particular about his final years (Maupassant died at forty-two), when although he became ill, almost blind, sometimes suicidal and eventually mad, he carried on writing to the last.

Babel's story concludes: 'I read the book to the end and got out of bed. The fog came close to the window, the world was hidden from me. My heart contracted as the foreboding of some essential truth touched me with light fingers.'

In Greece, in Thessaloniki in September, I didn't have that St Petersburg fog, but I had Babel's book and I had the palpable thrill of literary transmission. What Babel was describing in relation to Maupassant was exactly what I was feeling in relation to Babel.

I don't think I saw my five months with a rucksack as a Babelian apprenticeship—it came a laughably poor second, after all, to riding with the Cossack cavalry. But perhaps I did ask myself, conversely and rather shamingly: what might Babel have made of many of the sights, impressions, incidents, moments of vivid human contact and minor adventure that I'd experienced in those few months? The stabbing, for example, that I'd witnessed in central Turkey, a white shirt turning red; or that family in Izmir who simply let me stay in their little house as long as I wished and who when I left—for no other reason than the itch to be moving on—all *wept* to see me go and made me feel like the lowest creature on earth. Or that time in Bulgaria when I walked out of the forest and along a rutted track into a village where, I learned, no foreigner had ever appeared before and where the mayor, or elder, or whatever he was called, assembled the entire population to have its photograph taken round me, this historic phenomenon. And that village, with its wooden houses and carts and women in peasant headscarves, was like something out of Babel's Polish fringes.

Yet, by a strange twist, one of the most memorable adventures of my five-month journey, when I thought it was all over, was still to happen. My train home, which came from Athens, was due in at Thessaloniki in the early hours of the morning. The morning before this, I'd turned a corner of a busy square in the centre of the city to see, walking towards me, two school friends of mine. They weren't, of course, as I'd last seen them, in school uniform. They were dressed rather as I was and they were in the middle, as it proved, of a much shorter version of what I'd been doing since the spring. They'd left school at the regular time that July and they'd been travelling for less than a month. I admit to having felt an instant superiority: they were novices, not even travelling solo. And I admit, even before this, to a strong, immediate instinct, as soon as I spotted them, to turn the other way. I didn't want this 'intrusion'. It would, in fact, have been fortunate if I'd eluded them, but they spotted me and it was too late. The end of my reading of Babel.

We drank a lot of wine, and, as they were overnighting in Thessaloniki—I think they were heading for Istanbul—they insisted on coming to the station with me to see me onto my train. The upshot of their insistence was that by the time we were on the platform in the middle of the night we were behaving like—three schoolboys. I could feel all I'd learnt in five months' travelling seeping foolishly out of me.

A Greek army officer, with a particularly arrogant air, was striding up and down the platform, taking a dim view of our long hair, laughter and horsing around. He rightly took some of the laughter to be aimed at him. This went on for a precarious while, then one of my friends, who I remember had been quite big in the school dramatic society, took a knife from my rucksack and waved it at the officer, as if he might have been auditioning, badly, for one of the murderers in *Macbeth*. An utterly stupid thing to have done.

This was Greece under a newly imposed military regime. We were duly arrested by the station police, then carted off in a squad car by the town police. The fact that I'd had a train to catch and I hadn't been the one to wave the knife cut no ice. It was my knife. There was much shouting and thumping of desktops with fists. My train left without me. Then things had got a little worse. The car that took us to the police station, with two policemen in front, had travelled slowly and, it seemed, by a roundabout route. We'd all felt we might end up being beaten up in some deserted spot.

Any number of unpleasant fates might have awaited us. As it happened, though we spent the night in a police station, we weren't even thrown in jail, but it felt like touch-and-go. The fact that I'd bought the incriminating knife in Bulgaria and that it had a brand name in Cyrillic lettering didn't help. I could see the crude equation being made: I was a communist. I'd used the knife for little more than cutting bread and watermelons. I'd bought it to replace another I'd lost, and, like its predecessor, it had sometimes gone under my head when I slept to protect me from trouble. Now it had got me into trouble.

In the end I think the army officer, who'd also missed his train and had been required to come separately to the police station as a witness, began to resent the bother his indignation was costing him and backed down from pressing charges. We were released with our passports in the morning. This was fine for my two friends, who could continue their travels freely, with a good story to tell. I was left with the task of attempting to get back to London on an invalid rail ticket—a journey of nearly two thousand miles.

Somehow I managed to do it, all the way to Victoria. It was a somewhat hallucinatory journey, not least because it involved four nights, counting the night in the police station, without sleep. In those days the trans-European trains to and from Greece used to have whole carriages reserved by student travel companies, with couchettes and meals thrown in—but only once a week. I had to travel, with my rucksack and dud ticket, as a common passenger. In practice, this meant standing in the corridor, all the way from Greece to Germany (over thirty-six hours), as the north-bound trains were regularly packed with Greeks, then Yugoslavs heading for the then-booming German economy—heading there too, it seemed, with most of their possessions. The lack of personal space in the corridor can't really be described—it was *impossible* to sit— but I was a seasoned traveller, used to all kinds of privations, and might have breezed through it all, if I hadn't also been afraid of being at any moment chucked off. Officials periodically came, or rather clambered and squeezed, along. They were not generally in good moods. There were lengthy border stops. I invented several stories to excuse my incorrect tickets. None, of course, involved arrest by the Greek police.

It was, in fact, a good many Greeks and Yugoslavs, with their heaps of luggage, who got thrown off, at the German border. I don't know what became of them: another side of the booming German economy. I stayed on, still standing, but in ever less crammed conditions. After a while I could use my rucksack as a seat. I may even have nodded off as we threaded our way up the Rhine.

My principal remaining memory of that journey is of arriving after nightfall in Cologne, where I had to change trains for Ostend, and of finding myself on another railway platform with more military uniforms. I was pretty instantly befriended, in fact—one last strange upswing of that see-saw of fortune that travel brings—by a gang of young British squaddies, on the point of returning home on leave. They seemed to make it their purpose to fill me with beer. I've never forgotten their extraordinarily generous good company, when anyone could see we were different creatures, if not so different in age. There was I with the unkempt trappings of five months' very rough wayfaring; there were they with their uniforms and boots, caught in the still lingering ethos of National Service and of the Army of the Rhine. If I'd been born a few years earlier, I might have been one of them. But I was too tired, and then too drunk, to absorb another lesson in post-war change. I'd also lost by now all worries about my inoperative tickets. I felt I was assured of a charmed and invincible passage home.

I don't recall much about the train to Ostend or the night crossing to Dover. I remember that on the ferry my army friends deserted me for the bar below while I stretched out with my faithful rucksack on a bench on deck. I might have been all alone up there, but I'd slept in some funny places by now and I hadn't stretched out anywhere for four days. The cold and wet of the North Sea air in September were neither here nor there.

I recall waking up in Dover, because one of my military chums—who must have remembered me and been concerned—was shaking me. He looked rather green around the gills. He said simply, 'We're 'ere.'

So we were. There were the white cliffs. There was England looming through a murky early autumn morning. It looked extremely strange, my country; it looked very weird indeed. It continued to look very weird as we clacked through Kent. How ironic if I'd been finally turfed off that train at Ashford or Tonbridge.

But I heaved my rucksack at last onto a platform at Victoria. I realized that if I hadn't been detained by two idiot friends in Thessaloniki I might have thrown away a lot of what was in it—dirty clothes and no-longer-needed accoutrements—and spared myself some weight. But that sensible moment had passed me by, and anyway I'd got used to travelling with a sort of house on my back. In it, too, among the debris of five months, was a Bulgarian knife (it hadn't even been confiscated) and a copy of Isaac Babel's collected stories. In a two-and-a-half-day journey by train I'd never had the chance or been in a fit mental condition to read a single word.

But I still have the book. And Babel's photograph is the only photograph of another writer I've ever felt the need to place before me on my desk as I write.

GREECE AGAIN

1974

The following piece, to which a few details have been added, was originally written in 1993 for an anthology brought out to celebrate the twenty-first anniversary of the publishers Picador. The anthology was called simply *21*, and the idea was to ask twenty-one Picador authors to choose any year from the imprint's life span and to write about it from whatever angle they chose. I quickly nabbed 1974 (1967 would have been before Picador's existence) but the later year brought me back to a second, longer time I spent in Greece, working as an English teacher, with some summer months of travelling added on. The travelling was redolent of my earlier wanderings in the Aegean, though now I had rather more cash. The cash, in fact, had not been so easily acquired, as the commercial language school where I taught had a crude, if not actually corrupt, approach to commerce and my pay tended to arrive in small, unpredictable parcels of very used notes.

By odd historical coincidence I found myself in Greece for the fall of the seven-year military junta, when previously I'd been there at its start, and had even come close, in Thessaloniki, to feeling its bite. This piece refers back to that railway-station episode, but rather suggests I was the only one involved and to blame. To keep the original piece down to length, and perhaps to pardon their complicity, I omitted my two friends, but they were definitely and instrumentally there. Would that they hadn't been.

The years in between, from the autumn of 1967 to the autumn of 1973, were my student years, first at Cambridge, then at York in the somewhat fraudulent way, academically speaking, that this piece alludes to. It was from Greece that I wrote to York University, after their formal reminder was sent on, to say that I wouldn't be submitting my PhD thesis. The truth was that it would never be completed and it was a cover, anyway, by which I'd managed to wangle three years living on a postgraduate grant.

It was at York, nonetheless, by dint of this subterfuge, that I really did at last begin to write. That is, to practise writing or—though I never thought of it so formally and programmatically—to teach myself to write. I had no one else to teach me. Some people have assumed, because of the generation I belong to and because I wrote a novel set in the Fens, that I'm a product of the University of East Anglia's well-known creative-writing school. The reality is that I spent three years at York, pulling a fast one about my doctoral intentions while, as a novice writer, being entirely on my own. Creative-writing courses, which have now proliferated, can be valuable ways of giving aspiring writers useful time, temporary security and the company of like minds, but I retain a stubborn antipathy to the notion that writing can be institutionally and communally 'taught'. Like rough travelling, I think the learning's best done alone.

Though, like the travelling, it can be pretty rough. This piece mentions that—perhaps with excessive self-censure—I destroyed most of what I wrote at York. I certainly wasn't in the business of sharing work with anyone or of even thinking of getting anything into print. But it was a real, formative apprenticeship and when I came out of it, my ambition still intact, I could at least say to myself I was a writer, even if I still had no absolute faith that a writer in the fully fledged sense was what I would become.

Later events proved ironic. I was enormously touched, wrong-footed—and honoured—when in 1998 York gave me an honorary degree. I got my doctorate after all. It was twenty-five years since I'd last visited the university and my former, duplicitous association came embarrassingly back to me. It had been three years of false pretences, but also of a lot of hard work. Skivers aren't unknown among the postgraduate community, but I didn't feel like a skiver, and perhaps because, in those days at least, postgraduate students were an inconspicuous breed much left to their own devices, the success of my fraud wasn't really so remarkable. I didn't live in daily fear of being found out.

I keep fond memories of York in the early 1970s—of the city, principally, where I spent most of my time, rather than the university. This was before York was theme-parked and boutiqued, and it still had an easy, unpretentious relationship with the stony history you could see at almost every turn. Past and present rubbed shoulders naturally. It had a plethora of pubs, wonderful butchers' shops, a magnificent railway station: a working city that just happened to be extraordinarily picturesque. For a while I lived near Rowntree's chocolate factory, east of the centre. Whenever I walked to the university campus out to the west (I can't remember going anywhere in York except on foot), I'd slip through the huddled medieval gateway of Bootham Bar, the Minster towering just ahead, pass along High and Low Peter-gate, down the impossibly narrow and crooked Shambles, then, skirting Clifford's Tower and York Castle, emerge through the city walls on the further side—so taking in, in a routine twenty minutes, what tourists travel from all over the world to see.

Later, I moved inside the walls, south of the Ouse, where there were still some sleepy, almost forgotten streets of small terraced houses and, by the river itself, clusters of quietly deserted warehouses. I shared a two-up, two-down, which had an outside loo that in the extremes of the York winter became a no-go area in every sense and necessitated a resourceful use of old milk bottles. The shivering, coat-wearing and, frankly, urinous conditions in which I sometimes wrote then were a far cry from the donning of honorary robes or, indeed, from a jasmine-scented veranda in Greece.

Bootham Bar

The Minster from Bar Walls

York Minster and Lendal Bridge

L.N.E.R. War Memorial and Station Hotel

Micklegate Bar

YORK

1974

1974 was the year I failed to write my first novel. It was also the year that the military dictatorship in Greece collapsed almost overnight. The two events are not entirely unconnected. For most of '74 I was living in Greece, and it was in Greece, though I didn't know it at the time, that my literary failure occurred.

Having reached the end of my student years—the last three spent posing as a PhD candidate while I secretly began learning my craft as a writer—I'd answered a dubious advert for teachers with the Strategakis Schools of English, a chain of commercial language schools operating throughout Greece.

It was a fanciful attempt to embrace, or perhaps postpone, my future. It had precedents. There is the fairly well-known case of John Fowles, who went to teach on a magical Greek island and found there the inspiration for a successful novel. I don't recall if I saw myself as following his example. I certainly saw myself under some vine on a veranda, conjuring up that—for me unprecedented—thing, a novel of my own.

There was no magical island. I was sent to Volos, a port on the east coast, largely destroyed by an earthquake in the 1950s and unattractively rebuilt. And the general state of the Strategakis School in Volos can be characterized by the school manager, who met me off the Athens bus, strapped my suitcase to an ancient bicycle and spoke perhaps six words of English.

But I did find a veranda and a vine. They came with the rooms I rented on the edge of town. Thrown in was a little terraced garden with below it a straggly orchard of apricot trees where in the weeks before Easter, but not afterwards, grazed two innocent white goats. And there was a splendid view. Volos itself may lack glamour but its setting is genuinely inspiring. Before me lay the bay from which Jason set forth with the Argonauts. Behind me, cloaked in chestnut woods, rose Mount Pelion, home of the Centaurs.

And one day on my veranda I duly sat down and began to write a novel. There's no point now in disclosing its contents. My memory of it is happily dim. But there I was, fulfilling my vision, intently writing—in the early hours before I set off to teach or sometimes late into the night—my first novel.

Voluntary exile is an extraordinarily self-protective thing. Back home there'd been the tension between dream and reality. Because I feared the judgement of reality, I was my own toughest critic. I tore up perhaps more than I needed to of the stories I wrote. But in Greece I seemed to enter a state of suspended self-doubt. All questions of appraisal could wait till I returned. The important thing was just to do it.

It was a quiet spot, perched above the edge of town, where the built-up streets gave way to rough tracks and smallholdings. At night, along with the bark of dogs or the bleat of a doomed goat, the only sound would be that of raised human voices: children being scolded, husbands being called in to supper. Occasionally there would be a hooting from the hardly thick traffic climbing or descending the tightly twisting mountain road behind me. At one of the bends, not far above, was the site, it was claimed, where Peleus married Thetis, with all Olympus in attendance, and where Eris delivered the fateful Apple of Discord.

In the other direction was the village of Ano Volos, a place of steep, narrow lanes down which, depending on the season, donkeys carried huge panniers of chestnuts or olives. It lay alongside a ravine with a rushing stream which powered an olive press, next to the lay-by at the foot of the village where the buses into town turned round. When the press was busy, the lay-by and the sloping road would run with the purple-brown must left after the extraction of the oil.

The vine and the veranda were not always available. Autumn came, with spectacular thunderstorms, and the Greek winter is not as mild as Greek summers suggest. More than once I watched the snowline creep down Mount Pelion almost to engulf me. Even in a well-provided-for town like Volos, the Greeks seemed to have a standard, inexpensive way of dealing with winter: they attempted to ignore it. In one of the schoolrooms in the outlying villages where I also went to teach, it was my duty to light and manage the primitive stove. It would just about get going, and class and teacher would have recovered from the fumes, when it was time for the lesson to end.

But winter back home was hardly preferable—this was the crisis winter of Heath's three-day week—and I confess I wasn't particularly troubled at making my temporary home in a country whose own politics and social condition bore no scrutiny at all. Greece in those days was littered with propaganda, and radios or public loudspeakers regularly blared out martial music. The grotesque symbol of the junta—a soldier standing before a spread-winged phoenix—was everywhere, and if the infamous regime had in fact not long to last, it could still demonstrate what it was capable of. In November 1973 there were riots, bloodily suppressed, in Athens, and the whole country was placed under curfew.

Six years before, on a previous trip, I'd had my own vivid run-in with the Greek authorities when I spent a night in a police station in Thessaloniki after a Greek army officer had accused me (with some reason) of threatening behaviour towards him on a railway station. I was frankly lucky to have suffered no more than a night's detention and a missed train. But I was younger then, and I was not writing a novel.

Winter eventually melted into spring. After a few false starts, the air turned suddenly warm. The goats appeared and disappeared. A pair of nightingales took up residence in the jasmine bush in the garden. I carried outside the little fold-up table that was all I had for a desk and, once again, in the early hours I'd sit with my pen and notepad, listening to the nightingales, breathing jasmine and watching the pink light spread over the hills of Thessaly.

I don't know what happened to the Strategakis School in Volos after my departure in June. Its days were plainly numbered. Its finances and its classroom furniture were in ruins. In nine months I'd grown attached to its odd mixture of impoverishment, mercenariness and ingenuousness. I was fond of my students, who taught me more Greek than I taught them English and who boasted among them an Ares, a Socrates, an Adonis and at least two Aphrodites. I'd grown fond of graceless but not uncompanionable Volos. I knew the cafes and *ouzeria*, where to eat the best fish. I'd made good friends in town. And I would miss my veranda.

But the best of my time in Greece was yet to come. I'd always intended to stay on when the school year was over and, with what was left from my salary, to travel at will. I took the bus to Athens, left the bulk of my things with a friend there—including the now quite voluminous, if unfinished, manuscript of my novel (it could wait till I was back in England)—and that same evening took the night boat from Piraeus to Lesbos. On the darkening upper deck I met three girls, one English, one American, one Greek, rolling out their sleeping bags. They were going to stay in a little beach house on Lesbos owned by the Greek girl's uncle, and asked me if I wanted to come along. I rolled out my sleeping bag next to theirs. Sometimes life is very simple.

In the weeks and months that followed I was as happy, as free, as lucky as I've ever been. I hopped at random around the Aegean and, beginning with that charmed week in Lesbos, idyll followed idyll as island followed island. I went my own way when I wanted to, but there was no lack of fellow travellers. I fell in love, certainly in lust, more than once. I knew the country, could speak the language, and my saved-up drachmas seemed to last miraculously. I don't recall sparing a thought for literature or making a single note for my novel.

And none of this was greatly altered when in July, following the Turkish invasion of Cyprus and the intensification of the fighting there, all of Greece was mobilized. The life of vagrant hedonism went on, even as guards were mounted, rifles issued to every adult male and blackouts imposed. I remember sleeping one night on a beach on Kos—just across the water from the Turkish mainland—and being woken by the rumble of trucks and the shouts of orders as an army convoy moved along the island's perimeter road. If the Turks intended to invade, the beach was probably not a good place to be. In the troop-carriers were conscripts younger than me. I turned over and looked back up at the stars.

But before the summer was out even Greeks had cause for joy. In the wake of the threat of full-scale war, which never materialized, the seven-year dictatorship dissolved—a military tyranny brought down by military exigency. The realization that this had indeed happened spread, even in the remote Aegean, like some quickening breeze. I'd never before seen a whole people touched by political glee. I should perhaps have reflected that while Greeks had still been oppressed, I'd been having the time of my life and I had no right to share in *their* new happiness. But it was infectious stuff, and what I think I actually felt was that larger events had only crowned my own lease of bliss. It was nearly time to go home, but I would leave the country on a high note.

One afternoon that summer, on the island of Siphnos, I went with a bucket on a length of rope to a well, the only available source of water nearby, and though I'd been repeatedly enjoined by the Greek friends I was with not to let go of the rope when I let go of the bucket, I let go of the rope. There was the bucket suddenly winking at me from the bottom of the well and there was I at the top. I remember standing there and just laughing out loud at my glorious, consummate stupidity, at the whole fabulous carefreeness of my way of life at that time. The cicadas rattling in the hot hills all around me seemed only to be joining in my laughter too.

Some while after my return to England I got out the manuscript of my novel, began to read it and knew at once that it was awful. Irredeemably awful. Strangely, this lucid realization didn't devastate me. I've abandoned work since with much greater agony. I didn't feel that those days on the veranda had been wasted or that those weeks in the Aegean sun were a delusion. No, the judgement I could now coolly pass on myself would have poisoned those days. Those days were inviolate. Let life be lived.

Nonetheless, what I'd written was crap.

The future had caught up with me but I wouldn't let it trap me. I found work as a part-time teacher—teaching, again, by the hour—in various South London colleges. I've never had any vocation or training as a teacher, but for the next ten years this was how I survived. The part-time status was as vital to my self-esteem—I would never be sucked into full-time employment—as it was in giving me time each day to write. And during those ten years, without the aid of a single vine leaf or veranda, I did indeed write, and publish, not only my first novel but two others.

I remember standing one morning that autumn at a crowded suburban railway station on my way to one of my colleges. Barely a month before I'd been dallying in the Dodecanese and laughing my head off by that fool-making well. There can be few sights less exalting, more chilling to the soul than the sight of English commuters massing for the daily grind, and here was I—who'd once on another railway platform mocked a strutting Greek army officer—dutifully clutching my briefcase. But I had the oddly uplifting sensation of being at a turning-point.

After that winter of oil crisis and three-day weeks there were two general elections. In America, Nixon resigned. The aura, the taste of a decade lingers over into the next and I can't help feeling that the spirit of the Sixties, that surge of post-war optimism and liberalism in which I was lucky enough to have been young, really died in 1974. Perhaps for me it was artificially extended, its edges blurred, by my time in Greece. I'd entered my mid-twenties. When does youth end?

But if the chill was entering my soul on that railway platform it was partly because I had no inkling that wonderful things were still in store for me in that benign year, and they were to happen not in Kos or Kalymnos or Khios, but in Clapham . . .

As 1974 drew to its close I would understand that I was at a watershed. It was the year in which I more than once knew perfect happiness. It was the year in which I became aware, in more than one way, of historical forces. And it was the year in which, contrary to the immediate evidence, I knew for certain I would be a writer.

Ano Volos and slopes of Mount Pelion.

NEGRONIS WITH ALAN

KENSINGTON, 1976

Alan Ross was my first ever editor and publisher and, before either of these, encourager. I first met him in 1976 but I wrote this piece some twenty-five years later after his death in 2001 and haven't published it till now.

Negronis with Alan

Writing and claustrophobia, or rather the need to overcome it, go together. I'm aware of this in more than one way when I think of Alan Ross. If you can't stand your own company alone in a room for long hours, or, when it gets tough, the feeling of being in a locked cell, or, when it gets tougher still, the vague feeling of being buried alive—then don't be a writer. When you're a young writer, still struggling to get into print, the sense of confinement can be particularly acute. You have simply yet to *appear*. You exist—it's only your choice—in a sort of box, under a lid. You can sometimes wonder if the lid hasn't become sealed or turned to stone.

Alan did two things. He opened a door of welcome to the literary life as no longer a solitary business, but he also lifted the lid. He let me in and he let me out. He gave me that first, un-repeatable, unforgettable gasp of about-to-be-published oxygen.

I know that my experience—it's only to pay tribute to him—was far from unique. Alan died on St Valentine's Day, 2001. Speaking at a memorial service for him some months later, the novelist Will Boyd, first published, as I was, in Alan's *London Magazine*, gave a curiously familiar account of his first meeting with Alan. They'd gone, he told the congregation, to a restaurant for lunch and Alan had said, 'What will you have to drink? I'm having a Negroni. Would you like one too?' Will had never had a Negroni before and hadn't a clue what it was, but he'd also never before been taken to lunch by an editor and publisher and, desperate not to look out of place, he'd said as nonchalantly as possible, 'Yes, please.'

When the service was over I went up to Will and said, 'That Negroni thing, it happened with me too. Just the same.'

And Will and I can't be the only ones. If the number of cognoscenti of the drink were to be measured only by the number of writers whose careers Alan effectively launched, this would still make, I suspect, a significant clan, a whole authorial brother-and-sisterhood of the Negroni. For me it will always be the drink of initiation and liberation. I only have to sip it to remind myself of all that's enchanting—and it can be enchanting—about the writing life.

Red vermouth, Campari, gin, a twist of orange. Soda to make it long. A little ruby-pink fire of a drink, sunset in a glass. Its name suggests some magisterial head barman of long ago, but, as far as I'm concerned, it ought to be called the 'Alan Ross'. No one else I've known has become synonymous in my mind with a drink.

My first Negroni with Alan (perhaps Will Boyd's too) was in a now-vanished restaurant called Meridiana in the Fulham Road, opposite Sydney Place, a short walk from South Kensington Underground and the *London Magazine* office in Thurloe Place. As the Negroni will always be Alan's drink, so the knot of streets round South Kensington Tube will always be Alan's patch, and will always have, via him and the Negroni, a certain Latin, Mediterranean brio. Lunch with Alan was invariably in an Italian restaurant: Meridiana, San Frediano's, the Piccola Venezia . . . Coming up from the Underground, past the flower and news-paper stands, I still feel, as nowhere else in London, that I might be emerging into some sunny Continental city—a concourse in Palermo or Rome. And the sensation goes right back to that first feeling of being let out from under a lid.

I'm thinking back to 1976, when Alan published my first story, which happened to have the (misleadingly) airy title 'The Recreation Ground'. By then I'd been a writer in theory and spirit for some dozen years; in practice—if not in print—for some five or six. But for the slender link I'd formed with Alan and *London Magazine*, I might have felt entirely on my own. I was nearly twenty-seven. Not so young. Other people at that age can be well settled into more conventional, more lucrative and, so they say, more sensible careers.

I'd learnt by then that in order to write you have to persevere, but you also have to eat. I'd found scraps of part-time work at various South London colleges and I led a sort of shadowy, furtive existence—writing in the morning and emerging in the afternoons to teach day-release or evening-class students 'proper' English. For some of this time, out of the same economic pressure, I was still living at my parents' home in South Croydon and so still within the envelope of everything that entailed.

In straight miles South Croydon isn't so far from South Kensington. In other respects they could be poles apart. I may have ached to spread my wings, but part of me was still lodged in a world where, not so long before, the china ducks had been flapping up the living-room wall. Alan—poet, writer, editor, publisher, collector of paintings, mover in literary and artistic circles—was simply the first person with any of these attributes I'd ever met.

Though, strangely, I felt I knew him even before I met him and when I did meet him he proved to be one of those people who retain about them the lasting aura of when you first encountered them. I was actually in his company only a few times, widely spaced, over a period of more than twenty years. I can't pretend to have known him closely at all, yet he had a presence for me far exceeding the actual contact. When I met him he was fifty-four, more or less twice my age at the time, and he remains in my mind's eye a distinctly youthful fifty-four—offering me that remarkable drink.

The presence I'd known, or intuited, before that first meeting was gleaned mainly from rejection slips, which can, of course, be the most cruelly impersonal things around. Alan somehow had the art of making them converse. They would come with an individually inscribed 'Sorry' or 'Almost', a 'Not quite' or 'Very nearly'. Thankfully, they never seemed to have the tacit message, 'Go away'. I'm not sure how many stories I sent Alan before he finally took one, or if the gradient of encouragement was a steady upward slope (though I like to think so), but by the time the magic acceptance came I felt I had, or my work had, a friend.

No other editor I sent stories to in those days ever gave me that feeling. Though, again, I know I wasn't alone. Through *London Magazine*, which he kept going for over forty years, Alan was, quite simply, the best and most unsung supporter of young writers there was. Unsung, because trumpet-blowing was never part of his style, and he detested that appropriating aspect of publishing that likes to brag about 'discovering' talent. Yet style, in which modesty and reticence were mixed with eccentricity and even flamboyance, he had in plenty. You sensed a range of possible Alans, only some of whom you might see. There was a chameleon quality about him, even an alert, looming, chameleon largeness to his eyes. He was certainly capable of being many things at once, but you felt the essential being was never in doubt: he'd merely chosen for it a variegated and idiosyncratic wardrobe.

When I first met him, in his office at 30 Thurloe Place, he seemed, almost literally, a man of two parts. To the waist down, he was jacket and tie, slightly patrician, slightly raffish—a wispiness to the sideburns. Below, it was rumpled jeans and sloppy shoes. Perhaps he'd concocted this combination to cover his mixed anticipations of me. The expression and demeanour were also complicated and versatile: a sheen of affable panache, but a definite, innate hesitancy—a quiet smile, a watchfulness, a slight stammer, the dark eyes seeming to bulge as if he was always about to be, or ready to be, surprised.

I'm sure I disappointed him. I was nothing out of the ordinary. 'Hungry?' he soon asked, as if his first impression of me was banal: I was skinny.

His office was at the top of the building then. It had no separate entrance and you had to make an apologetic dash through someone else's office to get there. In subsequent years, during long battles with the landlords, it moved down to become a sort of cabin in the back garden, always adhering to the same address. But 'office' was never the word anyway. It was more a sort of miniature cosmos of Alan's passions and tastes. There was a lot of colour. Pictures covered the walls, mingled with photographs. Some of the photographs were of people I recognized but regarded then as mythological beings. Some of the pictures were of women naked and frank enough to seem to give off a musk. There were rows and stacks of books, and heaps of jumbled correspondence—some of it held down by a glass paperweight shaped like a breast. You felt the presence of other writers, great names, in that tiny room. There was the dog, supposedly trained to devour unwanted manuscripts, and there was Alan himself, a man not just of two halves but, clearly, if that crowded space was anything to go by, many sides: poetry, painting, publishing, cricket (he was the *Observer*'s correspondent), Italy, India (where he was born), dogs, racehorses, women. And more women.

We walked through Onslow Square: a bright spring day in 1976. I'd never been anywhere like Meridiana before. People came and greeted Alan, he greeted them. To the waiters he was 'Signor Ross'. In one sense clearly in his element, he retained, reassuringly, that characteristic look of subdued but appreciative astonishment. We sat down. He asked me what I thought of the women sitting at other tables, at least one of whom had kissed him on the way in. He asked me what I'd like to drink . . .

He was the same age as my father, and there were other parallels. They had the same name—my father taking the double 'l'. They'd both been in the navy in the war, serving on Arctic convoys to Murmansk, which had left in Alan's case (though I don't think my father escaped lightly) some terrible memories and a chronic need for southern warmth. They both had a quiet, modest core. But there the resemblances stopped, lost in that gulf between South Kensington and South Croydon, now filling anyway with a ruby-pink haze.

I wasn't alone, but that doesn't dilute the experience or stop the debt being immense. He published my first story and my first (and still only) collection of stories. If his book-publishing side arm, London Magazine Editions, hadn't fallen at the wrong moment into one of its occasional cash-strapped abeyances, he would have published my first novel. He was certainly the first publisher to read it and accept it. Not long after that first meeting, he wrote with uncanny perception (since I hadn't said a thing) to say he felt I must be working on something longer than stories. If I was, could he see it when it was ready? I was, he did see it and, within days, promised to publish it. It's not supposed to happen so simply, and when in fact it proved too good to be true, he swore to find me another publisher. Though it took four years, *The Sweet Shop Owner* found its way into print largely through Alan's efforts. The first story and the first novel were both thanks to him.

There was an unhappy aspect to Alan's chameleon nature, unseen and rarely alluded to—a dark suit hanging in the wardrobe. Sometimes he'd be compelled to put it on. He suffered from periodic bouts of severe clinical depression. I never knew, if he or anyone did, their origins, but the war was one possible source. He'd once been briefly sealed (though it can't have seemed brief and he might never have got out) behind a locked bulkhead amid the remains of two gun crews, in a burning, flooding ship, under fire at the time from a German cruiser. The ship was the destroyer *Onslow*, and I suppose Alan must have received a subliminal reminder every time he walked from his office to Meridiana by way of Onslow Square.

A pleasure-loving man, a lover of open, sunny places (cricket, racecourses, the Sussex coast, Italy), he suffered from intervals of mental torture and incarceration. Every so often he would 'disappear', and you knew he wasn't at Thurloe Place or in the real or the Piccola Venezia but somewhere in a pit of misery and drugs. Then he'd resurface, looking fragile but very pleased to be back in the world, and generally playing down the whole thing. I remember lunching with him soon after one such nightmare. He still looked shaky and medication-dulled. A friend of his entered the restaurant, looking too, for whatever reason, a little frail. There was an exchange of token 'how are you's' and 'oh, all right's'. Then Alan said, with a rush of cheeriness, 'Hard work, isn't it—being all right?'

Writers should count themselves lucky: merely to have their self-induced immurements, their self-imposed immersions.

Not long before he died Alan suffered a particularly dreadful onslaught of depression, triggered, it seems, by the news of the sinking of the Russian submarine the *Kursk*, not far from Murmansk. A trigger of a trigger, in Alan's case. He seemed to have got through it and was back on form again. In the last note I had from him there was the usual casual reference: 'Wouldn't wish it on anyone . . .' Then, two months later—there was no connection, it seemed—he died, of a heart attack, on St Valentine's Day.

Life offers us very few, if any, moments of real 'arrival', when we know that we've entered a domain that, however fragile our presentiments of it, however unfamiliar it may seem and however awkwardly we actually make our entrance, is yet where we belong: moments of arrival that are also moments of release. After drinking that first Negroni with Alan, I may very well have thought: I could use another of these. But I was also thinking: I'd like more of this please, more, please, of *all this*.

I knew something by then of the privations of the literary life. I'd never really known that it can also be, from time to time, intensely sweet. Alan introduced me to its sweetness. I was twenty-six and virtually penniless, but here I was, being published (how ridiculously puny it will seem to a non-writer: one story in a magazine) and offered a rose-tinted elixir. I was young enough and wise enough not to waste the opportunity for walking on air.

And that wasn't so hard to do. At this time, though I wouldn't have dreamed of sharing the fact with a fifty-four-year-old man —even as he invited my confidential comments on those women at the other tables—I was very much in love. I'd met, not so long before, the woman with whom I wanted to share, and have shared, my life. I'd 'arrived' in that sense too. Life can be doubly sweet.

St Valentine's Day, 2001 . . . Soon after Alan's death, on a cold, grey February afternoon, I was waiting in a London bar to meet a friend. There was only one possible drink I could order. My friend arrived. He said, 'What's *that*?' 'It's a Negroni,' I said. 'Have one.' I ordered another fiery-red glassful, then I told him the story that Will Boyd would tell too.

GUILDHALL FARCE

1983

In 1983 my third novel, *Waterland*, was nominated for the Booker Prize. After it was all over, *Time Out* asked me to write this short, irreverent but not unheartfelt piece. The television coverage of the award dinner reached new, grotesque heights that year, and I've been told that the recording of the programme was subsequently used in television training as a locus classicus in how not to present such events. The ineffable Selina Scott committed gaffe after smiling gaffe, of which the most conspicuous was randomly to ask one of the dinner guests, after the winner had been announced, for an on-the-spot reaction, only to be told by Angela Carter (for it was she) that she was asking one of the judges. The most brilliant tactical stroke of the evening was that of the winner, J. M. Coetzee, who, to the consternation of the TV people, was serenely absent.

Though *Waterland* was for a while the bookies' and the popular favourite, I'm not at all sorry it didn't win (though the newspaper clipping shown after this piece would have it otherwise). I think a win might have seriously unbalanced the rather unready figure portrayed in *Time Out*. When I did win in 1996, with *Last Orders*, I was much better able both to sustain and to enjoy the process of winning. And the atmosphere in the Guildhall was a little less out of hand that year.

Guildhall Farce

There's no real reason why a book, which is full of words, should require any other spokesman than itself, but try telling that to the assembled media when your novel has just been nominated for the Booker Prize. You won't get a hearing. For me the prime symptom of shortlistomania (rare form of schizophrenia) was this condition of fundamental absurdity: the requirement to deliver what I did not have to deliver; the repeated obligation to give the two-minute, half-hour or thirty-second version of what, in the case of *Waterland*, took three years to produce.

Don't mistake me. I'm not the total purist. A writer these days has to be either foolish or sublimely aloof not to accept that some extra-authorial hoop-jumping will help his book reach readers. And I *was* very chuffed to be shortlisted. But this doesn't alter the raw sensations. Now the jamboree's over, I hope I can get back again to the real thing.

The lesser symptoms were numerous—some just plain ludicrous. My diary, usually a white desert, became suddenly crowded. The phone rang a lot. Heinemann kept sending me pink bits of paper with my latest itinerary and timetable of interviews. To certain temperaments this state of affairs might bring euphoric illusions of stardom. For those of a nervous disposition it instils trepidation. With a four-week spate of it, I should have acquired the necessary glib techniques. Alas not. I bounced dazedly in and out of radio stations, not knowing what I had said but pretty sure it had been meaningless. LBC referred to me in my absence as the author of *Wetland*, then corrected it to *Wasteland*. After my fifth or sixth time behind the mike, I resolved not to worry and just to say '*Waterland*' as often as possible. I failed even in this resolution.

My television initiation, in some ways, couldn't have been gentler. *Book Four* came to the safely familiar territory of my publishers. But not even the efforts of my editor, David Godwin, who got me well tanked up beforehand, or the patient reassurances of my interviewer, Hermione Lee, could quell my panic. What do they want of me? Oh, just two minutes on what *Waterland* is all about . . . I sit in the hot seat. Words come out of my mouth. Editing miracles may have been performed for the finished piece (which I never watched), but I possess a transcript of the original: it shatters the notion that novels are written by articulate people.

I travelled a bit. I was actually *flown* somewhere by my publishers. Only to Glasgow, but I could still indulge in jet-hopping fantasies. I did readings and signings. I turned up for a session at the Arts Council Bookshop to find there was no audience. So much for hype. I got whisked off to Cambridge by a Celebrity —the bulky, lugubriously jocular figure of Clement Freud, MP for the region where my novel is (only partly) set. My book, it seemed, had acquired political value, and Radio Cambridgeshire provided a royal welcome—for Clement Freud. 'Nice to see you too, Mr Smith . . .'

I had high times and low times, got drunk a lot, missed a lot of sleep. My mantelpiece got stacked with well-wishes and I was continually touched by the support of friends and by sudden expressions of enthusiasm and sympathy from unforeseen quarters (along with their developed nervous systems writers have good noses for telling the genuine from the phoney).

I hired my penguin-suit from Moss Bros. After the four-week crash course—election campaign, paddock trotting, whichever metaphor you prefer—the Day, or Night, of Judgement loomed with sudden inescapability. I wasn't prepared for high comedy. I'd evolved my own philosophic assumptions about the outcome and I sweated less over that than the prospect of another turn before the cameras. In the event, the sheer farce of it all actually cured my nerves. The evening deserves full-length description—if it's not beyond it—and some serious analysis could be made of its contents, including what the cameras didn't show, particularly Fay Weldon's Chair-of-the-Judges speech. Since I'm trying to keep things light-hearted, I'll only recall the more laughable moments: the BBC man who came up to me and said, 'Ah, hello, Mr Rushdie . . .'; the extraordinary Selina Scott—was she there to ask questions or perform public seductions ('Mr Swift, I'm Selina Scott and I'm going to interview you on the floor . . .')? The spectacle of sloshed publishers living up to their image.

I congratulate J. M. Coetzee on his win. I congratulate him also on being well out of it that Wednesday night. The Booker Prize has boomed in the past three years. It has made a noise about fiction, which is no bad thing. I am thankful for the boost it has given to *Waterland*. The prize makes no difference, as John Fuller pointed out, to fiction-*writing*. It is certainly in danger of bursting its own inflated proportions. You cannot give something more prestige while turning it into more and more of a circus, or bring credit to writers by making public fools of them. Fay Weldon's statements on the abuse of authorship undoubtedly got home to five authors present. Why reduce the craft of words to the point where words fail? To return to the mirth of it all, let *my*

last word come from the end of that painful *Book Four* transcript
(before I go and burn it):

GS: . . . I'm drying up, can we stop . . . [*laughs*]
INTERVIEWER: Excellent, good.

Novel finalists

CAMDEN author Salman Rushdie was finalist in this year's Booker McConnell Prize for Fiction, the country's most valuable literary award. That's Salman, left, pictured with the eventual winner, South African writer J.M. Coetzee. The local man of words, who lives in Raveley Street, made the finals with his latest work Shame (Jonathan Cape, £7.95). He won the prize in 1981 for his novel Midnight's Children.

Surely some mistake.

TALKING TO PATRICK

NEW YORK AND LONDON, 1984–86

I made my first visit to New York in the spring of 1984 for the American publication of *Waterland*, my debut novel in the States. I later became, on rather tenuous, ill-defined grounds, a 'contributing editor' of the New York arts magazine *Bomb*, where three of the interviews reprinted in this book had their first appearance. They are the main evidence of my connection and contribution.

My connection with New York itself is also rather tenuous and hard to define. I recognize its force, energy and uniqueness, but it's not a place I could ever settle in, though some of my best writer-friends have done just that, and they're my real link with the city.

Patrick McGrath has now lived in New York most of his adult life and I've no doubt he'd say his heart lies in Manhattan, yet he remains, to me at least, remarkably untouched in person by anything New Yorkerish or indeed American. Meeting him in Britain, you'd never guess his home is across the ocean. New York can stamp itself pretty powerfully on even short-term visitors, and I've always found Patrick's capacity to love the place yet remain virginally untransatlantic both baffling and splendid.

He comes to England for a few months each year, normally in the summer, and usually starts to get twitchy long before this time is up. He once took the considerable trouble to have

transported to London an American-style air-conditioning unit
—one of those contraptions that take up most of a window—
and have it installed in the room where he works here in Ken-
nington. But though he has this New World affinity (and an
Irish name), his whole demeanour and speech could not be more
impeccably—and amiably, charmingly, courteously—English.
His Englishness even has its own mischievous nostalgia. The air
conditioner may be an American import but the car he keeps
in London is decidedly indigenous: a champagne-hued Jaguar
which he calls 'The Peckham Flyer', a name that reeks of Ealing
comedies.

And, based though he is in New York, Patrick's fiction has
always shown a strong urge for delving into an England, or
London, that's more morbidly and forsakenly behind the times,
lost in fogs and shadows and sinister human miasmas: all of
which Patrick can distil, like no one else, with grotesque relish.
It's as if he needs the brightness of the New World better to
explore, mentally, the Old World murk and pathology. In his
recent book of stories, *Ghost Town: Tales of Manhattan Then and
Now*, there were signs of his wishing to ship out some of the
murk—like that air conditioner but, in every sense, in reverse—
and implant it in his vision of New York. His latest novel,
Trauma, is a New York novel through and through, though its
ultimate domain, echoing earlier work, is the asylum. Perhaps the
truth is, and Patrick is attuned to it, that the New World can
hardly pretend to be new any more and for some time now it has
been acquiring its own accretions of pathology.

But let it be said at once that, despite his penchant for the
dark and spooky and though he was born the son of a Broadmoor
superintendent, there's nothing pathological or murky about
Patrick. He's one of the sanest, most good-natured souls I know.

The interview that follows, which appeared in *Bomb* in 1986, was the beginning of our friendship and was the first, as Patrick put it when introducing the interview in a later *Bomb* anthology, 'of many merry meetings'. (Would a true New Yorker, I wonder, have used that word 'merry'?) The interview occurred, as Patrick scrupulously noted, 'in a cold house off the Fulham Road', with an adjournment to the pub, and was mainly about *Waterland*.

One of the nicest letters I've ever received from a fellow author came from Patrick, from New York, in 1992—just to let me know, as it were, that he'd met the actress Maria Aitken and that they'd simply had to get married. So they'd flown in nuptial haste to San Francisco, got a connecting flight to Reno, bought a marriage licence for $35, then, for another $35, actually got married and finally 'emerged, stunned, but well and truly hitched, into the strong, clear light of a Nevada winter afternoon'.

For a man so keen on America, it was the perfect, breathless American escapade, the perfect stateside fairy tale. But in its principal human components it was a very English marriage, and a very fine one. I've seen Maria and Patrick on this side of the Atlantic and on the other. On either side they make a lovely couple.

An Interview by Patrick McGrath

PM: You make the point in *Waterland* that history moves in circles, or even spirals, our disasters worsening every time round. Have you been accused of fatalism?

GS: Not in any deeply offensive way. I tend to shrug that off anyway, because novels aren't statements, they aren't prophecies or philosophies, they're stories, and there's a great deal more going on in the novel than simply speculation about the fate of the world. I hope that what my novels give readers is an experience, not something from which they can extract messages. I rather shudder at the idea. I ought also to say that I don't actually say those things. You can call this sophistical if you like, but it's my character who says those things, it's Tom Crick who holds those views. And he says many things, he says contradictory things. He's a highly intelligent man but he's in a state of personal crisis and his once-cherished and fairly coherent views of history are being challenged. So he's voicing in the novel different views of history, of progress, the fate of mankind and so on.

PM: Yet Tom Crick carries moral authority in the novel. It is he who speaks, it is he who controls the narrative.

GS: He does exercise a great deal of authority. There is a tendency, I suppose, to take what he says as the last word on things, but against that there's the plight of this man who is heartbroken and reduced and lonely. What becomes of this man? What becomes of Tom Crick? I think he's a very sad and desolate figure, for all his intellectual powers.

PM: Tom Crick's half-brother, Dick, is a fascinating figure. He is inarticulate and retarded, it's implied that he's half machine, that he's half fish, half eel, even half vegetable, a potato-head; and he works with silt, which is another of those half-and-half things, water and land; and it's into the silt that he makes his final dive.

GS: I'm not sure that I know, and if I did I wouldn't say, what happens to him at the end. When he dives into the river, you could interpret that as an act of despair, a return to nothingness and so on, but it's also, I hope, a sort of escape, so there's some sort of feeling of liberation. It would seem I'm interested in inarticulate characters, characters who become silent, inert, vegetable. I think it may have to do with this question of whether knowledge is good or bad: Is it good to know the truth, or is it harmful? Are there situations where it's best not to tell, or not to know? Or not to remember? Dick Crick's a character who among his many 'semi' attributes has an ability not to remember. He lives in an amnesiac world, and while we pity him in some ways, can we be sure that because of this faculty, or non-faculty, he's not better off than we are? Henry, his grandfather, goes off to fight in the trenches and comes back without a memory. There's a great deal of irony in the book about recalling things or not recalling things. History is constantly confronting this basic choice: Why should we summon up the past? Why should we remember anything, whether it's personally or collectively? Does it do us any good? Does it hinder us? I don't attempt to come down on one side or the other, to resolve the issue, but I suppose you could say that Dick is a peculiar embodiment, among many other things, of this paradox.

PM: What is this thing beneath language that Dick has access to?

GS: I'm not sure that I know. It could simply be nature. Dick seems to be much more part of primitive nature and its primitive cycles than any of the other characters in the book, yet after all human nature does stand apart from nature, and I wouldn't want for one moment to share in that romantic view that going back to nature is a good thing. On the other hand, a complete loss of contact with nature—an inability to see that human nature, even if it is a peculiar and separate phenomenon, is part of nature—is I'm quite sure a bad thing.

PM: Nature at its wildest, the old, wild Fens, provides the setting for one of *Waterland*'s most horrific scenes: the abortion that Martha Clay, an alleged witch, performs on Mary Metcalf. It is evil, and results in septicaemia and barrenness for Mary. Yet Martha Clay is as close to nature as Dick Crick.

GS: The reactions I've had to that chapter have been interesting: it's a horrible scene; some people find it almost impossible to read. I've never felt that. I was conscious of wanting to construct a scene that was very sinister and strong, but with a fairy-tale feeling. It incorporates so many almost supernatural things. Even for Mary and Tom, the only way they can see it is as something out of fairy tale, in the gruesome sense of fairy tale. And I suppose there's no sense of there being any positive outcome. Given that Tom and Mary do want to get rid of the child, one could imagine an outcome where the abortion is successful, if any abortion is. But from the beginning you have the sense that everything's going to go wrong. It's a central episode of the book.

PM: Is the nature which Martha Clay, the alleged witch, inhabits, the nature to which Dick Crick is connected in his inarticulacy?

GS: I'd be reluctant to make these schemes, but if Dick somehow has this contact with nature which the other characters don't have, I wouldn't put Martha in the same category. Her realm is superstition rather than nature, and there's a great deal in the novel about superstition and its vices and virtues. Like many other things in the novel, superstition is paradoxical. I tend to have a paradoxical outlook. Superstition, when it creates an event like the abortion scene, is undoubtedly a bad thing. All the potions and the sheer crudeness, the unmedical nature of it all, this has disastrous consequences. But in another sense, in other areas of the novel, superstition, in terms of a need for something extra, is a benign thing. Even telling stories is a kind of superstition, an imposing of extra structure on reality. And it's something very much needed by these people who happen to live in a landscape which almost says to them, look, reality is flat and empty. All you can do in life is make something, and in so far as superstition is creative it's perhaps no bad thing.

PM: How was the idea of *Waterland* born?

GS: I think I started with the scene that opens the book, with a picture in my head of the corpse in the river, the floating corpse, and then certain things started to emerge around that, to do with location, setting, other characters, time. So it began as a kind of detective thing, a classic case of a dead body, a 'whodunnit'. The other crucial moment in the gestation was when, having evolved the narrator figure as the boy who lived in the lockside cottage— one of the people who discover the dead body—I started to feel for some reason that this was back in the Forties, in wartime. But I wanted it to be seen and told from a much later perspective, the 1980s. So the question is, naturally, what became of this boy Tom in later life? Then, when I made him a history teacher, there was a little—not so little—explosion of ideas. I thought of all sorts of possibilities, all sorts of things I could bring in. It was very exciting. I think that's when I said to myself, Well, all right, it's a novel and now I can start it. But we're talking about a process that went on for maybe a year before words got put down on paper.

PM: At what point did you decide to include a natural history of eels?

GS: Well, there's always a large element of serendipity and also— though we're talking quite seriously about this book—an element of fun. One does have fun when one's writing, although the issues at stake may be very grave. The construction of a novel can be enormous fun. I knew about eels. I didn't know as much as that chapter suggests, but I knew a fair bit about eels before I started writing *Waterland*. I'm a fisherman, I like fishing, I know a bit about fish. Eels have always fascinated me. The incredible life cycle they have, the mystery of it! And the extraordinary pseudo-science, through the centuries, of trying to find out how the damn things breed! And I thought, well, this is a wonderful little story in its own right, and wouldn't it be great to have the oppor-tunity to just fling it into the middle of some larger work? And the opportunity arose. I found generally in writing the book that I evolved a sort of form, or non-form, in which I could be totally digressive. I could have chapters in which the subject matter was virtually non-fiction, was no longer narrative, and the eels fitted superbly into that scheme, because after all the Fens are a region which abounds with eels. The eel has always had metaphorical overtones, like the landscape. And it suddenly seemed to me that the life cycle, the natural history of the eel, seemed to say so much about history generally and about our attempts to discover the origins of things, and so on. And all of that was quite apart from its being just an incredibly intriguing and amusing subject.

PM: You mentioned that *Waterland* was much more ambitious than anything you'd attempted before. Were you referring to this integrating of non-narrative, non-fictional material into the story?

GS: Yes, I think that was part of it. I suppose too I rather relished in anticipation a slight perplexity on the part of the reader— where the reader comes to the end of one chapter and then finds a chapter about eels, or beer, or something apparently not connected to the narrative. The reader would think, well, what the hell's going on? I rather delighted in that prospect.

PM: Will you do it again?

GS: I don't know. I think every book dictates mysteriously its own terms. It says to you, well, you can get away with that or you can't. And in any case it's never a good policy to repeat a pattern.

PM: Do you think it's all right for middle-aged men to run off with small female antelopes?*

*A reference to my short story 'Hoffmeier's Antelope'.

GS: Well, they don't.

PM: Uncle Walter did.

GS: It was all right for him. I might be wrong in saying they don't, there might be a case somewhere! I'm very fond of that story, I suppose because of the antelope. It was a fairly early story of mine, a story which wrote itself. One invents a totally unknown, totally specious species. That's just good fun.

PM: There's another story in *Learning to Swim* called 'The Hypochondriac' in which a doctor projects his clinical knowledge onto a young man, unaware that he's also projecting his own denial of pain; and then to his immense surprise the young man dies. There's a failure of medical knowledge, of scientific thought.

GS: It's a concern which is not unrelated to this business of 'Is it better to know or not to know?' It's an illusion that knowledge is always coupled to authority. Knowledge doesn't bring authority and authority doesn't necessarily imply knowledge. The doctor in that story is a good example of someone who feels that they have knowledge, and indeed they do, but of a limited kind. The crisis of the story is really a man's discovery that he has no authority: neither over people nor, as he once thought, over his own experience, over his own life. There's a great deal in the story about how he's dealt with his own marriage in terms of, 'I know what I'm doing, I can deal with this, my knowledge and my clinical cool will hold things together.' But it's blown apart by an incidence of the supernatural, since the patient, who does die, reappears for one moment. Of course, such an event is quite outside the doctor's range of experience. And he breaks down.

PM: It's a lovely, delicate ghost, a Jamesian ghost. It just flickers for a moment.

GS: Not really a haunting at all.

PM: Ghosts appear here and there in the short stories, and there's an important ghost, Sarah Atkinson's, in *Waterland*. Yet the earlier novels manifest no such magical or supernatural elements. Why is this?

GS: They were there inside waiting to get out, and they did in *Waterland*. But it's very hard to talk about the construction of a novel in terms of actual decisions to do this or that. Sarah does become a ghost, she returns in supernatural form, and she dives, as Dick dives; she returns to the water. She began as a solid, flesh-and-blood character who was the young wife of this very solid commercial man, and then I got to the situation where she's knocked unconscious, literally senseless, and remains so.

PM: She hits her head on a writing desk.

GS: Yes, falls and knocks her head against a desk. I see no signif- icance in the writing desk [*laughter*]. She's another inarticulate character and for the remainder of her life she says virtually nothing. It's as though she passes into ghostliness almost in her own lifetime. The people in the town turn her into this curious, angelic, saintly figure who's invested with strange powers, or so they believe. Then when she dies, almost inevitably you know she's going to come back, she's going to continue to have an influ- ence. But I don't think there was ever a moment when, before writing, I said, well, this is what the character is going to do. You just see possibilities. Some of them you pursue, and you fall flat on your face. Sometimes the pursuit's fruitful.

PM: Two of the observers of Dick Crick's plunge into the silt are American servicemen. It's sunset. Overhead, bombers are flying off to their targets. Is this an implication of Americans in some final apocalyptic moment, in some sort of global plunge?

GS: No, I haven't seen it that way, but I don't see why you shouldn't. I thought you were going to say, can you see the presence of the Americans just as some indication of a New World—Americans from the New World who've come into this old and in some ways inbred and failing English world. There was possibly an element of that. And I don't suppose I chose entirely by accident the state where those Americans come from: Arizona, the dry zone; and there they are in the wet Fens. One mustn't forget too that historically it's quite accurate; there were many American servicemen based in East Anglia at that time.

PM: Do you really see Dick Crick as an individual?

GS: Very much so, very much the character fiddling with his motorbike. I don't see him as a sort of cipher, symbol, representation—he's certainly very much there. Some of the little things he keeps in his bedside cupboard . . .

PM: A bird's nest?

GS: Oh, he has little bits of animals' skulls, and a pathetic sort of thing he made out of a tin for his mother on one of her birthdays.

PM: There's a fish hanging over the bed.

GS: A stuffed pike, which is quite important in the story. I like the concrete. Novels should be this mixture of the intensely concrete and the world of ideas.

PM: Many stories are told in *Waterland*, and one of the funniest is the story of Jack Parr's suicide attempt. Jack is a railway signalman, and decides to end it all by sitting on the railway lines. So he sits there doggedly all night, while unbeknownst to him his wife is up in the signal box, throwing switches and making telephone calls, and lights are blinking all over the eastern Fens as expresses and goods trains are rerouted to avoid the unhappy man.

GS: He's fallen asleep by this time, and he never learns about the subterfuge. And is actually convinced when he wakes up that he's been saved by a miracle. And nobody breaks this illusion.

PM: He goes on the wagon and stays on it. Many events in *Waterland* are seen to have two explanations, often one logical, the other superstitious. A live fish dropped into a woman's lap will make her barren, it's said; and this is precisely what does happen to Mary.

GS: Yes, you can imagine some of the old people in the Fens maintaining staunchly that the reason for all the trouble was the eel, the fish in the lap. There's a parallel in some ways between superstition and the way fiction works, the way fiction can produce these rather magical moments, which aren't entirely impossible, aren't entirely beyond belief. I think it's important for fiction to be magical, just as it's important for fiction to embrace the real world, to look really hard at the real world.

PM: Real world?

GS: Whatever the real world is.

PM: Now, this feeling for magic is quite new to the English novel.

GS: Yes, that's true, it's not at all a recognizable English tradition. The phrase everybody comes up with is 'magical realism', which I think has now become a little tired. But on the other hand there's no doubt that English writers of my generation have been influenced by writers from outside who in one way or another have got this magical, surreal quality, such as Borges, Márquez, Grass, and that's been stimulating and generally a good thing. We can be terribly self-absorbed and isolated, culturally, in this country. It's about time we began to absorb things from outside.

PM: What about France?

GS: I think there's always been a cultural antagonism between us and the French, but I think also that the French may have held the view, and justifiably so, that English fiction of the immediate post-war period, up to the Sixties and early Seventies, was terribly bound up by its own Englishness, that it just didn't travel. But they're more interested now in English writers than they used to be.

PM: Have they warmed to *Waterland*?

GS: Quite. I was asked to go over there. It was entered for some prize they have for novels in translation. It was shortlisted but it didn't win.

PM: Who amongst your contemporaries do you particularly enjoy?

GS: Well, I actually like very much a writer who's originally American, Russell Hoban, who wrote *Riddley Walker*. He seems to me to be completely his own man as a writer; I think he's got a real touch of genius. Then there's a writer who's originally Japanese, Kazuo Ishiguro, and he's about to publish a second novel. His first was called *A Pale View of Hills* and it's simply amazing. He's a remarkable writer in an understated, very quiet, unextrovert way. There's Timothy Mo, who's also about to publish a new book. His second novel was called *Sour Sweet*, which is a lovely book about the Chinese community in London. Some of these writers I know quite well as friends. One of the pleasures of having written a successful book is that you do get more opportunity to meet other writers. For a long time, really till *Waterland*, I knew virtually no other writers. Not that it changed anything fundamentally, and in some ways you can argue that knowing other writers is a disruption, a distraction. You can become more concerned about how other people write, which isn't necessarily good for your own work. I think in the end writing is a lonesome business. You have to go away by yourself to do it, whether you've got hundreds of friends or not. Nothing will ever change that.

PM: Would you like a glass of beer?

GS: Yes, please.

Beer bottle label—for the film of *Waterland*.

BUYING A GUITAR WITH ISH

NAGASAKI, 1954–60

Kazuo Ishiguro—Ish—was among the first novelists of my generation I met, though I forget exactly when. We'd certainly bumped into each other by the time we were both included among the 'Twenty Best Young British Novelists' in 1982 and group-photographed, all of us looking ill at ease, in a Chelsea loft by Lord Snowdon for the *Sunday Times*. The following interview with him—again for *Bomb* magazine—was made in 1989 after Ish had published *The Remains of the Day*. The work in prospect he tentatively refers to evolved into *The Unconsoled*, published in 1995.

We've been friends now for over twenty-five years and he's my only Japanese friend. That last statement needs immediate qualification, since I don't really think of him as Japanese and I don't think that, most of the time, Ish thinks of himself as Japanese either. The facts are that he was born in Japan in 1954, was brought to this country when he was five and grew up to be one of several novelists emerging in the 1980s who effectively challenged, by having their actual origin or their familial or cultural roots outside Britain, the meaning of 'British' or 'English' fiction.

Ish is in many ways as English as they come. Since I've known him, he's lived in such oriental locations as Goldhawk Road and Sydenham (very near, as it happens, to where my father and mother grew up). The facts of his birth and his earliest years must of course go very deep, and Ish's first two novels were set in Japan, but then his next novel, *The Remains of the Day*, went to the very quick of Englishness—or to its fossilized, emblematic shell—in the form of the fastidiously spoken, emotionally hampered butler, Stevens.

All of this has caused some confusion which I think Ish partly relishes, partly finds tiresome. There are those who were persuaded that he had latched on to some fundamental affinity between the English and Japanese temperament—both nations with a leaning towards reserve and formality (both nations also with imperial ghosts). Ish himself, while being one of the most easy-going of people, has a habit of not giving too much away, of being a little hard to 'read'. Given his origins and the quietness of his literary style, this has sometimes led by clichéd association to his being deemed 'inscrutable'.

I think Ish enjoys playing up to this notional enigmaticness. There's a mischievous gravity about him, or a grave mischief, which can be delightfully teasing. I think he even plays up sometimes to his Japaneseness. He once told me—mischievously but perhaps a little disingenuously—that he'd set his first two novels in Japan, not because his own knowledge of the country was so deep, but because for most British readers it was unfamiliar and remote enough to become a 'pure' zone, immune to close scrutiny, where his fictional purposes could work themselves out untroubled by issues of authenticity. It was like setting a novel in a made-up country.

But Ish's Japaneseness can't always be a matter for playful irony, and I suspect that one of the chief burdens of his life has in fact been in confronting the marked contrasts between England and

Japan, rather than in grasping the similarities. When he now visits Japan—there was a long gap before he ever went back—he does so as a celebrated author, but there can be moments when he finds himself, just as an individual, 'unmasked'. He looks Japanese, after all, and knows enough vestigial Japanese to order a meal in the language, but as soon as the waiter makes some off-the-menu remark, Ish becomes lost, a man apparently bewildered by his own country. And such moments of incidental confusion must surely reawaken the much deeper confusions of being a boy of, say, six or seven in England, when his first five years were spent in Japan. He once told me how he'd been horrified by the image he kept seeing of a tortured, bleeding man on a cross. This was how the English saw their god.

Ish's actual early memories of Japan must indeed be precious. It would be natural to guard them in a lasting habit of reticence. One such memory that he shared with me I've always found particularly affecting. He said he could remember lying in bed as a child in Nagasaki and hearing his father in another room, at the piano, 'practising the same phrase over and over again'. What strikes a chord, almost literally, about this memory is that there's nothing specifically Japanese about it. It might be a memory of England, or anywhere. Though for me what strikes the foreign note—and touches a rather jealous nerve—is that it's a memory of coming from a musical home.

It's perhaps not much known that Ish has a musical side. I was only dimly aware of it, if at all, when I made this interview with him, though I'd known him by then for several years—a good example of how he doesn't give much away. Ish plays the piano and the guitar, both well. I'm not sure how many different guitars he now actually possesses, but I wouldn't be surprised if it's in double figures. His wife, Lorna, sings and plays; so does his daughter. Evenings of musical entertainment in the Ishiguro household can't be at all uncommon.

One of the few regrets of my life is that I have no formal grounding in music. I never had a musical education or came from the sort of 'musical home' that would have made this possible or probable, though I was born at a time when an upright piano was still a common piece of living-room furniture. I need to be a little careful about what I'm saying. I never came from a 'writerly' home either: I didn't feel that was a barrier, and if I'd got involved in music at an early age, might it only have thwarted my stirrings as a writer? Or just left me with bad memories of piano lessons?

The fact is, I grew up very appreciative of music, but with no ability to make it, no knowledge of it from the inside, and always rather readily assuming that music was what those other, 'musical' people did. I've never felt, on the other hand, though a great many people who've grown up and read books have perhaps felt it, that writing is what those other, 'writerly' people do.

This dichotomy is strange, since increasingly I feel that a lot of my instincts and intuitions about writing are in fact musical, and I don't think that writing and music are fundamentally so far apart. The basic elements of narrative—timing, pacing, flow, recapitulation, tension and release—are musical ones too. And where would writing be without rhythm, the large rhythms that shape a story, or the small ones that shape a paragraph? I increasingly feel too that writing isn't about words in themselves, but about getting words to register and vibrate to things that might lie beyond them or just at their edge. Thus the spaces between and around words can have their unspoken resonances. And what else is music but a communication without words, in which the silences count as much as the notes?

As for that memory of Ish's, of the piano phrase being repeated over and over again, that will surely chime with any writer who's ever doggedly worked and worked over the same passage—trying, indeed, to get the phrasing right.

But that shared memory of Ish's also had its practical, stimulating effect. It's not quite true that I've had no dealings with music from the inside. When I was a student I bought a cracked Spanish guitar from a friend for five pounds and subsequently, with the aid of a guitar book but in a very on-and-off way, tried to teach myself classical guitar (not the easiest of instrumental choices, as I discovered). Sadly, I finally reached a point which seemed only to prove my ingrained belief that music-making was for those other, musical people. Like many lost causes, the guitar went up into the attic to gather dust.

Decades later, Ish's recollection about his piano-playing father made me get it down again. There were other factors, I'm sure. I was going through a bad patch with writing, I needed a diversion. But Ish's memory was a definite trigger. And, of course, I fully knew by now that Ish *was* one of those other, musical people. In awe of this fact, I didn't tell him for a long time about my cracked but reactivated guitar.

I'd been surprised, this time, by how my attitudes to learning, or to teaching myself, had changed, by how I persisted and even passed significantly beyond my previous point of abandonment. I'm not speaking of anything amazing, but there came a time when even I could recognize that the inadequate sounds I was producing were not just the result of my lack of expertise, but because I was trying to play on this old, cracked instrument.

I needed a decent guitar. The snag was that, such was my musical inferiority complex, I was terrified of having to go into a guitar shop and try out what they had, thus exposing my complete and lifelong lack of any real musicianship.

Ish came to the rescue. One of the best days I've had with a writer friend—though one of those delightful days when you value a writer friend for something that has nothing to do with writing—was when I met Ish one morning in Denmark Street, off Charing Cross Road, to shop for a guitar. I needed his trained ear, but I also needed his fingers: a direct and specific case of the author's personal touch. I was quite prepared not to find what I wanted (whatever that was exactly), though I was anxiously aware that I could hardly impose on Ish a second time to go so far out of his way for me.

But all went well. Denmark Street, with it several outlets, didn't come good, but in the basement of a shop in Rathbone Street, off Oxford Street, I found what I was looking for. 'Looking', of course, isn't the point with guitars, any more than a cover is a good guide to a book, but it did look very beautiful and I had Ish to demonstrate that it sounded very beautiful too. Only a few purchases in life seem to have been waiting expressly for you to buy them, but I knew, even before I nodded to Ish's nod, that I was looking at and hearing what had to be mine.

It was made by Amalio Burguet in Valencia and now it lives in my house. I know my ability with it is still elementary and that I shall never extract from it what it's truly capable of, but it goes with me, I go with it, we have our moments together, it's a friend. And it came by way of a friend.

While they put new strings on it in the shop and found a case for it, Ish and I went round the corner for a cup of tea and celebratory cake. This should have been the time to forget for a while the day's purpose and to ask after what was happening in Ish's life, but I confess I couldn't stop thinking about my new possession. A little later, my guitar and I travelled home together in a taxi, like some just-met couple, all the way from Oxford Street.

Though it was a present to myself, I put it on a par with just a few other, special presents, including the fishing rod my father gave me one Christmas when I was a boy. My father never played the piano—it would have been as likely as his speaking Japanese—though nor, in fact, did he fish. Fishing has its links and parallels with writing and in the mid 1980s I co-edited a whole book, *The Magic Wheel*, on the subject, but the links and parallels with music go deeper, to the very heart of why you have the unaccountable urge to make things up at all. Even a fumbling acquaintance with playing a musical instrument tells you quite a lot about the mysterious process of discovering what you have inside.

But there's also a simple matter of antithesis. Writers sometimes need to get away from writing, but since it's a thing in your head, this can be very hard to do. The trick, I think, is not to try to switch off or to empty the mind, but to do something else so engrossingly concentrating that all other thoughts, including those of writing, are suddenly gone. Fishing can certainly do this, but you can't fish in the next room.

In my very modest way I share a recourse that Ish has too. I have no delusions of performance-level mastery, but now and then, just now and then, I can make that sweet, clear, richly nuanced sound that only a guitar can make. I can make a kind of music. At the very least, after a hard or a bad day's writing, it can be a good and refreshing thing to go into that other room and, with the best and most devoted of intentions, murder Bach.

An Interview with Kazuo Ishiguro

GS: You were born in Japan and came to England when you were five . . . How Japanese would you say you are?

KI: I'm not entirely like English people because I've been brought up by Japanese parents in a Japanese-speaking home. My parents didn't realize we were going to stay in this country for so long; they felt responsible for keeping me in touch with Japanese values. I do have a distinct background. I think differently, my perspectives are slightly different.

GS: Would you say that the rest of you is English? Do you feel particularly English?

KI: People are not two-thirds one thing and the remainder something else. Temperament, personality or outlook don't divide quite like that. The bits don't separate clearly. You end up a funny homogeneous mixture. This is something that will become more common in the latter part of the century—people with mixed cultural backgrounds and mixed racial backgrounds. That's the way the world is going.

GS: You are one of a number of English writers, your contemporaries, who are precisely that: they were born outside England. Do you identify with them? I'm thinking of people like Timothy Mo, Salman Rushdie, Ben Okri . . .

KI: There is a big difference between someone in my position and someone who has come from one of the countries that belonged to the British Empire. There is a very special and very potent relationship between someone brought up in India, with a very powerful notion of Britain as the mother country and the source of modernity and culture and education.

GS: The experience of empire from the other end. Yet it's true that in two of your novels, which you could loosely call Japanese novels, *A Pale View of Hills* and *An Artist of the Floating World*, you have dealt with the ruins of empire, Japanese empire. These are post-war novels. Your latest novel, *The Remains of the Day*, is set in the Fifties, in post-war England. It seems to be as concerned as *An Artist of the Floating World* with mistaken allegiances and ideals of an imperial period: pre-war Britain in the Thirties, Japan in the Thirties. There is a similarity there.

KI: I chose the settings for a particular reason: they are potent for my themes. I tend to be attracted to pre-war and post-war settings because I'm interested in this business of values and ideals being tested, and people having to face up to the notion that their ideals weren't quite what they thought they were before the test came. In all three books the Second World War is present.

GS: *The Remains of the Day* has for its central character a butler. One tends to think of butlers in literary association with detective novels or comedy, stage farces, but your butler is a very serious figure indeed. How did you alight on his character?

KI: The butler is a very good metaphor for the relationship of very ordinary, small people to power. Most of us aren't given governments to run or coups d'état to lead. We have to offer up the little services we have perfected to various people: to causes, to employers, to organizations, and hope for the best—that we approve of the way it gets used. This is a condition that I want to write about. It struck me that the figure of the butler, the man who serves, someone who is so close and yet so very far from the hub of power, would be a useful person to write through. And there's the other reason that you've hinted at . . . It's precisely because the butler has become such a mythical figure in British culture. I've always found that bizarre and amusing. This has got something to do with the fact that I come from a Japanese background. There are certain things that are very exotic to me about Englishness.

GS: Although you could say that the butler is a figure who leads, by necessity, a very stylized existence. Dignity is enormously important to this character. There is a resemblance with Japan—that feeling of dignity, service, life as a kind of performance. There is a strong echo of *An Artist of the Floating World*. The central character of that novel, Masuji Ono, is also concerned with dignity. Yet Stevens is a much less self-knowing and more pathetic character. He seems to have this terrible blindness about his own experience. The only thing which redeems him is the enormous importance he attaches to dignity. Do you think of dignity as a virtue?

KI: I'm not quite sure what dignity is, you see. This is a part of the debate in *The Remains of the Day*. Stevens is obsessed with this thing that he calls dignity. He thinks dignity has to do with not showing your feelings, in fact he thinks dignity has to do with not having feelings.

GS: It's to do with the suppression of feelings.

KI: Yes, being something less than human. He somehow thinks that turning yourself into some animal that will carry out the duties you've been given to such an extent that you don't have feelings, or anything that undermines your professional self, is dignity. People are prone to equate having feelings with weakness. The book debates that notion of dignity—not having emotions—against another concept of dignity. The dignity given to human beings when they have a certain amount of control over their lives. The dignity that democracy gives to ordinary people. In the end, no one can argue that Stevens has been very dignified in one sense: he starts to question whether there isn't something profoundly undignified about a condition he has rather unthinkingly given all his loyalty to. A cause in which he has no control over the moral value of how his talents are spent.

GS: And that cause proves to be, however honourably it began, a mistaken one.

KI: Yes.

GS: There is of course a whole other area, even more extreme and even more poignant. Stevens seems to have suppressed completely the possibility he once had of a love affair with the former housekeeper, Miss Kenton. He is now taking a rare holiday, to visit her. He hasn't seen her for a long time. He's going back to this crucial moment in the past. Yet nothing he says actually constitutes an admission of his feelings over the matter. The novel succeeds in a very difficult area. That's to say, you have a character who is articulate and intelligent to a degree, and yet he doesn't seem to have any power of self-analysis or self-recognition. That's very hard to get away with. Did you find it difficult to do?

KI: He ends up saying the sorts of things he does because somewhere deep down he knows which things he has to avoid. He is intelligent enough, in the true sense of the word, to perceive the danger areas, and this controls how his narrative goes. The book is written in the language of self-deception. Why he says certain things, why he brings up certain topics at certain moments, is not random. It's controlled by the things that he doesn't say. That's what motivates the narrative. He is in this painful condition where at some level he does know what's happening, but he hasn't quite brought it to the front. And he has a certain amount of skill in trying to persuade himself that it's not there. He's articulate and intelligent enough to do quite a good self-deception job.

GS: You talk about the language of self-deception. That is a language that is developed with all your main narrator figures. It particularly revolves around the fallibility of memory. Your characters seem to forget and remember at their own convenience, or they remember things in the wrong context, or they remember one event elided with another. What is involved is a process of conscious or unconscious evasion. How knowing would you say this is?

KI: Knowing on their part?

GS: Yes.

KI: At some level they have to know what they have to avoid and that determines the routes they take through memory, and through the past. There's no coincidence that they're usually worrying over the past. They're worrying because they sense there isn't something quite right there. But of course memory is this terribly treacherous terrain, the very ambiguities of memory go to feed self-deception. And so, quite often, we have situations where the licence of the person to keep inventing versions of what happened in the past is rapidly beginning to run out. The results of one's life, the accountability of one's life, is beginning to catch up.

GS: After Stevens has visited Miss Kenton, the former house-keeper, he goes to sit by the sea and cries. This is a kind of facing up to himself, a kind of coming clean, but perhaps also a moment of another kind of dignity. There is a dignity that goes with the recognition of loss and failure. A dignity way beyond Stevens's scheme of things, and yet he acquires it.

KI: Yes.

GS: Painfully.

KI: It's the dignity of being human, of being honest. I suppose, with Stevens and with the painter, Ono, in the last book, that would be the appeal I would make on their behalf. Yes, they're often pompous and despicable. They have contributed to rather ugly causes. If there is any plea on their behalf, it is that they have some sense of dignity as human beings, that ultimately there is something heroic about coming to terms with very painful truths about yourself.

GS: You seem to have quite a complicated view of dignity. There is a kind of dignity in the process of writing itself. One could say that your own style has dignity. I wonder how much you think that for the artist or the writer there is a perennial problem, which is not unlike Stevens's. There is an inherent dignity, grace in art itself, yet when it becomes involved in big affairs, politics and so on, this can be both an extension of the sphere of art and very ensnaring. Ono, in *An Artist of the Floating World*, has been an artist in a very pure sense. The 'floating world' is all about beauty and transience, pure art. It's when he puts his talent in the service of politics that everything goes wrong in his life. Was he wrong to have done that? Is it bad for art to be put in the service of politics? Is it right that art should concern itself with social and political things?

KI: It's right that artists always have to ask themselves these questions, all the time. Writers and artists in general occupy a very particular and crucial role in society. The question isn't, 'Should they or should they not?' It's always, 'To what extent?' What is appropriate in any given context? I think this changes with time, depending on what country you're in, or which sector of society you occupy. It's a question that artists and writers have to ask every day of their lives.

Obviously, it isn't good enough to just ponder and sit on the fence for ever. There has to come a point when you say, 'No matter the imperfections of a particular case, it has to be supported because the alternatives are disastrous.' The difficulty is judging when. There is something about the act of writing novels in particular which makes it appropriate to actually defer the moment of commitment to quite a late point. The nature of what a novel is means that it's very unequipped for front-line campaigning. If you take issue with certain legislation that's being debated, you're better off writing letters to the press, writing articles in the media . . . The strength of the novel is that it gets read at a deeper level; it gets read over a long stretch of time by generations with a future. There is something about the form of a novel that makes it appropriate to political debate at a more fundamental, deeper, more universal level. I've been involved in certain campaigns about homelessness but I've never brought any of that into my novel-writing.

GS: Are you writing another novel?

KI: I'm trying to get going. I've got books out of the library. It takes me a long, long time to start writing the actual drafts. The actual writing of the words I can do in under a year, but the background work takes a long time. Getting myself familiar with the territory I'm going to enter. I have to more or less know what my themes are, what the emphasis will be in the book, I have to know about my characters . . .

GS: Do you find that in practice you actually adhere to your plan?

KI: Yes. More and more. Less so for my first novel. One of the lessons I tried to teach myself between my first and second novel was thematic discipline. However attractive a certain plot development or idea may be that you stumble across in the process of writing, if it's not going to serve the overall architecture, you must leave it and keep pursuing what you wish to pursue. I had the experience in my first novel of having certain things upstage the subjects I really wanted to explore. But now I'm beginning to crave the brilliant messiness that certain writers can achieve through, I suspect, not sticking to their map.

GS: From following their noses.

KI: I have these two god-like figures in my reading experience: Chekhov and Dostoevsky. So far, in my writing career, I've aspired more to the Chekhov: the spare and the precise, the carefully controlled tone. But I do sometimes envy the utter mess, the chaos of Dostoevsky. He does reach some things that you can't reach in any other way than by doing that.

GS: You can't reach it by a plan.

KI: Yes, there is something in that messiness itself that has great value. Life is messy. I sometimes wonder, should books be so neat, well formed? Is it praise to say that a book is beautifully structured? Is it a criticism to say that bits of a book don't hang together?

GS: I think it's a matter of how it stays or doesn't stay with the reader.

KI: I feel like a change. There's another side of my writing self that I need to explore: the messy, chaotic, undisciplined side. The undignified side.

Tea with Ish, 1990.

IN THE BAMBOO CLUB
WITH CAZ

TORONTO, 1986

That 'next room' where writers go to get away from writing can take many forms. I once met a Spanish author who said that his perfect writing circumstances would be these: a remote, idyllic desert island, on which there would be a single, peaceful house. In the house would be a room, with a desk, in which absolute, monastic calm would reign. But in this room would be a door, and it would lead to a nightclub.

Not all writers have such domestic dreams, but maybe most writers have the experience of discovering places—hideaway places, loud or quiet, bright or dim—where they've felt suddenly, temporarily at home, while in another sense gratefully absent from home: places they'd never have found, perhaps, if they weren't writers (and they're not always sure how they did find them), but once they're there the whole point, really, is that they don't have to be writers for a while.

Toronto may seem an unlikely setting for such a happy bolt-hole and, sadly, the last time I found myself there I discovered that the Bamboo Club no longer existed. Even the site of its former entrance, among the clutter of frontages on Queen Street West, was hard to discern, though it's true that the Bamboo had never given itself away. It was one of those Alice-in-Wonderland places you had to burrow into from the street. Once you were in, it opened up on you even as it gathered you in a surprise embrace. But, so I was told, it was gone, and since it was gone, I was rather glad there was no sign of its ever having been there. It preserved its mirage-like, iconic status.

I first met Caryl Phillips—Caz—in Toronto in October 1986 when we were both guests of the Harbourfront International Festival of Authors; but it would be fairer to say we met in the Bamboo Club. We certainly tracked it down. I actually first saw Caz when his head, under a baseball cap, poked gingerly round the door of the room in the Harbourfront Hilton reserved as the Festival's hospitality suite. The atmosphere when a lot of writers are packed into one room can be charged, and it sometimes became known as the Hostility Suite. Caz must have rapidly picked up on the latent tension, because his head quickly ducked back behind the door and it seemed some time before he steeled himself to try entering again.

Things were altogether more congenial in the Bamboo Club—on relatively shabby Queen Street West, in downtown Toronto, away from the showy aura of the Hilton and the new complex of buildings on the Harbourfront strip along the lake shore. So, throughout our visit, we stayed in the Bamboo quite a lot. This was no reflection on the Harbourfront Festival, which in those days was a well-organized, prestigious event which genuinely gave its invited authors the star treatment—I've never encountered a better literary festival, in fact. But it says something for the Bamboo Club. The writers at the Festival were required to give one solo reading and to take part in one or two other panel events. While there was no hard rule about attending events in which you weren't directly involved, there was a sort of understanding that it would be good to be around. Caz and I were among the more conspicuous truants.

The Bamboo Club, if you took it apart, was nothing special:

the bottleneck entrance, a long wooden bar, some tables, a dance space, a small stage for musicians, several tropically themed decorative touches which never quite toppled over into kitsch. It clearly aimed to create the mood, in the middle of often dour, often very cold Toronto, of some exotic and vibrant oasis—an aim that might have fallen on its face. But put it all together and it worked. You were in Ontario, but you were in that nationless place of magic refuge that could be anywhere in the world.

The guest musicians that week were from Ghana: Pat Thomas and his Native Rhythm Band. I can hear them now.

Ten years later, in 1996, I was in Toronto again for a book publication, to be celebrated, naturally—there was now an established link—at the Bamboo Club. But my publishers had kept back a surprise. At the bar when we walked in was Caz. He'd flown up specially from the States where he was now living. 'Couldn't miss the occasion,' he said, taking a nonchalant sip of his beer. He looked as if he'd been sitting there for the whole ten years.

In those ten years, and since, I've probably—no, definitely— had more beers with Caz than with any other writer-friend, and the Bamboo Club, transporting its spirit, has transmuted itself into numerous other haunts in many parts of the world. The territorial analysis of our friendship is interesting. I'm a more or less rooted Englishman and Londoner. Caz is a medley of influences. Born in the Caribbean, he was brought up in England and is a British citizen by way of St Kitts (as part of the Commonwealth), Yorkshire, Oxford and Shepherd's Bush. Anyone first encountering Caz on their travels will detect a puzzling, hard-to-place accent in his voice. I found it oddly hard to identify in Toronto. It's the accent of Leeds.

Caz now lives mainly in New York, but it might be better to

say New York is his base. When he shows up in London, every few months or so, you never quite know where he'll have been beforehand. He's the most peripatetic writer I've met, and, though I'm not nearly as ready or as frequent a traveller as he is, I may well have spent more time with Caz outside of Britain than in it. I haven't exactly totted it up, and the memories have a characteristic haze: Toronto, of course; New York and various other American cities; Scandinavia, the Low Countries (arguably, when with Caz, the High Countries); Amsterdam, Stockholm, Cologne, New Delhi, Singapore . . . But this is nothing to the ground Caz himself has covered.

Of the writers I know Caz has, in his mindset and his very way of life, the most openly, if always sceptically, global view. He's not Anglocentric, Eurocentric, America-centric or Caribbean-centric. Uprootedness, the disjunction of cultures and histories, is perhaps his abiding theme, but not merely as it might stem from the facts of his birth and the colour of his skin. Uprooted himself, he handles, adumbrates the condition of having no fixed abode, no single country, with style and poise. In his work he explores it with great insight and compassion. I know, or I can guess, that he's suffered from his uprootedness more than he's ever likely to say, and there's a way in which his self-made success and independence as a writer may have added their own twists and pressures to that uprootedness. But his writing, if it can be uncompromising, tough or sad, is without any underlying tone of bitterness, just as bitterness is absent from his personal repertoire. I know of no other writer who is so serious in his work while at the same time, in life, having such a serious sense of fun.

The interview that follows—published by *Bomb* in New York, but based on a public interview with Caz at the ICA in London in 1991—brings up in my final question this mixture of private fun and authorial seriousness, even pessimism. To some, such a mixture may seem not so much a mixture as an irreconcilable discrepancy, as if writers who take a hard look at the human condition shouldn't be allowed to have fun, as if a pessimist should be barred from enjoying life.

Caz and I are not of that puritanical school. Near the end of the interview I rather unfairly pin the label 'pessimist' on him, aware of its being sometimes pinned on me, and I share Caz's reaction of surprise to it. Elsewhere in these pages I say that all fiction, in its fundamental creativity, is affirmative—at most a celebration, at least a glow in the dark. This doesn't mean it should be a constant romp, or shrink from hard truths. And one effect of acknowledging those hard truths, along with respect for human resilience (Caz's answer is a good one) and the possibility of compassion, is that weight and warmth are added to the real joys of being alive. Anyone who looks thinkingly around for a while at the world and at human history will be a pessimist, but this isn't, as we all know, the end of pleasure and cheer. Even my namesake Jonathan Swift, whose work sometimes verges on the misanthropic, could make the distinction that he hated 'that animal called man, although I heartily love John, Thomas, Peter and so forth'.

And there remains the commonplace fact that writers, like anyone else, after their sessions of cooped-up toil, like to go out and have fun. With Caz the fun has often reached a high, anarchic, surreal pitch hard to recount and perhaps best not recounted. I think, for example, of another incongruously, exotically named club—the Kilimanjaro Club in, of all places, Washington DC. But this was only where we ended up late one night after a very long couple of days. We'd met, two days before, in Boston, when we were each on separate legs of US book tours.

I was near the end, Caz was halfway through, but we'd both clearly reached that point, not difficult to reach on US book tours, of having had enough. We then had to fly on to Washington where we had separate schedules the next day, but were due to read together in the evening at a well-known bookstore, best left unnamed. We decided to ignore our schedules, but we did make it to the bookstore.

For the audience and bookstore staff it proved to be a memorable evening of which Caz and I have very little distinct memory at all. Some years after the event I had a letter from the States from Caz saying that he'd revisited, with some caution, the bookstore in question and they not only still vividly recalled the event, but they *still had the glasses*. That is, the glasses we'd apparently been holding in our hands when we entered the bookstore and which belonged to the (again nameless) Washington hotel in whose bar we'd spent most of the day.

Further details are irretrievable, including how we got to (or left) the Kilimanjaro Club. But those two glasses had been preserved, it seems, in situ, as crystalline evidence of the grosser effects of a US tour. When I found myself in Washington again more recently, reading not at a bookstore but at the Press Club on 14th Street—and this would now be well over a decade since the original episode—one of the organizers gave me a strange look. She explained that she'd been there, '*that* evening', working at that bookstore all those years ago. 'You can't have forgotten,' she said. Well, yes and no.

I don't need that Spanish writer's special amenity—the quiet room with its door opening onto a nightclub. I don't think even Caz does. There are other ways, after all, of getting away from writing than nightclubs. Then again, there are plenty of sad, admonitory tales of writers who've made increasing use of the nightclub to the point where they can no longer get back to their desks. But I do need, as I think most writers need, to set alongside the seriousness of writing a place—or some ever relocatable territory—of forgetful fun. It shouldn't be a place (God forbid) where writers ordinarily convene, but it will be a place where one's happy to have the company of a like-minded (or like-mindless) writer or two.

Caz for a long time now has been such a companion, and the place, wherever it's to be found and though its archetype is no more, is called the Bamboo Club.

Bamboo Club flier, October 1986.

An Interview with Caryl Phillips

[The occasion of the original interview, before an audience in London in 1991, was the publication of Caz's fourth novel, *Cambridge*.]

GS: Caryl Phillips—Caz, as I've come to know him—was born in St Kitts in the Leeward Islands in 1958. He came to England when still a babe in arms and was brought up and educated here. He's since travelled extensively and made his temporary home in many parts of the world, including his native St Kitts. Nomadic himself, it could be said that one of the main themes of his work is that of the journey—or of human displacement in a variety of forms. The journey behind his first novel, *The Final Passage* (1985), was the one Caz himself took part in, albeit unwittingly—the immigration of the post-war years from the Caribbean to England. The journey that lies behind both Caz's last novel, *Higher Ground* (1989), and his new novel, *Cambridge*, is a more historic, primal and terrible journey; the journey of the slave trade westwards from Africa.

In *Higher Ground,* a novel in three parts, we travel from Africa in the slave-trade days to North America at the time of the Black Power movement, and finish in a Europe still nursing its wounds from the last war. In *Cambridge* Caz has reversed the general direction to bring a European consciousness face to face with Europe's global perpetrations. He does this through the person of Emily, an Englishwoman of the early nineteenth century, who escapes an arranged marriage by travelling to her father's estate in the West Indies (her father being an absentee landlord). There she is exposed to and indeed exposed by the effects of slavery and colonialism.

Cambridge is also in three parts, the first and longest of which is Emily's own account of her journey and her observations when she arrives. From what seems at first to be an inquisitive, self-consoling travelogue there emerges a drama revolving around a handful of characters including Emily herself; Brown, an Englishman whom we understand has somehow ousted the previous manager of the estate; and the Cambridge of the title, a negro slave who's suffered the singular but equivocal fate of having lived in England and having been converted to Christianity.

The second part of the book is Cambridge's own account of how he came to be Anglicized and Christianized. The third, written in the form of a report (which we guess to be far from reliable), describes how Cambridge comes to be executed for the murder of Brown.

A final brief epilogue tells us the effect of all this on Emily. These last few pages, coming at the end of a novel of enormous accumulative power, are particularly astonishing. Written in a prose of tense intimacy, they show how facile it would be to assess either Caz's heroine or his work as a whole by any simple cultural or racial analysis. Caz is interested in human beings. Emily's plight at the end of the novel plainly has its cultural or racial dimension, but it's essentially one of personal trauma—psychological, sexual, moral and (a word Caz will no doubt love) existential.

GS: How did *Cambridge* arise? What was the germ, the idea behind it?

CP: You know that period when you've finished a book and you don't know what to do? We generally have lunch during these periods in that place around the corner from the British Library, as one of us is pretending to be 'working' in there. Well, true to form, I was doing little more than scrambling around in the British Library, having just finished *Higher Ground*, and having a month and a half on my hands before I was due to go down to St Kitts. It was during this period that I happened upon some journals in the North Library. One in particular caught my eye. It was entitled 'Journal of a Lady of Quality' and written by a Scotswoman, named Janet Schaw, who at the beginning of the nineteenth century travelled from Edinburgh to the Caribbean. What attracted me to this story was the fact that she visited St Kitts. Right beside what was once my brother's place, up in the mountains in St Kitts, is a broken-down great house. Janet Schaw described going to dinner there when it was the centrepiece of one of the grandest plantations in the eastern Caribbean. I began to realize then that there was a whole literature of personal narratives written primarily by women who'd travelled to the Caribbean in that weird phase of English history between the Abolition of the Slave Trade Act in 1807 and the emancipation of the slaves in 1834. Individuals who inherited these Caribbean estates from their families were curious to find out what this property was, what it would entail to maintain it, whether they would get any money. The subject matter began to speak, but that's never enough, for there's another and formidable hurdle to leap; that of encouraging a character to speak to you. At the back of '88 when we used to meet, I was concerned with the subject matter and research, but as yet no character had begun to speak.

GS: And how did the character of Cambridge evolve?

CP: Actually, he came second. Emily, the woman's voice, came first, partly because for the last ten years I'd been looking for a way of writing the story of a Yorkshirewoman. I'd grown up in Yorkshire and I'd also read and reread *Wuthering Heights*, so I had this name in my head, Emily. Emily, who wasn't anybody at the moment.

GS: The novel's called *Cambridge*, but Emily certainly has more prominence in terms of pages. I wondered whether you'd ever thought of Cambridge as the main character, or indeed if you'd still think of him as the main character?

CP: No. Emily was always going to be the main character, but Cambridge was conceived of as a character who would be ever-present. He doesn't appear often in the narrative, in terms of time, but he's always in the background of what she's doing and what she's saying and what she's thinking. And then, of course, in the second section of the novel, he has his own narrative.

GS: There's a lovely irony to Cambridge's narrative. We've had many pages of Emily and then we get Cambridge's account: Emily figures in Cambridge's mind merely as that Englishwoman on the periphery—scarcely at all, in fact.

CP: There is a corrective in having Cambridge's perspective. Cambridge's voice is politically very important because it is only through painful application that he has acquired the skill of literacy. There are so few African accounts of what it was like to go through slavery, because African people were generally denied access to the skills of reading and writing. Reading and writing equal power. Once you have a language, you are dangerous. Cambridge actually makes the effort to acquire a language. He makes the effort to acquire the skills of literacy and uses them to sit in judgement on himself and the societies he passes through.

GS: Did your feelings about Cambridge change as you wrote the novel? He is a very ambiguous character.

CP: You know you cannot be too judgemental about your characters. Novels are an incredibly democratic medium. Everyone has a right to be understood. I have a lot of problems swallowing most of what Emily says and feels. Similarly, I have difficulties with many of Cambridge's ideas and opinions, because in modern parlance he would be regarded as an Uncle Tom. But I don't feel I have the right to judge them.

GS: Emily seems to be a mixture of tentative liberal instincts and blind prejudice. And it could be easy for us, with our twentieth-century complacent hindsight, to judge her quite harshly, but you are very sympathetic—and we can't do anything but sympathize with her, pity her. I wondered if your feelings about her changed as you wrote her long narrative.

CP: [*pause*] Maybe.

GS: Did you have the end in mind even as you wrote the narrative?

CP: No. No. I think she grows. She has to make a journey which begins from the periphery of English society. I couldn't have told this story from the point of view of a man. She was regarded, as most women of that time were regarded, as a 'child of lesser growth' when placed alongside her male contemporaries. She was on the margin of English society, and I suspect that one of the reasons I was able to key into her and to listen to what she had to say was the fact that, like her, I also grew up in England feeling very marginalized. She also made a journey to the Caribbean for the purpose of keeping body and soul together, which is a journey I made ten years ago. So in that sense, looking at it coldly now, through the prism of time, I can understand why I would have listened to somebody like her and why she would have entrusted me with her story. And through the process of writing . . . you are right, I did begin to feel a little warmer towards her. She rose above her racist attitudes.

GS: She became alive in her own right.

CP: Because she was courageous. It may be a small and somewhat unpleasant thing in the context of 1991 to find a woman expressing some warmth and affection for her black maid, but in the early nineteenth century it was remarkable that a woman, and particularly this woman, was able to confess to such emotions. A nineteenth-century man couldn't have done this. Men have a larger capacity for bullshit and for self-deception, even when they are talking only to themselves. I'm not sure that I would have trusted the narrative of a nineteenth-century man engaged in the slave trade. The only time I read men's narratives which seem to be lyrical is when the men, nineteenth-century or otherwise, are in prison.

GS: Emily, in a way, is about to be sold into a kind of slavery— her arranged marriage—which gives her a perspective on what she sees. Is that how you saw it?

CP: Yes. I didn't want to push it too hard, for the two things are obviously only analogous in a minor key. However, an arranged marriage to a widower who possessed three kids and a guaranteed income was a form of bondage. Emily finds the strength, the wit, and the way out of this. I admire her for this. What makes her grow are a series of events which are particularly painful and distressing for her. As I've already stated, part of the magic of writing is that you cannot be too judgemental about a character. You have to find some kind of trust, some form of engagement. You attempt to breathe life into these people and if you're lucky they breathe life into you. You love them with passion; then, at the end of two or three or four years, you abandon them and try and write another book.

GS: You said a moment ago that men could only become lyrical when they are in prison. The second part of *Higher Ground* actually consists of letters from prison in a very distinct male voice. In that novel generally you seem to depart from your previous work in using strong first-person voices. In *Cambridge* again there is an emphasis on first-person narratives. Was that a conscious decision or did it just happen?

CP: It was conscious. There are any number of stories to tell. You are populated with the potential for telling stories from now until doomsday; these things are circling around your head. But it seems to me that the real test of a writer's ability is the degree to which a writer applies him- or herself to the conundrum of form, to the task of imposing a form on these undisciplined stories. I'd written two novels in the form of the third person and somehow I couldn't address myself again to such a manner of telling a story. It was as though I had to find some way of expanding my repertoire. So the first part of *Higher Ground* is written in first-person present tense, the second part in a series of letters and the third part is in the third person, but with these rather strange flashbacks. Each segment of the novel demanded a different point of attack. It was a way of breaking out of what was becoming, to me, the straitjacket of the third person. We used to talk about this when you were writing *Out of this World*. I remember you saying there was an intimacy about the first person which you found attractive. Well, me too. And like you, I'm interested in history, in memory, in time, and in the failure of these three things. It seems to me, at this stage anyhow, that the first person gives me an intimate flexibility which I can't find in the third person.

GS: Nine-tenths of *Cambridge* are written in a pastiche of nineteenth-century language. Certainly, the final few pages of it are in your language, the language of the twentieth century. This sense of a language that can talk about certain things suddenly bursting through Emily's own language in which she can't, is very volcanic, it's a brilliant conclusion to a novel . . . I wonder if we could broaden things out and talk more generally about your writing. In your book of essays, *The European Tribe*, you say that you knew for certain you wanted to be a writer while sitting by the Pacific in California with the waves lapping around your ankles . . .

CP: All right, all right! The summer of my second year in college I travelled around America on a bus until my money ran out in California. And I went into this bookshop and bought this book, *Native Son* by Richard Wright. There weren't many black people writing in England. So it never occurred to me that writing as a profession was a possibility. But when I was in the States I discovered such people as Jimmy Baldwin and Richard Wright and Toni Morrison.

GS: Do you think it was necessary to go to America to become a writer?

CP: I was slouching towards a writing career. Being in the States shifted me into fifth gear and out of the very slovenly third that I was stuck in.

GS: How old were you when you first went back to St Kitts?

CP: Twenty-two. I'd written a play, *Strange Fruit*, in 1980, which was done at the Crucible Theatre in Sheffield. And with the royalties from that, I went back to St Kitts with my mother, who had left in 1958 when she was twenty. It was strange, because I'd grown up without any overbearing sense of curiosity about the Caribbean. My mother hadn't been back either. She held it in her memory. But when we arrived in St Kitts many of the things she remembered were no longer there: her school had burnt down, people that she knew had died, and someone she dearly wanted me to meet had long since emigrated to America. For her, it was like a ghost town. But for me, it fired my curiosity about myself, about England, about the Caribbean. Naturally, the 'rediscovery' confused and confounded me, but that was no bad thing, for, after all, writers are basically just people who are trying to organize their confusion.

GS: Your first two novels were very much about the Caribbean, coming from and going back to. How much was that actually paralleling your life and exorcizing your own feelings about the Caribbean?

CP: My first novel, *The Final Passage*, was published in 1985. I'd started some five years earlier, on the inter-island ferry between St Kitts and Nevis. I looked back at St Kitts and began to write some sentences down. I wanted to try to tell the story of the journey from the Caribbean to England, which seemed to me to be, in terms of fiction in this country, an untold story. People had written novels and stories about the journey, but not people of my generation. The second novel, *A State of Independence*, although not autobiographical, followed the emotional contours of my life in that it dealt with the problems of returning to the Caribbean and thinking, they are not sure if I am one of them, and yet feeling that I am not sure if I am one of them either. However, I have certainly not exorcized my feelings about the Caribbean. I have no desire to do so. The reason I write about the Caribbean is that the Caribbean contains both Europe and Africa. The Caribbean is an artificial society created by the massacre of its inhabitants, the Carib and Arawak Indians. It's where Africa met Europe on somebody else's soil. The history of the Caribbean is a bloody history. It's a history which is older than the history of the United States of America. Columbus didn't arrive in the United States. He arrived in the Caribbean. The Caribbean is Márquez's territory. He always describes himself as a Caribbean writer. It's Octavio Paz's territory. It's Fuentes's territory. The Caribbean for many French- and Spanish-speaking writers has provided more than enough emotional material for a whole career. For me, that juxtaposition of Africa and Europe in the Americas is very important.

GS: But now America has moved into your life. You are living in America now, teaching there. How do you feel about that?

CP: The reason I am living in America is because, like yourself, like many people, business occasionally takes me to the United States. When I'm not there, all I have to do is turn on the TV or open the papers and I'm bombarded with images of America. In other words, over the years I have come to think of myself as somebody who knows America because I have some kind of relationship with it. However, I'm not sure that anybody can seriously claim to 'know' a country as large and diverse as the United States. It seemed important, given the opportunity of spending a year or maybe two in the United States, to make a concerted effort to get to know a part of the country more intimately. That's really why I'm living there. Furthermore, the Caribbean is now, to some extent, culturally, an extension of the Florida Keys, and I really want to understand a bit more about American people rather than simply imagining them all to be characters out of *Dallas* or a nation whose soul is reflected in the studio audience and guests of *The Oprah Winfrey Show*.

GS: I've one last question and it's quite a big one. We always have a lot of fun together; whenever we meet we have some laughs. Yet your work doesn't exactly glow with optimism. You are very hard on your characters; most of your central characters are lost people, they suffer. Pessimism seems to win through. Is that ultimately your view of the world?

CP: I'm always surprised that people think I'm a pessimist. *Cambridge* is, to some extent, optimistic. Emily grows. OK, she suffers greatly, but she still grows. It's the price of the ticket, isn't it? The displacement ticket. Displacement engenders a great deal of suffering, a great deal of confusion, a great deal of soul-searching. It would be hard for me to write a comedy about displacement. But there is courage. Emily has a great amount of courage. As does Cambridge. And in *Higher Ground* there is faith. I don't necessarily mean faith with a religious gloss on it. I mean the ability actually to acknowledge the existence of something you believe in, something that helps you to make sense of your life. You are right when you say that the characters are often lost and that they suffer. But I would like to claim that the spirit and tenacity with which my characters fight to try and make sense of their often helplessly fated lives is itself optimistic. Nobody rolls over and dies. If they are to 'go under', it is only after a struggle in which they have hopefully won our respect.

In the Bamboo with Caz, 1986.

LOOKING FOR JIŘÍ WOLF

PRAGUE, 1989

In 1989 Europe underwent its most momentous succession of political changes since the end of the Second World War. In early December that year Bill Buford, then the editor of *Granta*, phoned me to ask if I'd be ready to pack a bag quickly and go to Prague to observe and write about what was happening there. Prague—and Czechoslovakia, as it then was—was in the midst of what was already being called a 'gentle' revolution and would later get even more cosily christened 'the velvet revolution'. In fact, at the time of Bill's call there was no real basis for believing that it would be such a mild affair, or even a successful revolution at all. I packed a bag and went.

I was almost completely unqualified for this mission, but Bill had a reason for selecting me. He'd heard that on a previous trip to Prague I'd taken an interest in the fate of an imprisoned dissident writer, Jiří Wolf, and he wondered if I might make it the object of my present visit to track him down and speak to him. Perhaps he'd now been released—that is, if he'd survived imprisonment.

I knew nothing about Wolf's current circumstances, next to nothing about Prague, and knew hardly anyone there. I thought the chances of my ever finding my man were virtually nil.

The piece was written back in London, in the last days before Christmas, with Bill eager for it to make, with an up-to-the-minute feel, the 'New Europe' edition of *Granta* that would appear in the new year. All the present-tense references that belong to the time of writing have been kept here. It's the only piece of reportage I've done.

Looking for Jiří Wolf

At the beginning of December 1988, I visited Czechoslovakia for the first time. I knew then about the case of Jiří Wolf, though it was not the prime reason for my visit. A month before, I had been in Stockholm, where my publisher, Thomas von Vegesack, is president of the International PEN Writers in Prison Committee. I told him that I had been invited to Czechoslovakia for the publication of a Slovak translation of one of my books, and he reminded me that Jiří Wolf was a prisoner 'adopted' by both the Swedish and English Committees. Perhaps I could ask some discreet questions.

I got some information on Wolf from the PEN Committee in London and did indeed ask questions during my visit. I discovered, rapidly enough, that the opportunity to ask questions was limited by the general constraints on talking freely. Also, for most of my visit I was in Bratislava, the Slovak capital, while Wolf was a Czech from Bohemia. I spent just a couple of days in Prague. The fact remains that when I did ask questions, I got the same response: genuine, not simulated, ignorance. No one seemed to have heard of him.

My visit made a strong impression on me, in part because I had read the dossier on Wolf, and some of Wolf's own words, just before my departure. Frankly, the country depressed me. I encountered a great deal of individual kindness, above all from my Slovak translator, Igor, a reservedly humorous man and a good friend, but I felt that I was in a land that had gone into internal emigration. It was cut off from its own best resources, and even the things that could be simply admired, like the beautiful buildings of Prague, seemed false and irrelevant.

Much of this may be the standard Western reaction. I felt a mixture of gladness and guilt on returning home and for some while I was haunted by my impressions and in particular—though here I had only imagination to go on—by thoughts of Jiří Wolf. I wrote letters on his behalf. I heard from the British Embassy in Prague that his case had been raised during the Vienna meeting of the Conference on Security and Cooperation in Europe, though to no apparent avail. It was only to be hoped that he would at least survive the remainder of his prison sentence, which was due to end during 1989.

I did not know if and when I might return to Czechoslovakia. I certainly felt, from my limited knowledge and from what I had picked up on the spot that, despite Gorbachev, the situation in the country was unlikely to improve. It might even worsen. A typical joke at the time of my first visit ran:

Karel: This perestroika is getting real bad.
Pavel: Yes, soon we Czechoslovaks will have to send tanks into Russia.

But we have all been surprised by the events of the last year. And, almost a year to the day after I had left it, I found myself returning to Prague in the grip of what was variously called, depending on your translator, a 'smiling', a 'gentle' or a 'tender' revolution. My chief purpose, with some five days to achieve it, was to find Jiří Wolf.

Wolf's case may be as unexceptional as it is awful. His is a history of harassment, imprisonment and maltreatment which has been documented—largely self-documented—and which seized my interest. There are many other documented cases, and time has yet to reveal, if it ever will completely, the extent of undocumented cases. Prisons are often the last sections of society to be touched by political reform and though, as I write, Czechoslovakia has a new government, it would be a mistake to suppose that the country no longer has institutions and personnel accustomed to the regular abuse of human rights.

Wolf was born in 1952. The facts I knew of his life were these. An orphan, he was brought up in state homes. He is of Jewish origin, with no living relative save one half-sister. He married, has a son, but was divorced in 1978. He has worked in the uranium mines at Pribram, also as a driver and stoker. Apart from his writings in and about prison, he has written an autobiographical work, *Mrtvá cesta* ('Dead Journey') and a novel, *Cerné barety* ('Black Berets'). In 1977 he signed the Charter 77 declaration and in 1978 was arrested for possessing 'anti-State', 'anti-Party' and 'anti-Socialist' documents, and subsequently sentenced to three years' imprisonment for 'subversion of the Republic'. He was committed to Minkovice prison.

At his trial Wolf complained that he had been forced to admit guilt under physical and psychological pressure, and his sentence was extended by six months for 'false accusations'. He was transferred from Minkovice to Valdice, a prison of the harshest category and perhaps the most notorious in Czechoslovakia. He was released in 1981. He remained active and was subject to harassment and arrest. In May 1983 he was charged with 'subversion in collusion with foreign agents' and 'divulging official secrets'—for allegedly passing information to the Austrian

Embassy about conditions in Minkovice. He was sentenced to six years' imprisonment and in 1984 found himself again in Valdice.

Wolf's prison writings, covering a ten-year period of imprisonment, are grim and harrowing. His 'regime' was one of terror, cold, hunger, isolation and deprivation. Prisoners are allowed one visit, of one hour only, and one parcel every ten months, though these minimal rights are often denied. They are exploited as cheap labour. They are denied clothing sent to them. They are subject to indiscriminate beatings, some of which prove fatal, and to medical neglect. They are forced to eat food off the floor, food which is in any case inadequate, as prisoners are known to cut their wrists in order to drink their blood. Or just cut their wrists. In 1988 Wolf was permitted a visit by two American doctors. They found him in poor shape but were not allowed to leave vitamins or medicines for ulcer treatment. Wolf told them he contemplated suicide.

I arrived in Prague with little more than a list of possibly useful names and telephone numbers. I had established from the PEN Committee in London that Wolf had indeed been released, in bad health, on 17 May 1989, but his whereabouts were unknown and information unforthcoming. I had recommendations and promises of help from various sources, and, via a BBC unit in Prague, the name of a man, Miloš, who might act, if needed, as interpreter and co-searcher. I had phoned him from London, along with a number of other people in Prague. Miloš knew nothing of Wolf, but, with only limited free time, was ready to help. Other responses, where there was not an immediate language problem, were cooperative, but no one, just as a year ago, seemed to have more than a dim notion of Wolf.

I had phoned Igor in Bratislava, who was prepared to meet me in Prague the following Saturday; also an editor in Prague, who again knew nothing of Wolf but promised to do what she could and in any case to arrange some meetings with other Czech writers. All these phone calls I prefaced with a wary 'Please tell me if I should not discuss certain matters on the phone.' This met with varying reactions, from 'Say what you like,' to 'It's probably bugged, but what the hell.' It was hard to tell if this was bravado or if a real barrier of caution had been lifted.

I arrived on Wednesday, 6 December. The 'gentle revolution', if it was to be dated from the ungentle night of 17 November, when police brutality had ignited the will of the people, was barely two weeks old. The opposition group Civic Forum was locked in intense negotiation with a government that still held a firm communist majority. The last big demonstration had been on Monday the fourth. A general strike was threatened for the following Monday.

It has to be said that on the streets the general impression was of calm normality—if normality is not an ambiguous term for Czechoslovakia. The Czechoslovak flag was everywhere. Unostentatious red, white and blue tags adorned hats and lapels. In the central part of the city, posters and information sheets, many of them handwritten and seemingly modest, were thick on walls and shop fronts. On Staroměstské náměstí, Old Town Square, a huge Christmas tree vied with a vigil of striking students beneath the statue of Jan Hus.

'Gentle revolution' seemed appropriate. But the gentleness was deceptive as well as touching. Optimism was being undermined by jitteriness at the extreme fragility of the situation. This was a week when things might go either way. The 'smiling' revolution might lose its smile or show its teeth. People admitted to violent swings of mood from euphoria to depression. Little things told a lot: a confusion in the use of the pronouns 'we' and 'they'; the tiredness in people's eyes; the hoarseness in their voices. They had been doing a lot of shouting, a lot of talking, aware of never before having been able to talk so much. But old habits die hard: a sudden glance over the shoulder or to the side would be followed by a self-reproachful but still worried laugh.

I made a round of phone calls, including one to Miloš, and arranged to meet the editor, Alžběta, that evening. She had done a great deal of homework since my call from London and had fixed meetings for me with the writers Ludvík Vaculík and Ivan Klíma, with the possibility of meeting other writers and dissidents. She had found out nothing further about Wolf but she had made her own list of contacts to compare with mine. My priority was to find Wolf, but, viewing things pessimistically, I wanted to keep my options open. If there was no trail to follow, I didn't want my time to be empty.

I confess to more complex motives. What drew me to Wolf was, in part, that he was unknown (in more ways than one, it seemed). He was a writer, but he appeared to have no standing in contemporary Czechoslovak literature. Quite possibly, he was not an exceptionally good writer, although very brave, and his literary career had simply been eclipsed by his activist and prison experience.

A certain myth of the 'Czechoslovak writer' seems to have arisen, at least in Western eyes: a figure automatically martyred and ennobled—banned, exiled—for the very act of writing. There may be both truth and justice in this sanctification: Václav Havel is a genuine intellectual hero who has won the spontaneous following of a people. But I suspected that the elevation of prominent writers into political symbols had obscured many 'unknowns'—writers and non-writers—and that it was perhaps unfair to the individuality of the prominent figures themselves. I wanted to test the myth, to discover whether writers resented or accepted their politicization and how they viewed a future which might restore their freedom but also remove some of their politically conferred cachet. To all this, Wolf's case would lend a rigorous perspective.

I met Alžběta at six. I gave her a copy I had of the PEN dossier on Wolf (unsure whether this was still a risky document to carry around), and we went to make inquiries at Civic Forum's new headquarters, a short distance from Alžběta's office. I anticipated the problem that, given the hectic pace of events, people who might otherwise be able to help would be too busy. I placed strong hopes on contacting members of the unofficial network VONS—the Committee for the Unjustly Prosecuted—which worked to monitor and publish details of such cases as Wolf's and itself included many ex-prisoners. The VONS network was inextricably connected with Charter 77, as both were now involved in the opposition movement. I did not expect to make much practical headway at Civic Forum.

I was surprised by the relaxed and low-key atmosphere of the Civic Forum office. I had imagined a throng of enquirers: there was a small knot of people. The staff all seemed to be of student age, smiling, casual, obliging; and if I was reminded of anything, it was of a university common room or a union office—an air of precarious organization. The word you were tempted to use—I thought of the handwritten posters and the single, small-screen televisions relaying information to potential crowds of hundreds—was 'amateur'. You had to remind yourself that a month ago the machinery of opposition and free information simply hadn't existed; and that, at a deeper level, all revolutions must appear to be started by amateurs.

Furthermore, if these were amateurs, who were the professionals? No doubt, when the communist leaders were first compelled to negotiate with Civic Forum, they must have stifled the thought (it was creepily instructive to have shared it) that the situation was preposterous—they were dealing with amateurs. But were they themselves professional in anything other than their official possession of power? Professional, in terms of expertise, responsibility, knowledge, education? The answer I got to this was to be repeatedly and vehemently 'No'. The constant cry—with a gush of relief now that at last it could be uttered openly—was that in a totalitarian regime stupidity floats to the top. At every level, control had passed for years into the hands of people with no qualification other than their Party allegiance. What Czechoslovakia desperately needs now is intelligence.

Jiří Wolf's name struck no immediate chords at Civic Forum. We asked after several of the names we had, some of them VONS people. Yes, one or two had been there, but they had gone. There was a little further conferring among the reception staff. Then someone disappeared and came back with a piece of paper. On it was written Wolf's name and a Prague telephone number. As simple as that.

It was well into the evening, but we went to Alžběta's office and phoned the number. No answer. We tried several times. Meanwhile we talked and Alžběta studied the PEN dossier I had given her. It was clear that she had not fully appreciated how central to my visit was the search for Wolf, but she was becoming rapidly involved in it. We had a phone number, and it was perhaps now a straightforward matter. But there was a puzzlement which Alžběta shared. Why had she never heard of this man?

And why had so many people, many of them on the circuits of information, at best only a vague knowledge of him?

As we left the office and walked to get a meal, I began to feel that Wolf was having a distinct psychological effect on Alžběta—on top of all the emotion that the present crisis had brought. Here was a man whose painful history had been unknown to her only days before, and here was the prospect that soon many other such secrets must come to light. I did not imagine for one moment that Alžběta's knowledge of what had been perpetrated in her country lagged behind my own. But the individual case was acting, rightly or wrongly, as a catalyst to the assimilation of events.

As we walked, she spoke of things which do not often get mentioned in the West. How Charter 77 was in certain ways, for all its courage and worthiness, an elitist and divisive body, exerting a tacit reproach against those who did not sign it, and throwing up within itself an inner circle of eminence at the expense of many an 'ordinary' signatory. It is generally true that in the West reference to Charter 77 evokes a handful of names. One forgets, firstly, that even by 1980 Charter 77 had more than a thousand signatories, and, secondly, that its total number of signatories was only ever a tiny proportion of the population. Alžběta was gently scornful of those now flocking to sign the Charter. She also spoke of the pressure that had surrounded the signing of other petitions, such as that for the release of Havel; of a contagious attitude of 'if you are not for us, you are against us', which she pointed out was exactly the stance of the Communist Party.

What Alžběta was revealing was perhaps the inevitable nervousness and complexity that follow the simple, inspiring and hardly believable fact of revolutionary action. You could see the mechanisms of suspicion and trust, immunity and risk, rivalry and resentment beginning to turn themselves inside out: how good a non-communist were you? Old, familiar emotions were starting to flow stickily in a new direction.

I phoned the Wolf number that night. No answer. The next morning I tried again: the same result. Alžběta had arranged a mid-morning meeting with Ludvík Vaculík; I was to go to her office first. I phoned Miloš to say we had Wolf's number and would keep trying it. Miloš was tied up for the day anyway. I then phoned a contact at the British Embassy Cultural Section to ask if someone could keep phoning the Wolf number through the morning. I then went to Alžběta's office on Národní Street.

Alžběta had had no luck with the Wolf number either. We tried again from her office without success, then walked to the Café Slavia to meet Vaculík.

Vaculík is a short, rather leonine-featured man in his sixties, with a thick, grey moustache and long, thick, grey hair. He is perhaps best known abroad for his novel, *The Guinea Pigs* (*Morčata*), written after the Soviet invasion, but his best work is considered to be *The Axe* (*Sekyra*), published before 1968. For a long time his work has been largely confined to essays, necessarily published in foreign and émigré journals. He is currently busy with volumes of diaries and correspondence. He remains one of Czechoslovakia's leading literary figures.

I had been warned that he was difficult, 'morose', that he might react contrarily to questions. In fact he was amiable, humorous, freely gave me his time and insisted on paying for the drinks. Vaculík rejected communism in the 1960s, but described himself as having had a 'lasting battle' with communism ever since he joined the Party. The Soviet invasion and subsequent crackdown meant the virtual loss of all previous freedoms. He spoke of his disbelief and despair at the time; a feeling—echoed by others I spoke to—that his life was lost, that the effects of the invasion would last and that he would not live (he gave a wry smile) to see them end.

He was forbidden to publish in Czechoslovakia and endured a kind of house arrest. His decision to publish regularly abroad was effectively a decision to be regularly interrogated, and, like so many Czechoslovaks, he was obliged to keep monthly appointments with the police. His refusal to do menial work led to the threat of criminal proceedings for 'parasitism', though the charge was never brought. He had lost his pension rights and he had no recourse to the assistance normally available for treatment following a gall-bladder operation. He was imprisoned once, for two days, for signing a petition to nominate Jaroslav Seifert for the Nobel Prize.

How did he view present developments?

He was a 'sceptical optimist'.

Was he bitter, did he regard the past as an evil joke?

No, it had to be viewed as a great, if terrible, lesson for world history and it should not be vulgarized.

How did he see the future?

There were two futures: one before and one after elections. Elections in the spring of 1990 seemed to him a reasonable possibility, with time enough to form parties and find personalities to stand.

Would he wish to stand himself?

No, it was his 'secret wish' to have nothing to do with politics.

In this last, frank admission Vaculík belied the stereotype of the Czechoslovak writer and perhaps expressed the inner feeling of many of his fellow authors. He exuded the dignified desire to protect his own independence. Our discussion moved on to the Czech Writers' Union, even then being denounced as a restrictive organ of the State. Vaculík, of course, was not a member, but nor did he wish to join the new free writers' association that was being formed. The scepticism in his optimism was apparent and even extended to some reservations about Civic Forum.

Did he think the perpetrators of repression should be punished?

An emphatic yes. But the punishment should be by law, not in the spirit of revenge, and those accused should include not only those responsible for the persecutions and imprisonments, but those who had wreaked economic and environmental damage. One might need to accept that the punishment would not correspond to the guilt, since the degree of criminality might never be properly determined.

What of the punishment for those personally involved in his own suffering?

Here Vaculík's individuality reasserted itself. He would like, he said, with a slyly wistful expression, to invite a certain police officer to his home, just as that police officer had issued many invitations to him. No one else, no publicity. A simple invitation to coffee.

Finally I asked Vaculík if he knew about Wolf. Once again there was the vague recognition of the name, but he could not help me further.

After lunch I called in at the Cultural Section of the British Embassy. Had they got an answer from the Wolf number? Yes. Would Saturday morning be all right for a meeting?

Mr Wolf couldn't give a precise time as yet, but would call back. And he only spoke Czech.

I was amazed. My goal appeared to have been achieved in less than twenty-four hours. And with all my readiness to pursue numerous Czech contacts, it was a section of the British Embassy that had made the connection. I was still baffled. How had he sounded on the phone? Was he genuinely ready to meet or perhaps a little cautious?

Oh, perfectly ready, perfectly positive about it all. And he sounded fine.

As it happened, I was able to hear for myself. They had forgotten to give the number he should ring at the Section, so a further call was made to him, in Czech of course. The voice I overheard issuing from the receiver was businesslike and robust. One image I had of Jiří Wolf, as a man physically and mentally wrecked and beyond rehabilitation, faded.

Back at the hotel, I phoned Miloš to tell him the news. Would he be free to act as interpreter?

Only if the meeting was early. Could it be on Friday instead—he had the whole day free?

I said Wolf had to choose the time. I could probably find someone else for Saturday. It looked as if I might never get to meet Miloš.

This was late afternoon on Thursday the seventh. There had been stories during the day that Adamec, the Prime Minister, was threatening to resign. A stalemate seemed to have been reached between Civic Forum and the government. Civic Forum wanted a reformed government (with a non-communist majority) by Sunday, otherwise the general strike would go ahead. Adamec's position was that he would reform the government but would not act under pressure and ultimatums. If they continued, he would resign. Since Adamec was, temporarily at least, a significant figure in negotiations for both sides, this was not a desirable outcome.

Alžběta had arranged a further meeting with another writer, Eda Kriseova, that evening between six and seven. Kriseova spoke English and would come to the hotel, but I was not to be surprised if she did not show up. I fully expected her not to appear, since she was closely involved with Civic Forum and was currently privy to discussions with the government. But she was also a writer, and perhaps sometimes it is true that writers like to meet writers. At six o'clock she phoned from the lobby, and, though we could have talked in the hotel, we quickly crossed the street to a cafe.

Obviously in a hurry and excited, but smiling and genial, she was the first person I met who seemed truly charged with the electricity of events. She was also the first person to convey a real shiver of fear. She had been on a tram just now and people were saying that Adamec had resigned. If this had happened, then everything was thrown into flux. There would be a 'constitutional crisis'. There might be a 'putsch'. She used this word several times, as if she had not chosen it thoughtlessly.

This was unsettling, to say the least. I shared the generally accepted view that the way ahead for Civic Forum was not easy, but that the current of change was essentially irreversible. Correspondents in the Western press, at least, were ruling out intervention by the army. But Kriseova seemed convinced it was still possible. 'I don't see many uniforms about,' I said, rather obtusely, remembering that a year ago it was hard to get away from them.

'Exactly,' she said. 'Where *are* they all?'

It was hard to get the measure of Kriseova. She seemed both to have acquired a special grip on events (given her closeness to the centre of things, you could not deny her privileged viewpoint) and to have lost some normal hold on them. She herself seemed to acknowledge this. Her language had a heightened, even ecstatic quality. She spoke of the 'existential' nature of recent experience, of being 'on a wave' and having no choice, of something working 'through her', of events moving so fast that you were 'racing after history'. She also admitted to an uncanny sense of being involved in the unreal, to having asked her old friend, Havel: 'Václav, are we dreaming this? Are we acting this?'

The question reverberates. Theatrical metaphors need to be applied with care to Czechoslovakia, where the theatre has traditionally involved itself very concretely in politics. It is no bizarre accident that the opposition movement was inaugurated by an actor (famous for his romantic leads), threw up as its protagonist a playwright, Václav Havel, and had its first headquarters in a theatre, the fantastically named 'Laterna Magica'. Yet here was Kriseova testifying to the actual feeling, as the Civic Forum leaders met inside a theatre, that surely they were in a play. No doubt all remarkable events may seem at first unreal, especially when they have the weight of twenty years to deny their possibility. For me, too, these days in Prague had an unreal tinge. But surely people *make* history, they don't act it (otherwise everything is excused). Nor do they run after it. Or do they?

Rapt as she seemed capable of being, Kriseova was full of earthy warmth and vitality, and she plainly had a bent for the practical. She described herself as Havel's 'fairy godmother', making sure, amid everything, that he got his medicine for the lung problems he has had since contracting pneumonia in prison. She was also, one guessed, a courageous woman. She spoke of the demonstration on the night of the seventeenth, at which she, her daughter and some five thousand others had been caught in the trap formed by the police in Národní Street, preventing access to Wenceslas Square. All sorts of accounts were circulating about this night. Some said that the police had been specially drugged; that they had used nets to snare small clusters of people; that bodies were seen lying under covers (this apart from the publicized rumour, later proved false, that a student had been killed).

What seemed beyond dispute was the ferocity of the police attacks and that this was a premeditated plan, executed to prevent the escape of a mass of people from a confined space. A public investigation (that unprecedented thing) was currently being conducted into the brutality. A neurologist had testified that the cases of shock were similar to those he had seen in people who had experienced bombardment in the war. Others pointed out that from sheer weight of numbers and from crushing and confinement alone, fatalities would have been likely.

Absolutely beyond doubt is that 17 November was a turning-point in events and a colossal mistake by the authorities. The world changed overnight.

Like Vaculík, Kriseova had found herself stripped of hope in 1969. Formerly a successful journalist, she suddenly had nothing, and had to wrench herself from despair. She took work in a mental hospital, which she says saved her from going mad herself. She saw that the inmates were 'free' in a way those outside were not. Her first stories arose from her mental hospital experience. In the 1970s she came under scrutiny and threats from the security police, and, after refusing to 'retract', had established, like Vaculík, a regular 'relationship' with an investigator and was, of course, prevented from publishing.

How did she get involved in Civic Forum?

She had once presciently told Havel that if he ever got drawn into things so much that he needed help, he should call her. He called soon after.

Was she bitter about the 'lost' years and did she want retribution?

You had to remember, she said, that the worst time was in the 1950s. The generation that had known those years was conditioned by its terrible memories, numbed into submission. Even now many of them were sceptical. The generations of the 1960s and after had not lost their hope. And you had to get retribution into perspective: one woman who had recently been assaulted at night in the street was found screaming, 'They are killing us now! They are going to kill us!' Her assailant was a solitary molester, but the woman was a Party member and genuinely feared an opposition massacre.

The Prague streets did indeed seem a little darker after speaking to Kriseova. In the cafe the talk on the tram had been confirmed: Adamec had stepped down. But even as she hurried to a possible constitutional crisis, Kriseova was making arrangements to meet me again, to give me some of her stories. I must read them, we must discuss them. Writers!

At the hotel there were no messages about Wolf. I phoned Alžběta to tell her that we seemed to have a meeting with Wolf on Saturday. Could she possibly be there to interpret? I also told her what Kriseova had said and discussed the evening's news. I could hear anxiety creeping into her voice. I could not tell if this arose from her own assessment of the situation or from my words, the garbled, intrusive words of a foreigner clumsily relaying inside information from one Czech to another. The palpable throb of rumour.

The next morning was bright and clear. There were no uniforms on the street and the trams were crossing the bridge over the Vltava as usual. I had to be at Alžběta's office at ten thirty to meet Ivan Klíma. (Alžběta seemed to have abandoned normal work, but a revolution was a good excuse.) I phoned the Cultural Section to see if there was a definite time for Wolf.

We're glad you phoned, I was told. You see, the thing is, there's been a mistake. The man we spoke to phoned back and said that, after thinking it over, it seemed a little strange that you wanted to meet him. You see, the fact is, whoever he is, he's the wrong man. He's not Jiří Wolf.

I called Miloš. I let the enigma of the bogus Wolf go. It was Friday, Miloš's free day. We were back to where we started. He was at my service. He would do some scouting while I went to see Klíma. I also called a number of contacts I had neglected to follow up, believing we had found Wolf. Those included a man called Hejda, a man called Freund and a man called Doruzka, a leading jazz figure (this a recommendation from Josef Škvorecký) who might put me on to a man called Srp [sic] who might know Wolf. Hejda did not know about Wolf, but suggested someone whom I had already tried without success. Freund was out, but his wife said she would pass on the message. Doruzka, in stylishly idiomatic English, sounded the keynote of my search so far: 'No, I am afraid this man's name does not ring any bells with me.'

Now that Wolf was once again a mystery, I could not resist indulging in dubious theories. Could it be that Wolf, on his release, had simply wished to disappear? Could it be that there was something about his personality that had kept him removed from the main circles of activists? Had he always been, perhaps, a little mad? Some of the names and phone numbers I had were copied directly from a typed information sheet on a window in Národní Street, giving details about Pavel Wonka, who had died in prison the previous year. It seemed extraordinary that, if such matters were now public, Wolf should be so elusive.

I told myself that my hypotheses were indeed indulgent. It was wrong to construct riddles merely out of my lack of luck in finding a man. I went to Alžběta's office to see Klíma.

I had met Klíma on my previous visit. He is a tall, rather gangling man, with straggly dark hair, a sort of misshapen handsomeness and a crinkly smile. He has the air of a veteran from beatnik days and speaks good English. Popular at the time of the Prague Spring, mainly as a playwright, he now has a high reputation, both in and outside his country, as a novelist. Much of his work, though perhaps not the very best, has appeared in English. His untranslated *Soudce z Milosti* ('A Judge on Trial') is considered, along with Vaculík's *The Axe*, to be one of the great Czechoslovak novels of recent times.

Comparatively speaking, Klíma has not been severely persecuted during the last twenty years, and I wondered whether for some this has slightly diminished his otherwise considerable standing. Despite the ban on his work at home, he has been able to survive on foreign royalties and to keep up a steady rate of production, and he emanated relative contentment. His life, on the other hand, has scarcely been easy. In 1969 he managed to visit an American university, leaving on the very day (31 August) before the borders were closed. His passport was confiscated on his return and he was not able to travel for eleven years, and then only within Eastern Europe. He ceased to write plays because of the impossibility of seeing them staged. He was harassed, his home searched, his telephone tampered with, but he was never arrested or imprisoned.

Klíma is neither complacent nor possessed of any false guilt at not being in the top league of the persecuted. He has a strong sense of his own individuality—I suspect that he shared Vaculík's 'secret wish' not to be involved in politics—and even a rather gleeful sense of irony about how his case goes against the grain of some received Western ideas. He pointed out that he did not sign Charter 77, but, as many of his friends were signatories and he moved in Charter circles, he was nonetheless subject to scrutiny. He also implied that not signing Charter 77 might have been a tactical advantage: you could be active without advertising the fact. He was not snubbed for not signing. His position was that as an author he wished to sign only his own texts.

Unlike Vaculík, Klíma did not disdain manual work. Rather, he took the view that doing other, temporary jobs could be valuable for a writer; and he told a story which was a perfect explosion of the Western 'myth'. A famous Czech author is seen cleaning the streets by a friend of his at the American Embassy. The American goes into a fit of outrage at how the authorities humiliate the country's best minds. But the writer (could it be Klíma?) is doing the job voluntarily: it is research for a book.

We discussed Havel, who conforms in paramount fashion to the Western myth and who at that moment was being tipped for president. There were two possible views of Havel in my mind. One, that he was a man moving willingly to meet his destiny as a leader of the people; the other, that he was being sucked into events at some cost to himself, a writer uprooted from his true vocation.

But it seemed that Havel did not have the 'secret wish'. Klíma said that Havel was, of course, exhausted right now, but underneath he was happy. He called him a 'childish' man (I think he meant 'childlike'). He was happy to be the great citizen. He was a brave man, yes, but he had political ambitions—they were not thrust upon him. Klíma had always found Havel's essays and political writings more impressive than his plays.

We spoke of other Czech writers, the exiles Kundera and Škvorecký. Klíma thought Kundera was a great writer but self-interested. He played up to Western preconceptions in terms of both his own position and his portrayal of Czechoslovakia, which Klíma found often superficial and too eager for symbols. *The Unbearable Lightness of Being* was not entirely liked in Czechoslovakia. Škvorecký, on the other hand, retained a strong following, particularly among the younger generation, and was seen as the exile with the greater integrity.

We turned to Czechoslovak writing generally and to what the future held. Both Vaculík and Kriseova had spoken forcibly about the discrediting of the Czech Writers' Union, and Vaculík had wished to hold back even from the newly established free association of writers. Klíma seemed to be directly involved in the founding of this new association (*Obec*—'Community'), but some of the harshest language of a generally gently spoken man was reserved for the old Union. He called it an 'instrument of national treason' which for twenty years had accepted without protest that hundreds of Czech writers were suppressed and persecuted, if not imprisoned. The Union, he said, was 'covered in shame'. However, there should be no 'craving for revenge'. Members of the old Union should be allowed, as individuals, to join the new Community. This was in accordance with the Community's overriding commitment to freedom of expression. But there was to be no 'fusion' between the two bodies.

What of the Union's money, its assets?

Klíma said, with some bitterness, that the Union had no assets, only tables and typewriters. Then he said there should be a calling to account for the 'abuse of literary funds'.

I half appreciated what he meant. I knew that all writers, Union members or not, were obliged to pay a percentage of income to a Literary Fund. In effect, writers who were banned were forced to pay for the privileges of the approved.

From my visit of the year before, I had a graphic illustration of what these privileges might entail. I vividly remember being taken from Bratislava on a snowy day to a 'castle' in the Slovak countryside, which was owned by, or rather allocated to, the Slovak Writers' Union. I have to say that those who took me did so in a spirit of hospitality but also with detectable unease.

The 'castle' was a grand country house, set in extensive grounds and approached along a magnificent avenue of poplars. I was told that for a very small payment writers could come here to work; though few of the many rooms seemed occupied. Nonetheless, we were greeted by a permanent staff and ushered into a building that was as warmly heated as it was immaculately decorated and furnished. I was given a brief tour and shown one of the best bedrooms—one of the most sumptuous and elegant guest-rooms I have ever seen. Brezhnev, I was told, once slept here.

For their small payment, writers were also fed. There were only four of us, and the place really did seem empty, but a table (dwarfed by the proportions of the room around it) was laid for lunch, complete with fine cutlery and glassware. While snow fell outside on noble trees, a waitress served us a meal worthy of any restaurant, in an atmosphere of Cinderella-like fantasy.

I asked Klíma what would become of such places and of the Literary Fund. He said the Literary Fund and all that it paid for—the 'castles', the Union buildings, offices, secretaries —all belonged to the Ministry of Culture. The Union owned nothing. He did not know what would happen now. He said that foreigners often overlooked the abuses in his country that were insidious and did not form neat or dramatic symbols. Of course individuals had been martyrs and suffered terribly and bravely, but the real damage was the gradual erosion of the self-respect of a whole people, the spread of corruption and the simultaneous ruination, by progressive mismanagement, of the economy and the environment.

It was perhaps the wrong moment, but I asked Klíma about Wolf.

No, Wolf's case was not familiar to him.

I lunched with Alžběta. I had told her about Wolf proving not to be Wolf. She seemed in a low mood. I was not sure if this was because she had entered the spirit of the search and felt thwarted, or because she was anxious at the uncertainty still surrounding Adamec's resignation. Klíma had a theory that Adamec had resigned with the hidden purpose of popping up again as president. The ultimatum of the general strike stood. The streets were still calm. I went back to the hotel and waited for a call from Miloš.

Miloš duly rang, in positive mood. He had inquired again at Civic Forum. No success. Then he had tracked down some VONS people and had been given an address for Wolf in Prague. No phone. He had gone to the address and found no one there. But he had left a note on the door, with a brief explanation, asking Wolf to call him or (if he spoke English) to call me at the hotel. So far, no replies. But we could only wait and see. I made a note of the address and we agreed to phone each other as soon as we heard anything.

I waited. The situation was a considerable improvement from the morning—at least I knew Wolf was in Prague. But, as time went by, I started to have doubts. Wolf did not have to be at the address at all. I also reflected on the wisdom of leaving notes on doors. Surely this was rash, even now. A forgotten fact came back to me: Wolf's sentence had included not only six years' imprisonment, now served, but also three years' 'protective surveillance'.

Late that evening there was a knock on the door. Surely not? No, it was Eda Kriseova, eyes bloodshot with fatigue, but smiling, dressed in a trench coat and chic black hat and clutching a folder of papers. The scene was straight out of a spy movie.

Would she like a drink?

No, she was too tired; she had been all day with Civic Forum; she had to go and rest. But here were the stories and extracts from a novel she had promised to bring me. We talked for a moment in the corridor. She told me that Civic Forum had reached provisional agreement for a reformed government and that President Husak would resign that weekend. I hardly registered the full import of these quietly spoken words. I took the folder and wished her good night.

Two things struck me. That despite what was clearly an exhausting and historic day, she was still writer enough to find time to bring me her manuscripts. Secondly, that this was one of Prague's 'international' hotels, much used by Western visitors, and three weeks ago one might legitimately have feared bugs and the ears of informers. But here was Kriseova announcing her momentous news in one of its corridors. Thus you learn of the fall of tyrants.

I began reading Kriseova's work immediately. The green light on my phone came on. Wolf? No. A message left by a Mr Freund, giving the same address for Wolf that Miloš had discovered.

It was snowing the next morning. I phoned Miloš, who had heard nothing and would be busy till four o'clock. I had an arrangement to meet Igor from Bratislava at two in the hotel lobby. Miloš said he could find time to call me around one-thirty. The morning was free and, though I was beginning to lose hope, I resolved to go to Wolf's address myself on blind chance. Since this might have been fruitless anyway without someone who spoke Czech, I called Alžběta. If Kriseova was Havel's fairy godmother, Alžběta was surely the fairy godmother of my search for Wolf. It was Saturday, I could hear a child in the background, but she agreed to come.

By a stroke of luck, the address given for Wolf was not far from where Alžběta herself lived, south of the centre of Prague, some three stops on the metro from Wenceslas Square. Alžběta met me at the station and, following a street map, we walked through the snow. Wolf's street was a quiet cul-de-sac (though all the streets seemed quiet), with family houses on one side and a run-down apartment block, where Wolf lived, on the other. A cold, gloomy landing. We knocked. No answer.

Jammed in the door frame was a pencil-written note on a scrap of paper, which, according to Alžběta, was to a woman and simply said, 'Wait for me here.' It seemed to have been written by Wolf himself and suggested he had been here recently. We knocked again, just in case, waited, considered; then knocked at a neighbour's along the landing. A burly man in a check shirt appeared, who did not seem unduly suspicious of us.

Yes, Wolf was around—he had seen him this morning. He had complained of not sleeping. Yes, he knew who Wolf was. Wolf was out and about a lot; he was still 'active', perhaps. My own son, he said, was with Charter 77.

Did Wolf look well?

He didn't look so bad.

We deliberated. Alžběta was for waiting; then for leaving a

note. I was unsure. This would be the second note from a stranger on his door in twenty-four hours. I was beginning to think that the truth of the matter was that, whatever Wolf was doing now, he did not want intrusion; perhaps he should be left alone. And I was beginning to question my persistence in seeking him out—the whole absurd folly of a Western visitor trying to find an elusive Czech dissident. Was I not conducting a grotesque parody of the 'protective surveillance' that, for all I knew, Wolf was still subject to? I had got carried away with the detective-hunt element of things and had somehow pushed to the back of my mind the terrible facts that had provoked my interest in the first place. As though merely finding him mattered.

Alžběta left a note, this time giving her phone number as a further point of contact. We walked back to the metro in a subdued mood. I would probably not see Alžběta again before I left. She was sorry that with all our efforts we had not met with success. The search had led us only to mutual self-searching.

At the hotel there were no messages. Igor was due shortly. I looked forward to his arrival. I had called him from Prague at a point when I illusorily believed that my task would be accomplished by Saturday afternoon: the time would be free. I would have to explain what had happened, but I felt the situation was essentially unchanged: I had done all I could. Just before I met Igor, Miloš phoned, as promised. No further news. I explained that I had been to Wolf's address myself and that my feeling now was that Wolf was a man who wanted to keep to himself.

'No, no,' said Miloš, with some emphasis, 'my information about him is that he would not find this intrusive, he would be ready to meet.'

I wrote a note for the reception desk, saying that if I had any callers or visitors, especially a Mr Wolf, I would be back at six. Then I waited in the lobby for Igor. He showed up, wearing the badge of Civic Forum's Slovak sister movement, People Against Violence, and we went off to a cafe on the Old Town Square. We intended to take a walk across the river to Hradčany, but the weather was bitter and, with much to talk about, we were still sitting there at five.

Igor's presence was a reminder of the elementary fact that Czechoslovakia is a federation of two states, the Czech and the Slovak. The negotiations to reform the government, going on even as we spoke, involved a good deal of juggling of Slovak against Czech as well as communist against non-communist representation. The Slovaks are proud of their Slovakness—in Igor's company you learn not to use the word 'Czech' to apply to the country as a whole. But Igor was generally sceptical of the notion that political changes might lead to an awkward upsurge of Slovak nationalism.

Events in Bratislava appeared to have run a parallel course to those in Prague, with the Bratislavs having the particular excitement of being suddenly allowed to travel freely across the Austrian border, less than five miles away. In practice, Czechs and Slovaks are still restrained from foreign travel by the lack of foreign money. But here was a chance to to-and-fro across a ghostly Iron Curtain just for the sake of it, East-Berliner style, several return trips a day.

Were there any problems peculiar to Slovakia?

Yes, eastern Slovakia was a notoriously 'remote' part of the country and the spread of information from the capital had proved difficult, meeting with confusion and distrust. (Vaculík and Kriseova had made the same point about the rural areas generally.) The authorities seemed to have colluded in the problem, since there was a remarkable incidence of power cuts at the same time as opposition broadcasts. But not all Igor's stories raised laughter. There was the one about the Russian soldier (the Soviet army was still there, of course, keeping a *very* low profile) found hanged near a railway station. Suicide? Or something else?

At five-thirty we walked back to the hotel. Igor was good company. My pensive mood of the morning had lifted and I was now sanguinely resigned to the fact that I would not meet Wolf. When we entered the lobby I could see there was a message for me next to my key. It said: 'I am tall with bushy hair and glasses. I am waiting in the lounge. When you read this Mr Wolf will probably be waiting too. Miloš.'

I am still confused as to how this small miracle occurred: whether Wolf and Miloš converged on the hotel by mutual arrangement or by some remarkable coincidence. Even after later hearing Miloš's account, I am not entirely sure of the exact sequence of events.

I walked, with Igor, round the corner into the lounge. There was Miloš, as described. There, introduced by him, was Wolf. And there was a third man, who spoke English and gave his name as Weiss. We moved to another part of the lounge which could accommodate us all, and the whole strange, short encounter began.

The first element of strangeness was the setting. To repeat, this was one of Prague's big hotels. It was a Saturday evening. The lounge was busy and hung with Christmas decorations. We might have gone to my room, or somewhere else—the choice was Wolf's—but we were sitting down to talk in a place that only recently would have been quite unsafe, and perhaps still was. I was conscious throughout that people *were* listening to us (who would not have eavesdropped?). I vividly recall the young waiter, with the face of a bespectacled sixth-former, who brought our drinks and stared boggle-eyed, transfixed by what Wolf was saying.

The second element of strangeness was the air of feverish, if businesslike, haste. From the moment he sat down, Wolf launched into a monologue, interrupted almost exclusively by Miloš's disciplined translations. There were no questions put to me about the nature of my interest and no opportunity for me to explain it voluntarily. Nor was there much opportunity for me to ask questions. The nearest thing to small talk came from Weiss, who was the third element of strangeness. I had not anticipated a mystery companion, though such a figure should not have been so unexpected. It became plain that Weiss was not just there for his English; he was looking after Wolf in some way. He said of Wolf at one point: 'He is part of my family now.' It emerged that Weiss had been a prisoner too, for several years, some of them in Valdice.

The contrast between Weiss and Wolf could scarcely have been more pronounced. Whereas Wolf was all contained nervous energy and concentration, Weiss was relaxed, smiled a lot and was ready, when he could, even to joke and digress. He apologized for his teeth, which had been damaged in prison, but the defect hardly marred a kindly, avuncular face. Weiss was dressed in a casual cardigan; Wolf in a suit and tie which, if it were not for a general dishevelment (the tie was quickly loosened), might have been called dapper. The clothes had been sent from America.

In the space of an hour, I learned a little about Weiss, the man: that his passion was aeroplanes; that he had a library of eight thousand books. I learned very little about Wolf. When Wolf said that his wife had divorced him because she did not wish to be married to a criminal, there was no emotion and the remark was made almost incidentally. Weiss chipped in that his wife, too, had divorced him when he was a prisoner, but, on his release, they had met up again and married for the second time; and he was evidently delighted to repeat the story. It was as though Weiss was there to give the picture of a man who had been a prisoner yet was restored to a benign, rounded humanity.

Wolf was short, with the sort of slight frame that often suggests an intense mental life. Afterwards, when I asked myself the question, 'If you hadn't known who Wolf was, what would you have taken him for?' I answered: I would have taken him for some distrait chess-player, an obsessive academic, a mathematician. His face was distinctly Jewish, and I wondered how this may have affected the treatment he received from prison guards. He blinked a lot, with a twitch to his cheek, a definite tic. He sat on my right, with Miloš to my left. He spoke rapidly, a little breathlessly, mostly looking straight ahead or at Miloš, but now and then turning to me with a sort of uncertain smile, which I rightly or wrongly took as a seeking of reassurance. His hands were in contrast to the rest of him: thick, blunt fingers, with very little spare nail.

What did he say? In one sense he said what I had already heard, since the substance of the monologue, elaborated and extended, was similar to the dossier I had read on him and covered much the same ground. It was the third-person, case-history Wolf of the dossier, rather than the direct, first-person, intensely pitiable Wolf of the prison writings. There was, of course, something utterly new and strange in hearing facts already half known issuing from the lips of the man himself. But I confess to more than once having the absurd urge to stop him and say, 'I think I know this. Tell me about *yourself*.'

There was also the sense that what he was uttering was prepared, rehearsed, had often been repeated. He had certain things to say, then he would finish. It did not take long to surmise that Wolf had probably been doing a lot of this recently. Telling a lot of different people or groups of people, if rarely stray visitors from England, the facts. This was his work now, his task, the way in which, according to his neighbour, he was still 'active'. It was also, at some deeper level, the way he wanted, and was able, to deal with things. Weiss later confirmed the intuition. He said, 'We are very busy politically.' He spoke of fears that the prisons would be slow to change, that there would be a conspiracy to destroy prison and court records, a general hushing-up.

The repeated note from Wolf was forensic and legalistic: the attestation to accumulated injustice. He was not interested in his 'human story', nor in sensation, nor, save when he referred to Czechoslovakia's 'Gulag', in rhetoric. When he stated that he had received ten days of solitary confinement and a halving of rations for having a loose button, and I had to ask him, in amazement, to repeat what he said, he did not dwell on the matter. When he remarked that a 'co-defendant' had been released after one year and was working 'to this day' for the state security, it was spoken without special stress or elaboration, like the reference to his divorce.

His release on 17 May had been at the full term of his prison sentence. He had been ill for a month and was treated by a neurologist. Necessary follow-up treatment proved unforthcoming, partly because doctors were afraid of his reputation with the secret police. When fit to do so, he was required to report to the police every day. There were problems with both employment and accommodation, and there was pressure on him to leave Prague.

He was held in custody twelve times after he was released that spring, with a flurry of detentions in August. Court proceedings were opened against him twice. The police entered his flat several times, sometimes at night. The last such visit was on 15 November, less than three weeks ago. In the same month, when he was working as a stoker in a boiler-room, he was visited by police who threatened to throw him into the furnace. On 17 November he was arrested at home and held till eleven that night to prevent his participation in the events of that day. Since 17 November he has refused to go to a police station, but since the seventeenth (the finality of that day), persecution of him has ceased.

Wolf spoke of his years in prison with the intent but impersonal tone of a man in a witness box. There was little actual description. In ten years, prison rations were cut by half, but the workloads of enforced labour were increased. Prisoners were required to *pay* for their maintenance in prison, but because of reductions in their wages for forced labour and because of other financial penalties, the 'bill' could never be met. Wolf is still technically in debt to the state for 4,200 crowns for the privilege of six years' brutal punishment.

Conditions for political prisoners were worse than for others, one aspect of their degradation being that they were thrown in with the worst criminals (Weiss's foreman at one time was a triple murderer). Political prisoners were selected for the worst work and were not allowed to associate with each other. They were subjected to close scrutiny of their behaviour and speech and to regular reports by warders, who were directed to destroy prisoners psychologically. All prison functionaries, medical staff as well as guards, colluded in the cover-up of breaches of law and human rights.

Wolf was manifestly a brave man, but his readiness to endure the worst showed a staggering single-mindedness. When his half-sister asked for remission for him, Wolf refused to sign the application, on the grounds that only those who were guilty could ask for remission: accepting remission amounted to retraction. When he received his six-year sentence he also refused to appeal, on the grounds that he did not accept the legality of the verdict. He annulled an appeal made on his behalf by a lawyer. Pressure was put on him to bring an appeal, to demonstrate the fairness of the courts, and he was promised one year off his sentence. Wolf did not comply. In the twenty-two-month interval between his two stretches of imprisonment Wolf had been offered political asylum in France. He had refused on the grounds that, if he were granted asylum, all other victims should be offered the same.

After making this last point, Wolf brought things to an abrupt close. I had been wondering how long he would continue, whether there would be a more flexible stage in which he would be open to questions. But now he gave a quick expulsion of breath, said something which I was sure was the Czech equivalent of 'That's it,' and made the knee-patting gesture of a man about to depart. I looked at Igor, who looked bemused, and at Miloš, who wore his interpreter's mask. There was a reaching for coats, some final hand-shaking, some pleasantries from Weiss, and then the two were gone, as if hastening to some other, similar appointment, leaving behind a vacuum of bewilderment and the consciousness that all around us were eyes and ears.

Why should I have been so stunned? Given Wolf's history, I had been ready for anything, so why was the reality so confounding? And why, beneath it all, did I have a perverse feeling of disappointment? I had met him; he had spoken, on his own terms, which were the only proper terms; I had listened. Why should I feel sorry that I felt I was nowhere nearer to knowing him? What right did I have to know him? If I could conceive at all of what ten years of his kind of imprisonment might take away from a man, how should I expect anything to be rendered to me in an hour?

I had never asked him about his writing. What happened to that earlier work? Confiscated, destroyed? Did he (absurd question somehow) still want to write? It was sobering that I had met three other writers who, each with their own personal nuance, had transcended the image of the 'suffering Czech', yet Wolf had given it back to me in hard, annunciatory fact, as if at a press conference, with scarcely a touch of the personal.

Miloš had to leave. I thanked him for all he had done. Igor and I had a strong desire to be out of the hotel. As we walked off, I, for one, could not resist looking over my shoulder. We began the process of analysing what we had just experienced, but this slid into the anaesthetic urge to find a restaurant that served Slovak food, to drink several glasses of vodka, followed by several glasses of wine. A radio was switched on in the restaurant. It confirmed what Kriseova had told me in the hotel corridor: a new government would be sworn in tomorrow; the President would resign. It was the end of an era.

Walking late that night across the lower end of Wenceslas Square, I was stopped, not by a secret policeman, but by a street huckster with a small, puckered, toothless face. I thought my English would deter him, but he grabbed my hand, studied my palm and, with a confident American twang, assessed my life and character as follows: I had been a naughty boy, oh yes, a very naughty boy, and I would live to be seventy-four. This cost me ten crowns.

My last morning in Prague—Sunday the tenth, the day communist domination would cease—bloomed brilliant and clear.

A huge rally was planned for the afternoon in Wenceslas Square when the new government would be announced. But I had to be at the airport at two, and in any case had the feeling I would be an intruder at someone else's party. On my last day I wanted to do what I had not yet done: to cross the river, to walk up to Hradcany, to the castle, and appreciate that Prague is beautiful. A year ago the beauty had seemed bogus, even sinister. What place did aesthetics have in politics? But now, perhaps, Prague could be truly, unashamedly beautiful again. And so it was, its valleys and crests of architecture rising out of the dazzle of the winter morning.

Igor came with me. We crossed the Charles Bridge, seagulls squawking around us. What place did aesthetics have in politics? Seifert, whose love of Prague was as fierce as it was gentle, and who did not live, like Vaculík, to see the end of repression, wrote, with his own terrible heed of aesthetics:

> When I shall die—and this will be quite soon—
> I shall still carry in my heart
> this city's destiny.
>
> And mercilessly, just as Marsyas,
> let anyone be flayed alive
> who lays hands on this city,
> no matter who he is,
> no matter how sweetly he plays
> on his flute.

The Czechoslovak people, the guidebooks say, have always honoured their writers. The road up to the castle is named after a writer, the poet Jan Neruda, from whom Pablo Neruda borrowed his name. Hunched against the castle walls is the impossibly tiny, fairy-tale house where Kafka wrote part of *The*

Trial. And all over Prague there were poems, of a kind, blossoming on walls and windows and statues. Someone will anthologize them, if they haven't already. Igor translated: 'Husak, you talked a lot, but you said nothing.' 'He has eyes but he does not see; he has ears but he does not hear: who is he?'

Writers, writers!

We walked through the courtyards of the Presidential Palace, where even at that hour, perhaps, Husak was enjoying or suffering his last lunch as President, and over which flew the presidential flag with its motto which, on this day, could not have been more ironic, more Delphically barbed: 'Truth Shall Win'.

Igor insisted on coming to the airport to see me off. With events just beginning on Wenceslas Square, this seemed a considerable sacrifice. Perhaps he shared the 'secret wish'. Did Wolf have—would he, could he, ever have that wish?

Later, on the phone, Igor told me he'd gone back and caught the last of it: he 'couldn't resist'.

A television in the airport concourse showed pictures of the jubilant crowds. The plane left on time, minutes after the President's resignation. There were several Czechoslovaks on board and I wondered how they felt, to be flying out of their country on the day of its deliverance.

Jiří Wolf, Prague, December 1988.

FILMING THE FENS

NORFOLK AND TWICKENHAM, 1991

The days are gone, if they ever really existed, when to have a novel adapted for film was like being touched by the gods. And anyway the gods can have a clumsy touch. For every successful movie adaptation—however one defines that—there are lists of clunkers that must have made the authors shudder. The analogy should really be the other way round. The books come first and it's the authors who are the gods to whom the film industry, with a massive inferiority complex about its own creative initiative, has to come beseeching. But try suggesting that to the film industry. And it's certainly not how it feels to the godlike but perhaps near-destitute author when the movie people knock on the door.

The instances of authors being launched into the stratosphere by a movie adaptation are rare. Among my own author-friends, Michael Ondaatje is the outstanding example, but I'm not sure that I envy Michael. Anthony Minghella's hugely successful film of *The English Patient* put into worldwide circulation oceans of copies of Michael's book, but in the long run it also swamped it. Minghella, to his credit, made a good film of a novel that was by no means an obvious or easy choice for adaptation, but the book is more wonderful than the film, though it's now very hard to extricate it from the film's phenomenal success. It's even harder to extricate from the film the other work of a writer who, by the time *The English Patient* was published and won the Booker Prize (another fact that the film has rather made forgotten), had already published two other superb novels and a memoir. And how many people, if they equate the words *English Patient* with a book or an author at all, would know that Michael Ondaatje has also written almost a dozen volumes of poetry?

When Jeremy Irons put himself up to star with Meryl Streep in Karel Reisz's film of *The French Lieutenant's Woman*, it was clearly going to be a big-number production of an already highly successful novel. When, ten years later, he agreed to star in the film of *Waterland*, something he very much wanted to do, it was clearly going to be a low-budget operation which, but for Irons's participation, might never have happened at all. I'm not sorry that the filming of *Waterland* was a modest undertaking (of a difficult task) or even that the film wasn't a great success. It certainly didn't swamp the book for me (a rather water-filled book anyway), and, looking back, what I feel is that, despite an inauspicious start, I had a good time during the making of it which I might never have had if it had got the really big treatment—or, of course, if it had never been filmed at all.

I've been generally lucky with the movies. I'm, manifestly, not a purist: I let my work be filmed, though I try to be careful in doing so. I've taken the gamble three times and it's twice paid off, at least in forging friendships and giving me some good memories. A film was once made of my second novel, *Shuttlecock*, which, happily for me and for the world, never got released in the cinema. In fairness, it began as a perfectly sincere and serious project—a film-maker's vision—then turned into a lesson in how, along the rough road of development, compromise and an expedient artistic blindness can set in.

While it's true that there's no correlation between the merit of a film and the amount of money spent on it, it's also unfortunately true that many low-budget films that struggle to find funding succumb to a basic corruption: the object of the exercise becomes, in the end, not to make a film that's true to the original source, but just to make a film. Pure intentions turn into corner-cutting. No career points will be earned by a movie that doesn't get made. *Shuttlecock* got made (and I've always thought it could make a terrific film), but it soon went to what I imagine is the rather large graveyard of duff movies. It starred Alan Bates, who may occasionally turn in his grave because of it.

The films of *Waterland* and of *Last Orders* were more benign experiences, and in the case of *Last Orders*—of which there is more in a later piece in this book—the result (though you're always going to feel that the film isn't 'your book') was as good as any author, in a world in which travesties are regularly committed, can reasonably expect. There was the bonus, too, of a wonderful cast. If someone had said to me long ago when I went to see David Hemmings as a baby-faced Sixties idol in Antonioni's *Blowup* that one day he'd star (without the baby face) in a film of a novel written by me, I'd have said that pigs might fly. Sadly, David Hemmings is no longer with us, but I hope that, in his grave, he has the occasional smile over *Last Orders*. He certainly enjoyed it while it was being made.

To come back to the film of *Waterland*. So ungodlike was my role that I knew very little about what was happening—I'd been assuming nothing would happen—until about a fortnight before the filming began. But suddenly everything *was* happening. A script had been written, a director had been found and a cast and crew had been assembled on location in Norfolk, where the cameras were starting to roll. Would I like to come and take a look?

It was only when I did go and look and talk to some key people that I discovered certain things that might have made a more wrathfully godlike author throw a fit. For example, that large chunks of the novel which are set in Greenwich (London, England) were to be transposed in the film to—Pittsburgh, Pennsylvania. And that while Jeremy Irons as Tom Crick would retain his Fenland childhood (hence we were in Norfolk), he would mysteriously become in later life a teacher in a mid-American school.

Looking back, I can see I was naive, as writers can be when first dealing with some dimension of their profession that's additional to the main one of just writing. When you first learn that a book of yours is going to be translated, you don't immediately think that it might be *badly* translated and turn out to be a permanent misrepresentation of your work. You're just delighted. My detachment from the actual process of adapting *Waterland* (while I got on with my real work) was all very fine, but I could and should have done more checking up; I should have had more scrutiny over the script.

Now here I was encountering the movie business at its crassest. But Stephen Gyllenhaal, the (American) director, and Jeremy Irons didn't seem crass. They seemed like intelligent people. And Jeremy Irons, who told me he loved my novel, surely wouldn't have chosen to act in a film that would just take cynical liberties with it. Surely he and his wife, Sinead Cusack, wouldn't have chosen not only to act together but to play husband and wife for the first time on screen (that's acting, but it's also rather personal) in a film which they thought would have no integrity or heart.

Though writers can certainly be innocent when they emerge, blinking, from their studies into some not wholly authorial zone, I think film-makers can be oddly innocent too (though it's not the standard perception), even rather winningly so. Innocent, I mean, in their easy exercise of the assumed licence of film—in what they can get away with or just choose to *do*. Somehow, films can perpetrate things which would never be forgiven in a book. Writers, who only have to worry about what gets from their heads onto the page and so into the reader's head (only that!), spend a great deal of time, I believe, wondering about what they can get away with or just convincingly, effectively do. They develop a complicated instinct in this area which is anything but naive. And maybe this is one reason why in the literary world at large cunning and circumspection aren't at all unknown. Film-makers, perhaps because they have so much bigger and louder logistics at their disposal, seem able to make the crudest intellectual decisions with blithe and ingenuous confidence. I once had a conversation with a good writer-friend who'd done a great deal of work for the screen, in which the question arose whether movie people were nicer or not than book people. My friend, with the weight of experience, came down on the side of movie people. 'I like movie people,' he said. 'They stab you in the front.' And sometimes, it seems to me, they can do so without even knowing they're stabbing you.

Anyway, I didn't throw a fit. I winced and bore it stoically. And, on the whole, though I wish a better film had finally emerged—a film that hadn't distorted basic elements of the book and a film that, as film, had lived up in all parts to the real strengths and sensitivity it had only in some—I'm glad I didn't kick up a storm. Whether or not I'd been calculatingly kept in the dark until this point, it was clear to me that even the most almighty tantrum couldn't reverse a process already under way.

If I'd marched off the set there and then, I'd have certainly missed some absorbing days, not only in Norfolk, but later on when the filming moved to Twickenham Studios, conveniently close to home for me. By an irony that, if my frame of mind had been different, might only have been galling, the interior scenes for the wholly spurious Pittsburgh household later in the story were shot in a house in south London just a fifteen-minute walk from where I live, and the American classroom scenes, with an imported cast of American teenage actors, were shot in an old school almost as near to my own door. I might have asked Stephen Gyllenhaal not to rub it in. But by this stage he and I were friends and I'd become something of a cinephile, a regular visitor at Twickenham, popping in to see what was happening and spending time afterwards with Stephen in the editing rooms or in the Chinese restaurant across the road, drinking and talking the whole thing over.

When directors are in the midst of making a film they live and breathe the whole process and you sense their need of some special interlocutor who can externalize a constant, obsessive interior conversation. When it's your book they're filming and when you're in the presence of a genuinely creative effort, it's not difficult to throw in your own measure of assistance. Despite that transatlantic aberration (and certain other strange aberrations in its handling of time), the film certainly wasn't made in a cynical or unconscientious way. In Norfolk, the director of photography, Robert Elswit, produced some haunting images of the novel's authentic locale and I watched several actors getting uncomplainingly very cold and wet in the cause of recreating my book.

I was genuinely sad when the shooting finished—or, rather, when it moved to America. I felt the best bit for me was over, and I was oddly uninterested in the final product. I missed going to Twickenham, or, more precisely, I missed the frisson of going to a present-day Twickenham but only, in a sense, to go to the Fens, to a lock-keeper's cottage in the 1940s. For me, it wasn't just visiting, but revisiting too.

Stephen flew back to California (via Pennsylvania), but we've kept in touch and have seen each other from time to time since. He's more than once invited me to Hollywood. I think Twickenham's more my sort of place. In recent years he's acquired a secondary kudos as the father of two ever-rising film stars, Maggie and Jake Gyllenhaal. One of the junior stars of *Waterland*, Ethan Hawke, went on to his own fully risen stardom and to become a writer as well—it can work the other way round. One day I received a copy of his first novel. The younger Maggie Gyllenhaal had a very minor part in *Waterland*, in one of those perfidious Pittsburgh scenes.

And it can be revealed that the author also had a part in *Waterland*—about two seconds' worth, heavily disguised in Edwardian costume and moustache, playing a drunk. Definitely no thoughts of stardom, but another form of clandestine revisiting. Several years later, when *Last Orders* was being filmed, its director, Fred Schepisi, would also rope me in to being an extra.

In one of the early scenes in that film, in the Coach and Horses pub, extremely discerning viewers may notice a certain figure in the background, propping up the bar. A clear case of typecasting, I think.

With Stephen Gyllenhaal and Jeremy Irons, Norfolk, 1991.

MAKING AN ELEPHANT

SYDENHAM, 1922–92

My father died in 1992. I wrote this memory of him, which also took me back to some of my own earliest memories, more than ten years later.

Making an Elephant

The death of a father is, in most cases, an inevitable passage of life. If you're a novelist, however open-mindedly or unwittingly you start out, you know that certain big personal events must one day be accommodated into your work. There will, for example, be the novel you write after your father's death. It won't be about his death or even about him, but it can't help but be informed by his death.

He had a battery of first names: Lionel Allan Stanley. Fortunately, he liked to be known as Allan or simply Al. I never heard the word Lionel pass his lips. He was born in London in the early 1920s and brought up in Lower Sydenham, SE26, in a street optimistically called Fairlawn Park. I'd never been there, but after he died I went, on a sort of a pilgrimage, to see where he'd come from. A little, squat, terraced house, like thousands of others, but distinguished by its standing at an odd slight angle to the house next door and by the fact that, though occupied, it was spectacularly neglected. The tiny front garden was a seethe of creeping ivy, and seated on or sinking, rather, into the vegetation were two immobilized, rusting cars. They filled the cramped space between front window and street. The ivy had taken hold and was creeping up into the wheel arches.

I was strangely relieved—elated even—by this conspicuous dereliction. The place wasn't just ordinary and anonymous. It was singled out, even by that crooked angle, from its unremarkable neighbours, and that ivy and wreckage (I'll never know the story) were like some mock-portentous, tongue-in-cheek acknowledgement of mortality and the grave.

Lower Sydenham. The name embodies more than one kind of stratification. Sydenham is a long straggle of a suburb ascending a hill. As you climb you go up in the world in both senses, or at least in my father's day you would have done; the gradations have blurred now. At a certain point, up from the railway station, things become leafy, comfortable, sedate. You pass the church, and the house where Shackleton the polar explorer lived. The top of the hill is where once stood, like some acme of human aspiration, the Crystal Palace.

When my father was still young, a teenager from the bottom end of Sydenham, he met my mother. Her family, which hadn't originated in Sydenham either, inhabited its middle slopes and in due course, after one house was bombed, would move further up.

I vividly remember, though it's gone now, my maternal grandparents' house, just off Westwood Hill—a tall, singular, spooky structure with massive steps, like a museum entrance, leading up to the front door. It stood in an odd, thin, isolated triangle of ground where two roads merged. The pinched ground-plan and the roots and shade of the trees that lined two sides were the bane of my grandfather's gardening.

As well as a persevering gardener, my grandfather was a haphazard collector of curios, and the house was dotted with strange little articles, some hidden away, the exact significance of which I never really knew. On a small round table in the hall was a wooden model of Drake's ship the *Golden Hind*. How it had sailed into the house or what it represented for its occupants was a mystery. Kept in a drawer, there was a watch that had supposedly belonged to another polar explorer, Peary. Inside my quiet-mannered grandfather, perhaps, was the soul of an adventurer.

I now own the glassily polished mahogany dining table that was my grandmother's pride and joy and that when not in use would be ceremonially draped, like a catafalque, with a heavy maroon-velvet cover. It too had made the journey up the slopes of Sydenham. When a flying bomb had fallen almost directly on the previous Sydenham house, with my grandparents, my mother and a dog (never to be seen again) cowering inside, my grandmother said two things after the dust and shock began to settle. First: 'Are we all all right?' Then: 'And how's my dining-room table?'

What I most remember about the house was its altitude. A cavernous stairwell took you up and up. There may have been only three or four flights, but I was very small, and they seemed to go on for ever and to climb through zones of increasing dread. It was a sort of grim challenge to mount them, all alone, to the top, but at the summit was a reward, a strange little perch. There was a landing with a window, next to a garret-like spare bedroom, and on the landing was a table and chair, and on the table an archaic typewriter.

My grandfather worked for the Oliver Typewriter Company. Why this particular machine, with its stiff epaulettes of spokes, was placed where it was is something else I'll never know, but it drew me magnetically, via that climb of terror. I was allowed to sit there with some sheets of paper and thump away. God knows what at that age I would have bashed out, but it kept me happy, if not exactly quiet. I'd forget, behind my back, the ordeal of the stairwell.

And from that landing you could look down, over the tops of trees, on a whole vista of Sydenham. Round the corner, past some grand Victorian villas, was Cox's Lane, surprisingly rural in appearance, with a clapboard cottage or two, a reminder of how Sydenham was once, like so much of London, just unsuspecting countryside colonized by the gentry. Next to Cox's Lane was Sydenham Wells Park, one of the lesser-known London parks, but with hidden charms. A little stream (from the 'wells' themselves) wound through one corner of it, feeding a duck pond, beside which my father, aged perhaps eight or nine, was once photographed, a swan in the background.

He wears a white shirt and shorts, held up by a thickly emphatic belt, and sandals without socks. His hair is the thatch that I too had when I was small and is pale like mine was, though while his became black and groomable, mine merely darkened. His face hovers between a frown and a smile.

The duck pond is still there. If you walk past it, then up and over the steep hill on the other side of the park, then—another hidden surprise—down a path through a thick oak wood, you come eventually to Dulwich College (the wood is Dulwich Wood), my school for six years.

Here my father took me to be interviewed one day when I was not much older than he was in that photograph, after I'd gone through the dubious selection process known as the eleven-plus. A scholarship boy, a child of the 1950s and now, just, the 1960s. I had the feeling, as never before, of being summoned by grown-upness.

My father had taken the day off work but wore his best suit and his hair was Brylcreemed. He may have thought he was under assessment himself. I sat with him, mute with nerves, outside the headmaster's study, waiting to be called. I was scrubbed and brushed, my own hair somehow plastered down, and absolutely aware that this was one of those moments when you had unconditionally to 'be on your best behaviour'.

Years later, as an unexemplary sixth-former, I would be hauled in and lengthily harangued by the same headmaster for letting the school down, even for being part of the process by which— I only quote—'the country was going to the dogs'. (I'd gone through a door marked 'No Entrance'.)

Shackleton, the man who'd lived just over the hill but had escaped to the ends of the earth, was Dulwich's most illustrious former pupil. The school preserved the famous open boat, the *James Caird*, in which he'd made his heroic rescue journey from the Antarctic to South Georgia. It stood, forlornly beached, in a sort of cage outside the sports block and wasn't so devotedly looked after. Dust, leaves and random litter used to blow through the wire grille at the front and collect inside its gunwales. Stuck to its side, next to an area of clearly patched-up woodwork, was a rather graceless label saying 'Hole Made by Ice'.

There, on my pilgrimage day, was Shackleton's house, with its blue plaque, on Westwood Hill. There was my father's old front garden, with its rotting cars.

The suburbs can be very strange. If you turn back from Wells Park and continue the climb out of Sydenham you get to a broad ridge and the site of the Crystal Palace. Over the other side of the ridge, in the former grounds of the Palace, there used to be, and perhaps still are, some vast—and vastly inaccurate—stone replicas of dinosaurs, rearing up among the rhododendrons. For some reason this whole area—Sydenham, Dulwich, Norwood—was once favoured by rich Victorian tea merchants, and much of the surviving evidence of wealthy idiosyncrasy, the crumbling Italianate mansions among the trees, owes itself to that banal British institution, the cup of tea. One of the merchants, Horniman, endowed an eccentric museum: musical instruments, tribal masks and (living) tropical fish and amphibia. A favourite place, naturally, of my grandfather's, with his curator's yen for the exotic.

Memories of the original Palace, particularly of the night in 1936 when it spectacularly burnt down, were part of my parents' and their parents' lore. To me it was just a bare plateau where in the 1950s they built the TV mast—symbol of a new age as the Palace had been of an old—which still towers over south London. 'Crystal Palace', the name, remained, robbed of its wondrous resonance: a location, a bus terminus, a middling football team. But when I was small, coming back in our car on winter evenings from visits to my grandparents—by now we lived in South Croydon—it still had a fairy-tale aura. Driving along the broad hilltop beside the site of the Palace was like driving along a vast shelf, from which, on the opposite side, you could look down towards central London, London proper: a sea of lights, a black bowl of jewels.

The car would have been our first, a Vauxhall Wyvern, curvaceous and thickly chromed. To my father it was not just a coveted emblem of mobility, upward and general, but, with his instinct for things mechanical that I've never inherited, an object of ceaseless devotion. He drove it with a coaxing sensitivity as if it were a sentient being.

No doubt that view from the Palace would seem commonplace now. London itself, the inner core, was unknown to me then. I know it now, but I still have a sense of it—elusive, glamorous, a dark phosphorescent lake—that comes from those journeys, sitting behind my dad in the marvel of our car.

He grew up and met my mother in Sydenham. Perhaps no great social elevation was involved, since my impression is that my mother's family, on her mother's side, had come down in the world. Once immigrants from the far side of Europe, they'd lived prosperously—they were tailors—in Whitechapel, which, as my grandmother kept reminding me, was not all shabby East End. How much the former graciousness was just wishful thinking, I don't know. I remember being taken to see one of her eight siblings (though quite possibly he was of the *previous* generation), known to me as 'Uncle Cotton Reel': a wizened, pin-eyed man, the incarnation of a Phiz illustration in Dickens, who looked as if he'd spent all his life hunched over needle and thread at the back of some dark, crooked little shop.

They would have met in the 1930s. They married in 1943. When the war began my father was only seventeen, barely out of school, but he seems to have volunteered pretty promptly, opting not just for the navy but for the Fleet Air Arm, to train as a pilot—a precise and daring choice, which nothing in his obscure family history points to. I have to assume it came from his own gallant volition. At the same time he made a much more mundane commitment. He entered the civil service at the lowest possible age and grade. The understanding was that he would work till his call came, then his job would be held for him till he returned. His civil service and his military service would clock up together.

It seems both provident and reckless: the simultaneous choosing of aerial danger and earthbound security, and must surely have had about it the feeling of a bet—or of incongruous trust. Till he returned? In 1940 he was selected to become a naval pilot. For a year or more before then he'd been that lowliest of creatures, a messenger-boy.

Then the extraordinary period began. He was sent to Florida to learn to fly, to the air base at Pensacola on the east–west strip of the Florida coast, close to Alabama. Warmth, sunshine, ease: America hadn't yet entered the war. At home civilians, including my mother-to-be, were enduring privations and, in London, regular danger. It must have all seemed mockingly upside-down. Back there, rubble, food in short supply; here, watermelons, palms, shimmering heat.

There is a photo album, together with some boxes of loose photos, from which I get much of my sense of these years. The sections aren't always extensive, the photos are the small, often unrevealing productions of a cheap camera, but everything is assembled with my father's characteristic meticulousness—little captions in white ink on the thick black pages—as if from the start he'd made it his purpose, his project, to chronicle this special time of his life. The Florida section contains just a few snaps, all of a holidayish, sightseeing kind. Trips into the heart of the state: the Everglades, Spanish moss, bleached wooden sidewalks like those in cowboy towns, alligators in show pools. Nothing to do with planes.

But at some point in those months in Florida, perhaps relatively early on, he would have done that terrifying and exultant thing, the thing he'd put his name down for: flown solo for the first time, over the gleam of the Gulf of Mexico, taken off and landed all by himself. I never heard him speak directly of the sheer thrill of flying, of being airborne and alone, the rapture for which the word exaltation seems exactly made. But I can't believe he didn't feel it, over and over, as anyone performing that miraculous trick must feel it. Or that the exaltation, the privilege, even the lust didn't stay in his blood. In fact, I know it did.

In a still-neutral country they couldn't wear uniforms, at least off base. After Pearl Harbor that changed. His group came back not only commissioned but wearing officers' uniforms made with superior American cloth and cut with American style. The naval officer's uniform wins hands down for handsomeness over all others and, fed with Florida food and still tanned perhaps from Florida sun, they must have made quite a stir.

Home again, to Sydenham. And after the exaltation—bathos. An officer and a pilot, but for the time being kept from the skies, one of his duties was to attend a course at the Royal Naval College in Greenwich, to be instructed in the niceties of being an officer—and gentleman. Literally, this included how to sit at table, how to manage a knife and fork. Greenwich is only four miles from Sydenham. So for a strange interlude he would have boarded every day not a plane but a 108 bus, to join other novice officers under the famous ceiling in the Painted Hall of Wren's college building. Perhaps while he waited with me for my interview at Dulwich, which in those days had a sort of officer-and-gentleman atmosphere, all this came back to him.

I was finally called in, for inspection. He squeezed my arm.

Table manners, knives and forks—in the middle of a war.

He was sent, with his squadron, to South Africa—another long journey to faraway sunshine. The eventual destination was Durban, to join an aircraft carrier returning from the East. The carrier, I think, was the *Hermes*, and, had he joined it, my father's war would have been with the Japanese and might have been short. As it turned out, the East was the one part of the world his war didn't include. His ship-to-be was sunk before it, or he, reached Durban.

So, in the album, he once again appears in holiday mood—sitting on the rocks on top of Table Mountain, no doubt with a reinforced sense of the goodness of being alive. More palms and casuarinas, the surf of the Cape coast. 'The Rocks at Hermanus.'

He and his fellow officers wait to board their train to Durban: they stand around, hands in pockets; one of them licks an ice cream. Snaps from the train window. 'Karoo.'

So much of my father's 'war' seems, in fact, like an extraordinary slice of fortune, a gift—seeing the world. He might have been on the *Hermes*. He might have been somewhere amid the havoc of the North Atlantic. Planeless and shipless, his squadron was sent to Kenya, to an airstrip halfway between Mombasa and Nairobi. There they stayed, in the semi-bush, living in tents, flying, training, awaiting further orders, for I'm not sure how long. Africa and its baked interior (he could hardly have envisaged this, opting for a life on aircraft carriers) entered his consciousness. Four years before, he'd been a schoolboy in south London, then the humblest of minions in a government office. Now here he was, in the clear brilliant mornings, flying round Mount Kilimanjaro, watching the great herds fan out from the shadow of his wing.

Eventually, Mombasa again: a carrier, and all the way back to Europe by the long Cape route. And here was another sort of gift. The carrier was the *Illustrious*. Most of the carriers my father would later fly from were dumpy little escort vessels, some of them converted merchant ships, with gruff, doggy names like *Tracker, Chaser*. But the *Illustrious* was a true fleet carrier, a great ship with a name going back to Nelson's time. And over the decks of such a carrier, however outranked by non-flying officers, its pilots must have walked like lords, the creatures for whom the whole floating edifice was made.

Northwards from Cape Town, through tropical waters, bound in fact for the Mediterranean and Malta, and a grand entry into the Grand Harbour of Valetta—a marine band playing, the ship's company paraded in 'whites'. By then Malta, battered and scarred, had been freed from its terrible siege, and through its rescued streets a squadron of British naval pilots must have walked, again, like lords. And here was another blue and sun-struck sea for my father: the Med.

At some point on that voyage north from Cape Town someone took a photo of him. He stands on the flight deck in the middle of a little group of fellow pilots, all of them towered over by the crowding bulks and huge propeller blades of aircraft. Full hot sunshine. My father, in khaki shorts (I think of the boy by the duck pond), is bare to the waist. It's one of those not-so-typical moments when he's the centre of attention, so much so that he's heedless of the camera. Everyone is listening to him, heads bent forward. He has something amusing to tell, it seems, since his face is breaking into a smile. The moment is all his and it seems, too, as if caught in it is all his prime—all the extraordinariness of his being where he is on the deck of a great basking warship in the middle of an ocean, and all the nonchalance, that only youth can give, of occupying the scene as if it were the casualest thing in the world.

The *Illustrious* took his squadron to Malta to provide air cover for the landings at Salerno: the only time my father's war career coincides with one of the names that have gone into the history books. But his war had begun in earnest now, lapsing into a kind of unnoteworthiness and routine, which perhaps is largely what it was. Scapa Flow: convoys to Russia, Murmansk, alternating with convoys to Gibraltar and into the Med again. The long, perilous, icy run into the Arctic and the shorter, southerly, sun-nier one. A period stationed on land in Northern Ireland; then, in the last months, in Yeovilton, Somerset: an instructor, a trainer of pilots himself.

It all sounds, compared with some wars, rather flat—or rather lucky. But I have to remind myself how he was always one of that select and ever-vulnerable few, a fighter pilot, and that there was a constant heroism in what he regularly had to do: to land an aircraft on an absurdly small surface, perhaps pitching in a strong sea or suddenly cloaked by evil weather. In the Arctic, if you ditched you had only seconds—and aircraft frequently ditched, flipping over the end of the stubby decks, missing, as they landed, the crude system of wires and barriers that was supposed to clutch them from the air.

All that and, of course, an enemy. Among the loose photos are several of a U-boat, on the surface, under air attack, taken close enough so that you can see a single brave figure on its deck, handling its spindly gun, firing back. It's all blurred, ill-composed and without drama, nothing like how such a scene would be recreated for a film. It has the strange, grey quality of the incidental, the inconsequential: the little man, in the middle of nowhere, his little gun, its little whiff of smoke. But it's war, and the little man may be about to die.

Another index of those years, along with the photos: my father's pilot's logbook. It's mostly full of tedious, repetitious entries, seemingly written in half-code. It records his shifts round the globe, the changes of ship or squadron. At intervals there are appraisals from senior officers: so many marks according to a laid-down scale, as if the war is really a progress through some second school. 'A competent pilot.' Seven out of ten . . . But you turn a page and read, in the usual neat hand: 'One Focke-Wulf 190 shot down in sea in flames.' I can't help wondering what was going through my father's head as he wrote that.

The son, of course, has the obvious thought. In the one-to-one of aerial combat the odds can't have been so complicated.

That time, it was the other plane, the other man. But it might have been him. I wouldn't be here to know.

With some of his comrades, it was them. The one who went missing north of Norway. The one who crashed into a mountainside in Ireland—when I was small, we used to see that one's widow. Her son, named after his father, once came to stay, to be shown the sights of London. I can't remember at the time really putting two and two together, really understanding. He had no father. Killed in the war. If not in action, just a mountainside.

But my father survived. Enemy fire, accidents, all the possible disasters of sea and air. No wounds, no obvious scars. Several leftovers: his leather flying jacket, some canvas parachute-bags, turned into innocent domestic articles. Memories, certainly, mostly undivulged. Photographs. His special time came to its end. He never harped on it or went to squadron reunions. I'll never know how much it stayed inside him.

Not long before his death, when I got word that he was badly ill, I was in Australia—a bit of the world he'd never see. I broke off my trip to come home (part of me, I think, already knew), flying from Sydney airport, over the harbour, on a brilliant golden August afternoon: one of the great take-offs. But what you see, looking down from a jumbo jet, can hardly match the glory of the solo pilot, knowing all the poise, all the power and achievement, is his. The landscape of central Australia, like some rippled red-brown sea, seemed never to end.

He flew, mostly, a heavy, thick-nosed American fighter, the Grumman Wildcat, known in the British navy as the Martlet. It has none of the fearsome grace of the famous fighter planes. It looks quite hard to get off the ground. His most favoured individual aircraft, 'P for Peter', decided how my older brother would be christened. He had, of course, as I do, the aerobatic surname.

The war, or the Fleet Air Arm, didn't give him up easily. By some quirk, his formal demobilization failed to arrive till long after others like him had received theirs. Though he was back in Sydenham he was still officially a naval officer and—one very useful side-effect—still drawing an officer's pay, considerably more than his civilian earnings would have been. It was a tricky dilemma whether to spend the money or save it, in case the Admiralty wanted it back. Word eventually came through, and he wore his naval uniform for the last time in June 1946, to visit my mother who had just given birth to his first son. It had quite an effect, my mother says, on the nurses. On that same June day the Derby was run for the first time since the start of the war and a horse called Airborne won. The pun could hardly be richer. My father, with all that navy pay, never placed the bet.

In the same nursing home, three years later, I was born. Then we moved to a new house in South Croydon where my memories really begin.

He went back, six years older, to the job he'd left. An ex-naval officer, his uniform consigned to mothballs, now a clerical officer in the civil service: not a high-flier by any means—as if for six years he'd put on fancy dress. But he was in one piece and in employment. His providence, or bet, had paid off. And these were the days—the war only reinforced it—when you didn't look to your work for anything so colourful as excitement or fulfilment; you looked to it for safety. That was the deal. You'd had your thrills.

I don't know what my father, if he'd had a real choice, would have wanted to be. For many of his generation it was an unasked question. You fell in with what was required. Nonetheless, among the many things he might have wanted to be, he'd been one: a pilot.

He spent the rest of his working life in a department of the civil service that had a name Dickens might have invented: the National Debt Office. He toiled in and for the nation's debt, a task of some immensity and the source of many jokes. But neither his office's grandiose name nor the imposing sums of money he had to deal with could hide the fact that for not quite forty years he was essentially a bookkeeper, a clerk.

The National Debt Office no longer exists, absorbed into the murky workings of the Treasury, perhaps on the skulking principle that the national debt is best kept as unlocatable as possible. At least in my father's day it owned up to itself. It was housed then in a grey stone building in Old Jewry, just round the corner from the Bank of England, of which it was an official annexe. This meant that it was accorded, just inside its faceless entrance, a magnificent flunkey of a doorman, dressed in a bright pink tailcoat, waistcoat and top hat with cockade. All Bank of England departments had these florid sentinels and they all seemed to be tall and broad-chested and to have flamboyant moustaches.

Inside was a sort of essence of bureaucracy. I can still make the smell of my father's office tingle in my nostrils: the smell of waxed wood is in it, and of some standard-issue floor polish and of various kinds of standard-issue stationery. Something rubbery too (rubber stamps?), and, beyond that, the smell of cool, stony, featureless corridors that are mopped every day, and of sternly carbolic washrooms.

It all blurs somehow with the daunting smell of the corridor outside the headmaster's study at Dulwich—with the smell and clanging echoes of all those corridors of life of which we can never be sure if we have chosen them or they us.

My father, who had reserves of humour, once wrote against 'Occupation', when filling out a form, the single eloquent word 'Drudgery'. I only ever went a few times to his office and so rarely glimpsed him, in the professional sense, 'at work'. But I saw him any number of times at home, hanging wallpaper, painting, fixing the car, doing this or that job with the zeal of a natural, versatile handyman. His office was always to me a vague, walking-through-the-wrong-door shock.

For over thirty years after the war, like countless others, though not with the bowler-hatted, square-shouldered aplomb of those who made real money there, he travelled every day up to the City and back. The absolute paradigm: the new house in the outer suburbs, the job in town, the train to and from. It was the train at first, for many years, even when we had the car, then at some point in the car-owning era he acquired, through promotion or sheer luck, that priceless thing, a parking space in his office's tiny, hemmed-in car park, and so abandoned the misery of the jam-packed trains for the more independent torments of the crawling, swearing car journey.

Sometimes, in school holidays, I'd travel up with him—he always left very early to 'beat the traffic'—and, while he went to work, I'd wander at will, as day broke, round the City. For me it had romance: a great grey beast stirring in the winter dawn. To him it was just the Smoke, the Grind.

As a contented child, I saw none of the costs, personal or financial, of my contentment: that it was my father's lot to administer the nation's debt while constantly steering us out of the red, his accepted task to endure a daily tedium, to scale the ladder of promotion—executive officer, senior executive officer—so we might have all we had.

Which wasn't so little. Ours was the quintessential post-war package with all its fresh-faced promise and amenity. A brand-new semi-detached house built on the very edge of the suburbs and bought (as I later got to know) through the combination of a subsidy from my grandparents and the concessionary price offered by the developer to ex-servicemen. There was another former navy lieutenant turned white-collar commuter in number eight.

A short distance away in one direction were open fields and farmland: the literal edge of the country. London was moving outwards, and behind all the bland domestic trappings of suburbia there was an odd, spit-on-the-palms pioneering spirit. We had a fair-sized back garden which I can only remember in its finished state, but it had needed to be worked from a virgin plot. My father, with his joy in physical tasks, must have loved nothing better. There's another photo of him pausing in his labours, sitting on a wicker chair that has been carried outside, with a mug of tea and a cigarette (Senior Service). He could be an early settler in Nebraska.

For years our hillside cul-de-sac remained unmade-up, just a rough broad track worn into the chalky subsurface of what were really the lower slopes of the North Downs. In summer it turned white and dusty. Clumps of flowering vegetation would sprout up along the edges, crowded, in my not-so-fanciful memory, with butterflies. Across the road, below where the houses began, was a tennis club, behind a strip of fence, where my brother and I, when we were old enough to become junior members, could pretend to be Laver or Hoad. Summers went with the pok-pok of tennis balls.

Beyond the tennis courts was my primary school, St Peter's, another paradigm of the new age: newly built, cleanly architectured and lawned. Rowans and silver birches waved in the breeze beyond the classroom windows. We were all told we were the New Elizabethans, and, apart from having to eat every bit of your school dinner, I barely remember a bad moment there.

It all seems, in fact, a kind of dreamland, a modest little attempt at heaven on earth, though by the time I was in my teens, having been thoroughly nurtured by it, I'd naturally had enough of it.

Between school and university I took myself off, as many of my generation did, across Europe with a rucksack towards Asia, though the hippy trail petered out for me somewhere in eastern Turkey. My father at the same age could never have done or even contemplated such a thing.

A small incident stands out from my childhood. I still keep its physical relic—which I realize now has acquired the totemic status of those mysterious odds and ends in my grandfather's house. My father was the happy handyman I could never be; I became the willing pen-pusher he never was. But once, in spontaneous deference to his handyman skills and wanting to please him, I made a wooden elephant.

He must have seen real wild elephants in Africa during the war. He must have looked down from his cockpit and spotted them lumbering through the bush—dipped his wing and swooped to get a better view, but none of this would have occurred to me when I made my wooden one. Three pieces of thick plywood cut from a pattern with a fretsaw (I was good at twisting and breaking the blades): one for the body, head and trunk; two for the legs either side. Glue them together, rub down the joins and if you'd done the cutting well you had an elephant that could stand up by itself.

I didn't do such a bad job and my father had watched progress keenly, encouragingly. Then the time came to paint it. What colour, he asked. Yellow, pink?

I found these suggestions ridiculous. Grey, of course. Elephants were grey, weren't they? He counter-argued, ready for me to choose from his impressive array of paint pots, but I just didn't get it. Grey it was.

The strange reversal stays with me, as does the sad object of it all: that I should have been the realist, he the fantasist. It's not even a true elephant grey. It was the only grey available, the one used in finishing off Airfix kits, battleship grey.

As I stood, years later, outside his boyhood home, seeing those derelict cars, I thought: would he really have got this joke? Two cars, just left to decay in the front garden, the front garden itself gone rampant: such things to him would have been sacrilege, surely?

I wish I'd painted it pink.

In the late 1970s, because of some civil-service shake-up, he was offered early retirement. For some in those days this could have been a sort of execution, a knell, but he snapped it up. By then he'd not quite notched up the all-important forty years of service, but a full pension, temporarily on ice, was part of the package. He was fifty-five, my age now. He turned his back on the National Debt, sold the house in South Croydon (with surprisingly little sentiment or ceremony, I recall) and moved with my mother to the Sussex downs near Hastings.

Another paradigm: the house on the hill, the view of the sea —though I don't remember his retirement being particularly retiring; there was always some task, some scheme, some enthusiasm on the go. Here he had fifteen free and contented years, till one summer when I'd gone to Australia, when he was seventy, an otherwise fit and full-of-life man, he developed stomach cancer and died.

Now I do the bookkeeping, actuarial sums. He might have worked till he was sixty-five. He had those fifteen years. Therefore he was lucky. As he was lucky to have lived through the war. As he was lucky, as he himself often said, that all those blandishments of the Sixties didn't just favour the younger generation. This was the time, after all, not only of the hippy trail but of the package tour: sudden affordable foreign travel for all. So, from the mid-Sixties on, there he was, with my mother now, seeing the world again, back again in the blue Med just for pleasure this time, and the photographs now in colour. Good times. The kids off their hands. In the cupboard under the telly, a regular stock of duty-frees.

At some point in the Sixties he made a small but historic decision. He switched from his old-sailor, non-filter Senior Service to cosmopolitan, jet-setting Peter Stuyvesant—to which, so the slogan insisted, people were changing in 'city after city'. Even in Croydon. It always seemed to me a telltale, watershed moment, a throwing off of the past, a throwing in of his lot with the new.

I see him in the porch of the Sussex house when I arrived on visits, a beam on his face—the gin-and-tonics soon to be poured —looking like a man on permanent holiday.

His end was quick and cruel. He handled it as he handled so much of his life: practically, without fuss and with the usual recourse to humour. He was always, in those last weeks, concentratedly *there*—always, insistently, himself. Though how much of a life, at its end, do you see?

He made little notes and memos—what the surgeon had told him, what to ask—the handwriting a little shaky, but unchanged from the captions under the photographs, from the entries in the pilot's logbook. He might have lived to ninety. But, of course, death had been close to him—he knew more about it than I did—long ago, before. Others had had their turn then.

Only once, in those last few weeks, did we 'lose' him—I mean, other than when he was simply unconscious—only once did I almost not recognize my father. The end was inevitable, but certain procedures, interventions, were still offered, disruptive in themselves but designed to ease his suffering. He agreed to undergo them, more in a spirit of workmanlike cooperation —little last projects—than anything else, though he didn't agree to them all. One of his refusals produced, as he was dying, one of the best jokes of his life: 'Doctor, I don't think I'd have the stomach for that.'

But one procedure he did assent to left him—because of the drugs involved, I suppose—babbling, agitated, even thrashing about in his bed. It passed soon enough; the nursing staff were reassuring, but while it was happening it was genuinely frightening. The sidebars had been raised on the bed and for a while he was actually like a creature in a cage. I remember him trying to bite the hand I put out to him.

You'd have thought he'd gone mad.

Not completely mad, however. There was a thread of desperate intention to it all. It seemed he saw us—his family—as people trying to overpower him, to prevent him, prohibit him from something. In his ravings the word 'plane' kept coming up. 'My plane.' It seemed he believed he was being kept from his plane.

Everything had been twisted into this terrible conspiracy of restraint. Why wasn't he allowed to get to his plane?

How do you interpret such a thing? Hold it in your memory? Next day he was himself—his dying self—again. But right there and then he was a man I didn't know, couldn't ever know: my father, before I was born. And the situation was clear, no subtle interpretation was needed. He was being grounded against his will.

POEMS

In the misty and often lengthy periods which I later come to realize are the preludes to my starting a new book, I've noticed that my reading can shift from novels, or anything large, to poetry, as if I'm aware that whatever I do next will arise not from any grand design but from some small, insistent vibration; a blink of light through the fog.

I'll often concentrate on the poems of just one poet and even be drawn (though there's not such a wide field) to poets better known for their prose. Raymond Carver's poems, for example, have sometimes been my companions in the mist, and it would be true to say that I've derived more from them than from his widely admired stories. The poems give me that feeling of being in the same space as the man, which in these obscure intervals seems to be what I need.

Just once, so far, has this temporary inclination for reading poetry toppled over into writing it. Some months after I completed *The Light of Day* I found myself, unexpectedly, writing little else. One poem seemed to lead to another, so that I acquired, until it suddenly stopped, the cautiously darting momentum (quite unlike the momentum of writing a novel) with which you hop from stepping stone to stepping stone. That suggests it all had some transitional purpose, though I think it was more a case of not wanting to feel, while I waited for a new novel to loom, creatively becalmed. Perhaps it was just refreshing to be making those quick, frequent leaps. Novels come with gaps between them too, and I wouldn't want to say that there's any particular purpose or pattern to the way they're interspersed, just as I can't really explain how I make the larger leaps—or rather, slow, tentative journeys—between them. In the end, after a gap, they just happen. These are some of the poems that, in one of the gaps, just happened too.

This Small Place

The world is big enough,
Though getting smaller, they say,
And as for the universe—let's not think of that.
But there's always this small place, close to hand,
This place of small talk and whispers and memories
And small mercies and small blessings,
And small comfort, true enough, sometimes.
We started here, and now and then
We've come back, only half meaning to,
But thankful enough to find it still there,
In the small hours,
With only some furniture and our thoughts.
And it's where we'll be at the finish,
We know this too,
Sure enough, true enough, big enough.

Waves

When we all gather together,
Get thrown together, at bashes and dos,
I think of the seaside, the gleeful light,
Of how we've all gone in for a dip and, beyond the
      sparkling froth,
There are big waves running and
Up and down we go,
Up and down.
Those moments when we laugh at each other to see it:
Up and down!
Those moments when a wave slaps us, mid-laugh,
And we gulp and panic a little but laugh again.
Those moments when between the crests and troughs
We lose sight of each other altogether.

Our Childhoods

They pluck us on the shoulder sometimes.
Remember us?
And we think of them
Perplexedly, if fondly,
As if we don't know who they really are.
And yet we know something they don't know:
That really they're orphans, all orphans.
Look at them there, up to their old tricks.
When will they find out?
And then, when they have, who will they become?

Rush Hour

The fog of their massed breath,
The still-sleepy glitter of their eyes.
So this is their life, what they do every day,
Funnelled into work like hour-glass sand?
No, no, look again. It's not what it seems.
This smoky-blue dawn
That hasn't yet torn them from dreams,
These lights on their faces.
Not regulars, but extras, taking their places,
Here for this one, unrepeatable scene.

To His Dead Father

Their age freezes, but we go on,
Burning the years.
If I could meet him now
There wouldn't be that gap between us.
I'd say, 'I'm catching up,'
Like someone adjusting
To the other's brisker pace.
I'd say, 'I see it now like you saw it.
The thing is, I just lagged behind.'
We'd walk, we'd talk, we'd know each other.
We'd be like equals, brothers, friends.

Inmates

School dormitories, barrack rooms,
Hospital wards and, by a stretch,
Prison wings too.
All of a muchness and all grim.
But imagine them empty,
All the narrow beds unburdened.
Thrown in, we learn the hard way to muck in too,
All fondly supposing there's some other free place
Where we're all tender autocrats,
All sweet, proud exceptions to the rules.
And so it should be.
But, still, imagine them empty:
The long spaces silent,
Not a door being swung,
The beds simply waiting, as if no one's said,
The cold sheets taut, undented,
All the meaningless lights-outs.

History

The child is father to the man, they say,
And sometimes you can have the fancy
That all the creatures of history are children.
We are the only sad, wise grown-ups now.
To have lived in their day!
On a sledge, say, in St Petersburg, in 1904.
Or on the old ranch, out west,
Before Pearl Harbor, chasing the kicking maverick,
Watching the still wet foal find its legs.
Those simple, carefree times!

Borrowers

Who'd have credited it fifty years ago?
This genie in our wallet:
Yes, O master, it shall be so.
Was it a trick perhaps, we thought at first,
But, 'Live now, pay later,' came the cry
And, not to be left out, we took it up
With interest. Look at us living now.
So does that mean for those who came before
The rule was: Pay now, live later?
So it seems. Poor fools.
Life was always over the rainbow then.
And some of them paid the highest price
And never lived later at all,
Lying where they do
In Africa, Burma, Italy or France
Or where all the dreamed-of treasure lies,
If not over the rainbow, under the sea.
Credit where it's due, but they never knew
The sweet scam of living on it.
Judy Garland made them cry,
Madonna made us buy.
And the ones still left from those sad days
Shuffle now round Happy Homes, or,

Worse, wait bedless in some corridor,
Their cheated faces saying, I paid, I paid—for this.
So how shall it be for us
When our day of reckoning comes?
Having had our run of plastic bliss
Shall we all topple nobly,
Smiling fair's-fair smiles,
Into the black pit? Singing as we go,
Oh but we lived, boy, how we lived,
Bye-bye.

The Virtuoso

Sometimes, now it's impossible,
Now it's all useless,
He pines not for the great days,
The tours, the concert halls,
The roar of orchestras and applause,
But for days, long ago,
When he'd make his way
To the Academy. Some crisp morning
In autumn that seemed there
Just for him. Leaves on the cobbles.
The sun glittering along alleyways.
People passing, muffled, gloved,
In little clouds of steam.
His own hands, of course, were mittened,
And held, before he left (his mother
Filled the bowl), in hot water.
He'd hug them, even so,
Under his armpits. On Wilhelmstrasse
The tram bells rang.
Mornings he'd feared and loved.
One of those mornings (it was all still a dream)
When he'd climb those stone stairs,
Enter that tall, stern, merciless chamber,

Take up his instrument,
Take up his bow,
And (why *this* morning, what
Was magic about *this* morning?)
Everything sang.

We Both Know

We both know, we both knew.
It hovers now around us when we meet
Like some trick of light.
And those images of what might have been
Can't be so different now
From images of things that really were,
Memory and longing amounting to the same.
Our eyes meet. We never say, we never will.
Is this the sweetest, surest thing, in fact?
A poise, a tact unknown to the young.
We burned but never were consumed,
This soft ash keeping in the fire.

Breadcrumbs

Once, just glancing through the window
(Why should it have fixed him in his place?)
He saw his wife, with breadcrumbs for the birds,
Standing at the kitchen door.
Just a woman in a doorway with a breadboard,
A streak of sunlight, on a dull day, touching her hair,
But also his wife.
She never looked up to catch his stare.
Now that she's gone from his life
And he doesn't know what to do with the years,
He walks round galleries, and before
Those pictures painted by the Dutch—
Bits of yards, bits of rooms, a door, a figure,
Bits of nothing much—
He finds it hard to choke the tears.

The Trespasser

He never could quite grasp it,
A boy in school assembly:
'Forgive us our trespasses . . .'
What kind of word was that?
He only understood the sense
That had to do with property,
Or with not being on it.
Trespassers were people
Who *weren't supposed to be there.*
And wasn't that, he knew by then,
Exactly where he was at?
An intruder in this place:
Common mishap of us all.
And wasn't that the simple trick of it,
To know that you'd be always
On the wrong side of the fence?
He knew it even as he mumbled
Through those morning prayers,
Meek expression on his face.
It led him to a life (as he would call
It later) of 'adventure':
Con man and wife-stealer to the gentry,
Maestro of the sham,

Always creeping over someone else's carpet,
Always stealing down someone else's stairs
(Always stealing anyway).
Not a 'stranger in this world', as some
Weird people liked to say,
Oh no, but just a trespasser.

Chekhov at Melikhovo

Of course, a doctor, he knew.
He'd never grow old.
All through those quick June nights
The yellow light burned in his window
While the moths danced in and out
And the scent of hay and honeysuckle
Failed to distract him.
As if he needed, for his true mania,
These mere remissions in the summer fever,
This cool, dark flavour of brevity.
And he'd sleep, anyway, like a dead weight,
Like some useless *thing*,
Through the long boring fire of day.

Watched

Once, there were our parents to watch over us
And God, of course (we were told), looking down,
And it was a comfort bigger than we knew then,
Not to know the loneliness which we know now
Of our own devices.
To be watched. Isn't that the trick?
Isn't that the knack of those characters
Up there on the screens,
To whom we glue our eyes?
They are watched—we ourselves confirm it.
They have us to turn to, us to thank.
If only *life* had an audience, a theatre for each one of us.
Watched. Saved.

Extinction

What do ten vanished species of moth or mollusc
Matter to you or me?
The world will have gone before it is gone.
Or the hieroglyphics of the ancients?
Or even the quaint anachronism of a still-current phrase?
'Changing horses in midstream.'
Leave all that to the specialists and saddos.
We're not special, you and I,
Or sad.
The world will have gone before it is gone.

The Anatomist

Of course he remembers it,
The funeral, the procession, the crowds
And (as if by command) a weeping sky.
In those days even the weather adopted style.
Of course he remembers. The great weight
Of importance, like those pressing clouds,
That somehow he had to shoulder now—
'Brave little man', as they called him.
Only six, but how could he forget?
His mother's hand clutching his (everyone
Noticed that), as if he had to steady *her*.
And later, in private, her hugs, her tears,
As if he were some leftover part of *him*.
But she married again inside two years.
And that, really, was the whole story:
The young wife, from the beginning,
There to adorn her husband's glory.
And that's why there'd been that gap not just
Of decades but of pretty well everything
Between himself and him. Six years!
'But aren't you proud?' they'd say. 'You must
Be proud to have been his son.' And yes,
He'd say, for decency's and simplicity's sake.

Though pride never really came into it,
Except, maybe, on that grey, wet morning,
The plumed horses stamping and steaming
(How like a fairy tale it would one day seem).
But mostly what he felt was the great, grey yawning
Of his own decades stretched before him.
How could they be anything but lesser, small?
Not pride, not pride at all.

And when, later, they came, the biographers
And researchers, asking for his memories,
His 'child's-eye view', he had the perfect
Excuse. It was never exactly like lying.
I was only six, he'd stress, and he was always—though
Don't get me wrong—a rather distant figure.
He didn't say: What I remember is a man dying.
That house, that dreadful room, that bed.
It was a long slow illness, you know,
Not a 'valiant battle' like the papers said.
What I actually remember is a wasting, shrinking
Body, what happens (but I was only small)
To any mortal human animal.

Later, as it turned out (raised by a grudging
Aunt, who had her secret viewpoint too),
He took up medicine. Or not medicine so much
As that strictly scientific stuff: anatomy, pathology.
Became not undistinguished in his way.
Students would whisper now and then
(There was nothing he could do about the name):
Yes, he's the son. But he would always say,
Offering them his prefatory remark or two:

What, ladies and gentlemen, is our study?
It's the study, ladies and gentlemen,
Of how we're all the same.

Civilization

Would you have it any other way?
This cosy collusion in the trivial,
Much fuss and much indecision,
Then much preening
Over a new pair of shoes.
You want drum rolls and proclamations
And noble leanings?
Would you have it any other way?

Unlooked-for

These moments that come like gifts,
Ordinary moments that aren't so ordinary at all.
Like the sun on a cool day
Suddenly warming your neck.
My God, this is all you could wish,
Simple unlooked-for heaven.
While a thousand engineered occasions,
A thousand worked-at culminations fail.
Once, perhaps, you'd hardly have noticed.
You'd have rolled your shoulders, pettishly,
Under this unsolicited kiss.
Just life, for God's sake,
It's just what life brings,
Plenty more of this.
Now you're not so foolish.
You do the second, the double-blessed thing,
You heed it, mark it,
This unremarkable bliss.

Affection

And affection too.
Not love, it's true, no fires within,
Just simple affection, flickering from skin to skin.
Not lust or seduction or desire or possession,
Just simple affection,
Warming the air in between.

There Without Us

We've all been to such places,
Where the brambles shudder in the wind
And the branches creak up above
And rain batters the leaves.
We went there once when that sudden squall
Held up our summer walk,
And waited, watching everything
As you eye the furniture in a stranger's room,
And thought: we're here now and might never have been
And soon won't be, and places such as these,
Pierced with birds and secret life,
Must hardly ever get or need a human visitor.
It must be there still, while this rain beats
On the window. We think of it suddenly:
That place where we stood once
Under sighing trees—
The smell of roots and deep earth,
As if our nostrils were required for it—
And think of all such places
That are there without us now,
All the places where we've been but haven't.

Homings

Salmon still passage through the estuaries,
Geese arrow the heavens,
Turtles tunnel the oceans.
When shall we tell them we have ravaged their mysteries?
Whom shall we choose as our spokesman?

Priam

Maybe we all end up like Priam,
Not one of the heroes wreathed in glory,
Just the man who gets to be king of Troy,
Father of a hot-headed, cock-happy boy
Who steals a wife and starts a war.
The usual wretched soap-opera story.
But at your level it has to mean more,
So just when you've made your pile and settled down
And built your topless towers of Ilium,
You've a siege on your hands and now, what's more,
This crazy *horse* outside your front door.
Was it for this you strove and pushed your luck,
Just to get pulled back into the muck?
Who, given the choice, would be a king?
But you were, and you took it.
Now here's this weirdest thing:
A lull, a silence everywhere. A horse.
You look around, you stroke your royal chin. Of course.
Maybe you had your glory all the time,
And this is what it means: you win.
A horse. It's not your common sort of offering.
Maybe it stands for you, for Priam in his kingly prime.
Best take a look, best take it in.

The Bookmark

All the books you meant to read
Or reread or try again,
Having tried once long ago and failed:
There they sit, spurned, on your shelves.
And one wet weekend you actually reach
For an old crinkly-spined paperback and settle down,
But something stops you before you've begun:
The bus ticket falling from page thirty-one.
A bus ticket, yellowed and frail,
Like the pages themselves.
And what do you do?
You read the bus ticket, not the book,
Marvelling at its weird historicality,
The story it seems to want to tell.
Bus tickets don't come like that any more,
Nor at that price. You wonder what
The journey was for such a fictional fare.
From where to where? And when?
But mostly you puzzle who the person was
Who bought this ticket and instead of doing
All the annihilating things that are done
To bus tickets, slipped it casually
Yet fatefully, like a message in a bottle,

Between the pages of a never reopened novel.
You're lost in the bus ticket, you forget the book.
You know, of course, it must have been you.

Touch

Where do we really live?
Where is the centre of command?
In our eyes? Our brains?
In this thing that beats in our chest?
Or is it in our hands?
Those canny little twins,
So good at fending for themselves,
We can almost forget they're there.
Nothing speaks more
Of our time here than our hands.
Look how they weather and gnarl.
A hand is like a face (and sometimes lovelier)
And what can a face *do*, make, mend?
A hand has a mind, a memory surer
Than that stuff in our heads:
Ask any musician or draughtsman.
And what, in a word, do all wise masters teach
Their daunted apprentices?
Your hands will do it, give it time,
Your hands will tell you what to do.
Aren't we all apprentices to our hands?
And isn't the true mastery in touch?
Think of it, now you've come this far.

Look at your faithful hands.
Aren't *you* the faithful one, led like the blind
By those things before your eyes?
Think of all the moments, all the tests.
How many times, over and over,
Have those dumb creatures
Instructed you in the art of life?
How to reach out and do exactly what is needed.
How to comfort, caress, cherish, punish, beg.

The Dead

They cry to us, never finding the words
To tell us what we already know,
That our own lost voices will one day
Be as theirs, the mouths of our souls
Gaping like graves, gaping for reunion
With those we have preceded.

On the Bridge

Three girls on a bridge
(A subject for a painting—Gauguin or Munch).
Three girls on the old, quiet, stone bridge
At the edge of the little town
Where he, an English academic driving south
(Some summer thing in Nîmes),
Decided to put up for the night
And after a meal and a *pichet* of *rouge*
To take a stroll in the late, soft light.
Swallows skimmed the little river,
Then on the bridge (the obvious place,
After crossing, to turn back),
Those three girls in a huddle at the centre,
Leaning on the parapet.
That moment of polite hiatus when
Two worlds meet and agree upon
The brief suspension of each.
A bridge. *'Bonsoir.' 'Bonsoir monsieur!'*

He felt an intruder, of course.
Should he have crossed at all?
Their bridge, not his. But then
He was hardly Actaeon

Crashing on the forest pool.
And which, in any case, was Diana,
Which the attendant nymphs?
The fact is they were, all three, beauties—
And perhaps, somehow, he should have *said*.
Not intrusion but privilege.
Not Actaeon but Paris, come to judge.
(What was in that *pichet* of red?)

'Bonsoir monsieur!'
He crossed, walked on,
Turning along the farther bank,
Daring only once to twist his head
And see their faces still perched there,
Looking back at him, neither playful nor stern,
Just something in between.

Schoolgirls-no-more, he guessed:
The summer after the very last term,
And now they hung somewhere
Between girlhood and what comes next,
Looking for their futures perhaps
In the slow slide of the river.

The soft splash of a fish.
Their soft, indecipherable voices
Reached him over the water, and yes
(Somehow he knew it for them):
All their lives, they'd never forget.
These in-between places
Where all seems yet to come,
Which yet turn out to be the thing itself.

Do you remember, when we met?
Those evenings, that summer,
On the bridge.

GRAHAM SWIFT

Allotments

I used to tease out the word
Before I knew what it meant.
How could it be a lot when it looked so little?
A strip of soil for beans or cabbages,
A cold frame, a compost heap.
Hardly the Earth.
But look at the love that has gone into each.
The careful rows of canes,
The sheds magicked up from old offcuts,
Each one architecturally unique.
Look at them here on Sunday afternoons
Lost in their little worlds.
I never knew what a lot meant, or a little.
Then I was let in on the meaning.
'Allotment': it's what you get,
It's what you're given to get on with.
Didn't you understand?
Your little patch, your little place,
Among all the others.

Perspective

The desire to be in and out of your skin,
That soft fatal voice, yours and not yours,
That says even as you walk down the street:
'He walked down the street.'
This damp paving, these walls,
These rooftops, drying against a brightening sky,
Aren't of now, and only ever will be
Of some time that was.
Understand your position.
Understand the anguish of the painter
Who long ago in some Flemish town
Looked from his window and painted what he saw
So it would remain, in its frame,
Like another window on another world.

Relapse

These things that were still *there*,
Like scorched flowers under winterloads of ice,
These things that, surely, you could never relive.
But most of his life had fallen away
Like meaningless waste,
Memory caving in, an avalanche of the brain,
And he was back there again
Among that mountainous furniture,
Among those towering creatures,
Like some small, pecking bird
Hopping among buffalo, elephants.
Adults. What great, alien beasts they were.
And he'd been one once!
Their huge, crashing weight
And their thick, leathery stink of time.

Another

To see ourselves as others see us:
That's one thing.
But to see others when they don't see us,
When they aren't just part of our own grey penumbra,
In their own sweet, bright, unshadowed space:
That's another.

This Is the Life

'This is the life, eh?' some cheery oaf said,
In cravat and blazer and seaside flannels.
And of course we thought he was a fool.
But is *this* the life then, this life we've settled for?
No (we half know it), this isn't the life either.
And there he stands, that oaf, on the jetty,
Getting smaller.
He hasn't realized yet: we're *leaving*, not arriving.
There he stands, still grinning and waving
And rubbing his hands in readiness,
Trousers flapping in the wind.

Bookmark.

SANTA AGAIN

CHRISTMAS WITH MR BROWN, 1989–99

We don't see each other now, but for ten years or so we were in pretty close contact, at a time when it was very difficult to have any contact with him at all. It's one of the ironies of my memories of Salman Rushdie that I knew him most when the world was least able to know him. Of course, that statement can be turned on its head. The world knew him very well. Though he was in deepest hiding, he couldn't have been more conspicuously, glaringly in the news, and though he'd become invisible he was far from silent or uncommunicative. By temperament, Salman is a man who wants the world to know him. Setting aside the absolute seriousness of his predicament, there was a bleak joke in such a person being driven into seclusion. Still, during that dreadful time, I don't think the world knew Salman himself; it knew the figure, not the man. For his enemies, clamouring for his murder, it was important to do just that—to turn him into a monstrous figure beyond human delineation. But even those of his defenders and supporters who saw only the projection of events through the media often lost sight of the human scale.

It's hard not to get solemn in recalling that time, and solemnity is the last feature of his writing. But his situation then gave no quarter to the novel's customary playfulness with human gravity. It demanded deadly earnestness. It demanded, under pain of death, that a novelist shouldn't be a novelist. Salman, to his credit, was having none of it and, to his credit, he never turned solemn himself.

I hardly knew him before the fatwa was issued. I'd met him a few times, once at a Booker Prize dinner, not an ideal occasion for meeting anyone. I know I'm far from alone in having befriended him subsequently and having found that the friendship blossomed; and I know I'm not alone in having frequently made him, during the years in hiding, a guest in my house, along with his retinue of protection officers and their (usually) concealed weaponry. But quite early during that bizarre time a tradition grew up that he and his wife would spend Christmas Day with me and my wife, sometimes with other guests, either at my place or at a place that old habit, even now, makes me not want to specify. There was a general cloak-and-dagger avoidance of careless talk. I still think of Salman as 'Anton'. Caz Phillips and I sometimes arranged to meet him covertly, and it was Caz's idea that for this purpose, though for reasons not entirely to do with security, the three of us should be known as Mr Black, Mr White and Mr Brown. So Salman also became Mr Brown.

I shan't forget those Christmases with Special Branch upstairs (turkey and pudding for them too). It sounds odd, but they rather restored Christmas for me. I mean the feeling for Christmas that really goes with childhood and that we grow out of, even though we continue to celebrate the day: a feeling for Christmas that in my case has nothing to do with religion—and perhaps that was just as well. I'd frankly hate to think that on those days when I most intimately enjoyed being with him some religious point was being made. They were very merry occasions. The merrymaking may have had a touch of special, conscious defiance (how could it not, with armed police officers sitting in?), but it usually passed into a happy forgetfulness of the strange conditions under which it was occurring. And, for me at least, beneath it all, there'd be this feeling of Christmas that I'd last had decades before—a pagan feeling, really, of hearthside warmth and magic, of a glow in the dark days. Well, they were dark enough for him.

He was good, affectionate company. He may have been dominant company—he may always want to be dominant company—but in those days you could certainly forgive him that. You would have forgiven him, after all, if he'd arrived an exhausted, drained and haunted figure, but he was the life and soul. And that phrase, 'life and soul', wasn't just in those days a token epithet. Not the least of his achievements during that time was the preservation of his sense of humour. He must have had some blackest of black private moments, but he scarcely spoke of them. It was at one of those Christmases, I think, that he gave me his brief word—his rubric—on fear. He said that the thing was that you had to quell it, crush it *at once*, as soon as it arose, give it no further space, otherwise you were lost. Easily said. I've never experienced fear of the kind he must have felt, but it's the best and most convincing advice I've had on the subject.

Another irony, or simple fact, persists from those times. A great deal has been written or said about Salman by those who never knew him or who knew him only slightly. Empty or scabrous comment is one of the risks of seeking the limelight (fatwas apart). But the truth was that the smaller the audience, or the company, the better he was to know and the more good-heartedly, funnily and intelligently human he became. Some of the best conversations I've had about writing—writing from the inside, its personal demands and challenges—have been brief one-to-one exchanges with Salman.

Here was a man who would gladly, in ordinary circumstances, have faced the Albert Hall, for whom the term stage fright meant nothing, but now he had a price on his head and other things to fear. And here he was sitting at a small if groaning table in an entirely domestic setting (some cops with guns upstairs), and he and all of us were having a high old time. Salman, too, at Christmas, was thoroughly capable of feeling like and being a kid again.

As a writer, he's always been an overt enjoyer, a master of revels, only following a tradition that goes back to the novel's origins in Rabelais and Cervantes, of the novelist as a lord of misrule. But that rich literary pedigree could barely be mentioned at that time with impunity. He was a maker of fun, and righteousness lacks a comic register. The defence, the plea of fun, is to righteousness like a self-damnation.

Fun was certainly had at those Christmases. Once you've played charades with the author of *The Satanic Verses* or heard his imitation (not quite as good, in my opinion, as Kazuo Ishiguro's) of Bob Dylan, your view of things is fundamentally improved. Many writers—maybe most writers—are an assemblage of opposing forces. Outspoken or extravagant on the page, they may be reticent and shy in private. Or, spare and chaste when they write, they will let their hair down in company. Salman Rushdie, who contains his own incongruities, is nonetheless the most consistent writer-personality I've known. Never anything but a *force*, never anything but an intense bundle of energy and combustion, sometimes crackling, sometimes flaring, sometimes just emitting warmth.

I was a supporter anyway. The monstrosity of his plight was infinitely worse than any of the monstrosities of character alleged by his enemies and sometimes even by an otherwise rallying press. I went to meetings of a quickly formed group of defenders, though if the followers of the Ayatollah Khomeini had known that the International Committee for the Defence of Salman Rushdie consisted of a few people sitting round a table in a cramped office near London Bridge their gleeful scorn might have known no bounds.

I supported him, but it would be equally true to say he supported me. There was more than usual human sustenance, as there was more than usual festivity and entertainment, round those Christmas tables. We would wait for his clandestine and carefully monitored arrival, conscious of the theoretical gist of the situation: that we were giving shelter to a fugitive. But an opposite interpretation was at work. It was an absurd notion and in the light of what was going on and with its cartoonish element, it was only foisting on him another monstrosity he could do without—but he was just a *bit* like Father Christmas. You could imagine him donning the red costume, the cotton-wool beard, and doing it rather well. And he'd already, out of necessity, had to don an actual, partial disguise.

Once upon a time, I'd believed in (or at least happily absorbed the make-believe of) Father Christmas, as superstitious in that respect as any other five- or six-year-old. Scepticism set in for me around the time I received my polio jab, but in any case there had never been in my family one of those jovial, extrovert adults who was actually prepared to play the part. A good thing too, I think. Some parts play best in the mind. And anyway you grow up, you grow out of all that stuff.

Yet we would wait on Christmas morning for Salman Rushdie to appear, for the man under threat of death and under special police guard, and what I couldn't help feeling, if I never quite dared tell him at the time, was: it's Christmas morning and we're waiting for Father Christmas to arrive.

READING ALOUD

CHELTENHAM AND EVERYWHERE, 1991

Before I visited the Cheltenham Literature Festival in 1991, the *Daily Telegraph* asked me to write the short piece that follows, expressing my thoughts on reading aloud.

When I first began writing, writers very rarely read in public. Generally speaking, they were neither seen nor heard. The now-proliferating business of putting writers before audiences has various virtues and vices, though the common claim is that it allows writers and readers to meet. True up to a point, but incomparably the best time for this is when a reader quietly sits down to read a book. Most of the time, I hope, I meet my readers without ever being aware of it. I believe in this unseen contact.

My readers are certainly the most important people in the world to me. I need them and I trust them. Yet, strangely, while I'm writing I hardly think of them at all, it seems a folly and a presumption even to imagine who they are. And of course the one thing no writer will ever know is exactly what it's like to read their own book. Readers are essentially invisible too— or, rather, the actual experience of reading, what goes on in an individual reader's head, is for no one to be privy to, unless invited, but that reader. Very few book readers (I imagine) ever try reading aloud, and only a small portion, perhaps, of their silent reading is done in public. I've only occasionally observed someone reading one of my books, and then I've felt vaguely like an intruder. Conversely, when I've chanced upon someone reading a book by a writer-friend of mine, I've sometimes had the bizarre urge to phone them up and say, 'I've seen it, it actually *happens.*'

When I finish a book I seldom revisit it, except for practical purposes. By this time I'll probably have read it, in effect, a hundred times or more (though not in ways, I hope, that a general reader would read it) and the idea of *my* sitting down comfortably to read one of my own novels would just be ridiculous. It's the one experience a writer can't have. But public readings can give you a meaningful pretext for slyly revisiting your own book, or parts of it; and with the aid of a favourable audience of readers, or potential readers, and if the atmosphere is right (it so often isn't), you can even trick yourself into the feeling of being a reader of your work in both senses, of having sneaked up on it like a third party, as if you'd never actually written it yourself.

Reading Aloud

The programme for this year's Cheltenham Festival of Literature states that 'Graham Swift much enjoys reading aloud.' No doubt some bluster of mine on the phone to Cheltenham led to this blithe hyperbole, but I hasten to correct any impression that I am a Liberace of the lectern.

I can certainly claim experience as a public reader. This doesn't mean I have ever got used to it—I seldom give a nerveless reading—but I've done it enough times and under diverse conditions. I've read in a giant plastic tent in Adelaide, Australia, when the temperature outside was 43°C. I've read in another tent in Edinburgh when a howling gale threatened to tear the whole, flapping edifice from its moorings, leaving audience and author in astonished *in flagrante*. I've read in bookshops, libraries, theatres, pubs, town halls, colleges and disused churches. From Aberdeen to Adelaide, from Winnipeg to Wagga Wagga.

The author as one-man circus? Hardly. Ninety per cent of my professional time is spent at a desk, but over the years the 'author reading' has become the expected thing. It's not a perfect way of bringing writers and public together, but not a bad one. Authors are not necessarily the best readers of their own work, nor does all writing lend itself to reading aloud. Novelists are disadvantaged since they have to find passages of appropriate length which will work well out of context—not always easy. But in any case,

I don't write to be read aloud. I write for the inner ear of a silent reader. When I give readings I nearly always have to adapt the text.

Against all this it can be argued that readings are the 'purest' form of book-advertisement: the book speaks for itself. True in theory, but readings are rarely just readings. According to how they pitch their introductions, authors can lard their renditions with as much baloney as they like. There are also the questions which follow the readings. Some authors avoid them; having submitted yourself to public exposure, why submit yourself to public dissection? But in for a penny in for a pound. Since it's often beyond me to discuss my work in any structured way—spare me the straight 'author talk'—I prefer to be drawn out by questions. But it's a perilous procedure. It's here that you encounter the lunatic fringe of your readership, or the man who has wandered into the wrong event, or the unrecognized figure from your past . . .

I suspect most people go to readings out of curiosity. Authors are not very visible and the reading public has an urge to witness these usually closeted creatures (there are exceptions: I once read to the English staff of an illustrious university, plainly flummoxed to behold a *living* author). And the process is reciprocal. I like to see my readers, it's good to know they're *there*. That they should appear at all on a wet winter's night is really quite miraculous. And an encouraging word from one of them is worth more than anything the literary pages can afford.

Enjoyment, for both author and audience, perhaps depends most on the physical space provided. The cosy notion of the casual, huddled storytelling with perhaps some mulled wine on offer, invariably results in embarrassed discomfort. Then there are the noises off. Did nobody know there would be that thronged reception in the adjoining chamber of the Civic Suite? Bookshops, favoured for obvious reasons, often make appalling auditoria. So do tents.

The solo reading is really a species of theatre, which, given the right accompaniments—good acoustics, good seating, stage, lighting, microphones, *concentration*—can work wonderfully well. The best venue I know, the annual Harbourfront Festival in Toronto, provides all these things, attracts large audiences, and I believe no author appears there without feeling their work has been paid the immense respect of being offered a sense of occasion.

This is no Carnegie Hall complex, just a plea for professionalism. I suspect that the reality of readings will remain makeshift and multifarious, a thing of unpredictable splendours and miseries. How marvellous to read to this packed house in Canada—while forgetting that night in Covent Garden when no one showed up. The ego is fleetingly boosted. But the main lesson, which perhaps you can't so rapidly learn at your desk, is humility. I shall always remember a question from a youngish member of an audience in Yorkshire. Why had I chosen that particular passage to read? I gave an adequate answer. 'No, no, what I meant was, why did you choose that particular *author?*'

Required reading for John Major's government, 1996.

I DO LIKE TO BE BESIDE
THE SEASIDE

NICE, 1997

Whenever I'm asked to speak or to write in broad terms about my work, or to give my views about writing in general, I find myself saying much the same things. Every interviewed writer knows the experience of having to give yet again a familiar answer to a common, familiar question: on the one hand it can be tedious; on the other, to concoct a different answer would be arbitrary and flippant. My repetitions haven't altered much over the years, and, whether this is a good thing or not, it has the virtues of consistency and economy—writers can perhaps say too much about writing.

In 1997 I was asked to give the formal 'plenary' address at an annual conference, to be held in Nice, of French academics—the Société des Anglicistes de L'Enseignement Supérieur; a somewhat intimidating request softened by the appeal of the location, which also helped me to my subject matter. The theme of the conference was '*L'esprit des lieux: passages et rivages*'. I'd recently published *Last Orders* and it seemed to me that there might be a pleasant frisson in talking about the English seaside, which in my novel really means Margate, while visiting the French Riviera and, as it turned out, staying in a hotel on the Promenade des Anglais.

It remains my only formal lecture. I've redelivered it since, in slightly changed form (sometimes with the subtitle *The Place of*

Place in Fiction), at Oxford and at Yale, and I've drawn on it in part, whether in speech or in print, on other occasions and in other contexts. It proved to be a useful exercise in gathering together my thoughts at the time about the writing of fiction, but I don't think these have changed much since, or indeed were ever greatly different before.

I've made some small alterations for the purpose of this book, but have kept mainly to the format of the original spoken address to an audience in Nice. As it was then my latest novel, the lecture dwells particularly on *Last Orders*, but in subsequent versions it's not been difficult to incorporate something about *The Light of Day* and *Tomorrow*.

One of the lecture's articles of faith is a belief in the local as the route to the universal, combined with a belief that in the local (including those seemingly familiar localities, ourselves) the strange and the dislocated are never far away. *The Light of Day* is arguably an even more local novel for me than *Last Orders*. It's set in Wimbledon, just one postcode away from my own patch of London, and as settings go it could hardly seem more unthreateningly normal. But the novel deals with some radically dislodged worlds—the world of prison, for example, and of refugees. In any case it deals with that capacity in us all to step, without physically going anywhere, into unsuspected zones; to cross, for better or worse, lines of inner geography.

Tomorrow is set in Putney—also adjacent, in another direction, to Wimbledon. Despite appearances, no territorial programme is at work here. In fact there's little about Putney in *Tomorrow*, rather more about Herne Hill, and about several places beyond London. But what's true of Wimbledon is also true of Putney: it's a commonplace enough setting for two factors to be at work—both the sense of specific location and the sense

that, within the broad range of suburban existence, we might be anywhere.

The suburbs, which, even more than the seaside, seem to exert a hold on my work, aspire to be indistinguishable and unremarkable, as bland as each other, but, whatever else they are, they're densely populous: the great dormitories of humanity, rich with its privacies and dreams. This is the essential atmosphere of *Tomorrow*, which could be said to be set not even in Putney, but all inside one home, even inside one bedroom in that home, where, as a wakeful wife lies one night beside a sleeping husband, both dreaming and an intense nursing of secrets are going on.

Between Wimbledon and Putney is the beguilingly named Putney Vale. Most of it actually consists of a cemetery (next to an Asda supermarket). It's here that George Webb goes in *The Light of Day*, charged with the far-from-normal task of placing flowers for Sarah Nash on the grave of the husband she murdered. When I went there myself to check out the topography, I don't think I had any intimation of being, literally, on the edge of my next novel, but, looking back, I wonder if a passage in *The Light of Day* wasn't a kind of prefigurement. George, as a private detective, is a fairly nocturnal animal, and there's a moment when he wonders, if at night we could 'lift off the roofs of houses', what we might see:

> What would the aggregate be? More misery and hatred than you could begin to imagine? Or more secret happiness, more goodness and mercy than you could ever have guessed?

Tomorrow is certainly a novel that lifts the roof off one particular house to expose—via Paula Hook's thoughts—its contents. It's sheer fancy (though I confess I do sometimes think of my characters as having a life beyond the bounds of my books), but it would have been perfectly possible for George, based in Wimbledon, to have sat outside the house in Putney and asked those questions, as he actually asks them parked in the dark outside the very similar house in Wimbledon, where once a murder occurred. Quite unconsciously, I gave both houses the same number: 14. How different the inner geographies and the contributions to 'the aggregate' under their seemingly interchangeable roofs.

In the following lecture Montaigne makes the first of two appearances in this volume. As the lecture itself hastens to point out, this was not just a sop to my French audience. Montaigne already meant a lot to me, though I had no idea at this time that I'd one day have the opportunity to write the introduction to Montaigne, as anglicized by John Florio, that forms the last piece in this book. The lecture includes a long quotation from Florio's translation of the essay 'Of Exercise or Practice', which was left out when I was in Nice. I felt that Florio's Elizabethan English might have been a bit tough on my French audience, *Anglicistes* though they were—or, despite their being *Anglicistes*, might have come across as just plain cheeky, given that I was talking about a great French writer in France. So it never formed part of the lecture as originally delivered, but it was too lovely a passage not to be inserted in the lecture's later airings; or here.

241 — NICE — PROMENADE DES ANGLAIS

I Do Like to Be Beside the Seaside

The title of this talk borrows one of two epigraphs I gave to my novel *Last Orders*. The innocuous piece of alliteration is the first line of a music-hall song, written in 1909, which may be little known, if at all, outside the English-speaking world, but is still perfectly familiar in Britain today and still conveys, for all its Edwardian origins, the jaunty, fancy-free image we retain of the seaside. The full first verse goes like this:

> I do like to be beside the seaside,
> I do like to be beside the sea!
> I do like to stroll along the prom, prom, prom,
> Where the brass band plays, tiddly-om-pom-pom!
> Oh, I do like to be beside the seaside,
> I do like to be beside the sea,
> And there are lots of girls, besides,
> I should like to be beside,
> Beside the seaside, beside the sea!

You get the gist. The other epigraph to my novel is from Sir Thomas Browne and is a little more grandiloquent.

Last Orders takes as its main narrative a journey to the seaside —a special journey, since one of the travellers is no more than a heap of ashes in a plastic jar, though it's he who has instigated the whole trip. A journey to the seaside, though specifically to the seaside town of Margate, a now-scruffy, tawdry, if once-popular resort on the north coast of Kent. The contrast between Margate, facing the North Sea, and Nice, on the glamorous Côte d'Azur, could hardly be stronger, yet both Nice and Margate represent, if at different pitches, the same dream: the dream of worldly delight, of life as sheer holiday, sheer play. And they both embody a peculiar conundrum: that we should most seek out, most seek to fabricate this worldly delight, where our natural world and habitation—land—ends.

'Place' suggests land—solid geography—but when I look over my work I see that it features quite a lot this shifting, beguiling zone at the very edge of land. In my collection of stories, *Learning to Swim*, the title story is set almost entirely on a beach, and there's another story called 'Cliffedge', which begins with this paragraph:

> What is it about the sea that summons people to it? That beckons the idle to play and ponder at its skirts? What was it that built these ice-cream-coloured colonies, these outposts of pleasure along the cliff tops and shingle of the south coast? Pleasure in being on the brink? Pleasure in the precariousness of pleasure? How would they have become so strangely intense, so strangely all-in-all, these little worlds (the pier, the lifeboat station, the aquarium) we once knew for two weeks out of every fifty-two, were it not for their being pressed against this sleeping monster, the sea?

The 'Cliffedge' of the title is the narrator's invention, to hide the real name of the seaside resort in the story. The place Cliffedge doesn't actually exist; nor, in its compound form, does the word, but it's plausible enough and it suggests, graphically enough, that dangerous fringe where one element encroaches on another. And of course it's a short leap—if that's quite the right metaphor—from 'Cliffedge' to that other title of mine and invented compound word, *Waterland*.

If I'm interested in place, and I think I am, then it seems that I'm also interested in the opposite of place, in no-place—or in places where fixture and definition give way to indeterminacy. It's all there in that ambiguous, amphibious title. The world not just of *Waterland* but perhaps of most of my fiction is a world in which, sometimes casually, sometimes critically, the familiar surrenders to the unknown, the tangible to the illusory, the present to the past, the solid and safe to the uncertain and confused. But then—and don't we all know it?—isn't life itself always like that? Don't we all live, more or less, in this perpetual borderland, on this shoreline where the sand shifts constantly under our feet?

A feeling for place can be found in pretty well everything I've written, and yet for a good part of my writing career I would have said that place, in the sense of geographical setting, was one of the least important aspects of fiction. Novels have to be set *some*where and that's an end of it. But many years ago now I found myself writing a novel that would be called *Waterland*, in which the physical setting, a flat, wet region of eastern England known as the Fens, would play, ironically, a dominant role; would come to have the force, almost, of a principal character. I say 'ironically' for more than one reason. When I try to explain why I set that book in the Fens—and this is frankly something I've failed to do satisfactorily ever since it was written—one possible reason I give myself is that the Fens may have first attracted me precisely because they seemed like an *absence* of setting: their flatness and apparent emptiness were like an unobtrusive, uncluttered stage on which I could set my drama. And the novel itself at one point characterizes, or rather de-characterizes them, in just such a way:

> . . . what is water, which seeks to make all things level, which has no taste or colour of its own, but a liquid form of Nothing? And what are the Fens, which so imitate in their levelness the natural disposition of water, but a landscape which, of all landscapes, most approximates to Nothing? Every Fenman secretly concedes this; every Fenman suffers now and then the illusion that the land he walks over is *not there*, is floating . . . And every Fen-child, who is given picture books to read in which the sun bounces over mountain tops and the road of life winds through heaps of green cushions, and is taught nursery rhymes in which persons go up and down hills, is apt to demand of its elders: Why are the Fens so flat?
>
> To which my father replied, first letting his face take on a wondering and vexed expression and letting his lips form for a moment the shape of an 'O': 'Why are the Fens flat? So God has a clear view . . .'

But this passage itself already amply hints that the simple, empty stage is not nearly as simple or empty as I'd supposed. The stage itself has become fascinating. The apparently vacant physical landscape is full of metaphysical implication.

Yet the Fens are, after all, a real place, and the Fens of my novel are, I hope, real—that is, authentic. A fair number of people who live or have lived in the Fens have told me, much to my relief, that, yes, I've pretty well got it right. And ever since the novel was published, there has been quite a contingent of people who believe I must have been born in the Fens or at least have lived there; whereas the truth is I have never lived there and have no personal connection with the region whatsoever. I was born in London, SE23.

But *Waterland* taught me two things about place. First, that, almost in spite of myself, I do have—it's most apparent in *Waterland*, perhaps, but it's there in other work of mine—a genuine affection for English landscape, which I don't think has anything to do with the chauvinistic, or the picturesque or the sentimental. I think it's more the case that whatever I might find *wrong* with my country—and I could compile quite a list—I think its bone structure is good, the land itself is good, and I recognize in myself and in my work this rather bony, primitive instinct we call love of the land. So, just as *Waterland* pays its tribute to the Fens of East Anglia, and *Ever After* pays its tribute to the West Country of Devon, so *Last Orders* pays its passing tribute to the landscape of the so-called 'Garden of England', the county of Kent. Yet—to stress again that for all this feeling for the countryside, I'm a city-dweller—*Last Orders* ought also to make it clear that my affection is not just for landscape but for townscape too; and, since I'm a Londoner, that townscape is principally London.

The second lesson *Waterland* taught me is this. When I'm forced to disabuse those people who think I must have been born in the Fens, they can be surprised, disappointed, even sometimes a little suspicious, as if in setting a novel in a place I don't come from I've carried out some kind of fraud. This reaction seems to me to betray a very common misconception about fiction: that it is, after all—isn't it?—some sort of disguised fact. It's the writer's own experience dressed up, or the result of some deliberate documentary research. Whereas, of course, if fiction is really going to be fiction, it must involve some sort of imaginative act. And what else is the imagination than a means of mental transport by which we can move from familiar to unfamiliar territory?

Thus, although the landscape of *Waterland* reflects a real, existing external landscape, the world of that novel, like the world of all novels, is nonetheless an imagined world, and its landscape is to some degree a landscape of the mind.

But then, of course, when people, Fenlanders or otherwise, say to me that the world of *Waterland* feels real, I'm actually very gratified, since fiction can't do its convincing work unless it is *taken* as real. But that very margin of mysterious transition by which fiction can become 'real', by which the merely imagined can yet spring to life, only reminds us of that other borderline near which we all dwell, yet which, as writers of fiction constantly learn, is virtually impossible to chart: the borderline of reality itself—the borderline between what actually exists and what exists, yes, but only somewhere in our heads.

Which brings us back to the seaside, to where two different, if interpenetrating, domains collide. 'What is it about the sea that summons people to it?' One reason we go to the seaside perhaps is because it's there that we hope, if only for a week or two, that dreams might become real or reality might turn into a dream. In Margate there is a well-known amusement park called Dreamland. It has certainly seen better days and its brick entranceway now looks more like the gate to some prison than to a land of dreams. But then that wishful, seaside dream—of sheer amusement—can in any case quickly turn thin. As Ray, one of the characters in *Last Orders*, reflects:

> It aint much. It aint much to write home about, if it's what you get. If the sea's just the sea, wet desert, and the rest is knick-knacks. A pier, a postcard, a penny in a slot. Seems to me you could say that Jack and Amy were spared, after all, Amy was spared. It's a poor dream. Except all dreams are poor.

So there are deeper reasons. We go, we return, to the seaside because once, if we were lucky, we were taken there when we were small and we never quite outgrew that primal thrill. So perhaps, as Jack and Amy in *Last Orders* belatedly intended but never achieved, we retire there, late in life, in order to discover, maybe, a second childhood, or because it seems only appropriate that we should end our days where the land itself—the land of the living—stops. Whatever else the sea is, it's not us, it's the beyond. It makes us feel, and even be reconciled to, our insignificance. It's the great place which is no place, where no one lives. The sea is destiny, eternity, oblivion, death.

Jack Dodds in *Last Orders* has his own particular and precise reasons for wanting his ashes flung into the waves at Margate. They have to do with Margate. But all the characters in the novel register that this journey towards the sea is a journey we all make. The four men who travel to Margate Pier are drawn there by their allegiance to Jack, but also by the tug of their own inner tides of memory and longing. When they arrive, one of them observes that the sea actually smells 'like memory itself, like the inside of a lobster pot'. Even Amy, Jack's widow, who mysteriously decides not to join the men on their mission, absents herself, among other reasons, for seaside reasons, seaside memories.

The sea is destiny, and is present in *Last Orders* not just as a physical destination. More than one character in the book has been a sailor. And one of them, Vic, who served in the navy in the Second World War, is the cause of a whole detour in the novel's central journey in which the four men, with Jack's ashes, visit the naval memorial at Chatham, where are listed the names of those who, in the proverbial phrase, 'have no grave but the sea'. It's Vic who most broadly equates the sea with death. And he should know, since Vic is an undertaker. His business, literally, is death, and during the war one of his duties was to prepare corpses for that abrupt ceremony known, with its poignant verbal attempt to transpose two elements, as burial at sea. But in equating the sea with death, Vic also equates it with something, positively, more: with our mortal democracy, our common human denomination, with the fact that we are all, in the end, not so different from each other:

> But Jack's not special, he's not special at all. I'd just like to say that, please. I'd just like to point that out, as a professional and a friend. He's just one of the many now. In life there are differences, you make distinctions . . . But the dead are the dead, I've watched them, they're equal. Either you think of them all or you forget them. It doesn't do in remembering one not to remember the others . . . And it doesn't do when you remember the others not to spare a thought for the ones you never knew. It's what makes all men equal for ever and always. There's only one sea.

I'd like to stick for a while, or digress for a while, with death— if death can ever be a digression. Reviewers and critics have noted that death crops up rather a lot in my work. One English reviewer of *Last Orders* went so far as to christen me, good-humouredly, the 'terminal novelist'. In one sense I accept, cheerfully, this description. Mortality runs through my work: *Last Orders, Ever After*— those titles tell you something. *Last Orders* is about a man's last wishes; *Ever After* deals with a husband's grief for a dead wife. The main action of *The Sweet Shop Owner* occurs on the last day of the protagonist's life. And throughout my work there's a fair amount about that wholesale supplier of death, war.

But against all this I would say, firstly, that my work deals with many *other* things too; secondly, that an interest in death is a natural, rational, even healthy concern of anyone in any sense *alive*; and, thirdly, that in none of this do I think I'm in any way exceptional. Literature, after all, from Homer onwards, is littered with the recounting of deaths and with the fascination for death, and in this it only expresses what we all repeatedly dwell on but do not necessarily or readily voice. So far as death goes, I don't claim any oddity. There is only one sea: I'm in the same boat as everyone else. And that seems, more generally, to be the position that every novelist, unless they are possessed of a peculiar arrogance, should take: I am mortal too, I am human too. I too, like you, share life's joys, pains, confusions. We're all in the same boat.

One of the writers of the past I keep coming back to, and I say this not just because I'm here in France, is Montaigne. And I hasten to add that since my French is pitiful, I read Montaigne in English translation, particularly the marvellous contemporary one by John Florio. Montaigne was plainly fascinated, amid much else, by death. The very titles of some of his essays betray this: 'Of Judging of Others' Deaths'; 'That to Philosophize Is to Learn How to Die', and so on. But there's one essay of Montaigne's in particular that I keep coming back to, called, in English, 'Of Exercise or Practice'. In it Montaigne makes the unassailable point that though there are a great many things we can practise, and perhaps perfect, there's one thing we can never practise: death. But, he suggests, we can get close to doing so. He then vividly describes an incident in his own life—or you might say, near-death—when he fell from his horse and, as a result, also fell into a state of apparent unconsciousness during which he was assumed by those around him to be dying, though all the time he himself was aware, as in a kind of vigilant trance, of everything that was happening. It gave him the rare opportunity, he says, actually to observe what it must be like to die; and, he concludes, it was, really, not so unpleasant at all. It's worth quoting a little from Florio's version:

> Me thought, my selfe had no other hold of me, but of my lips-ends. I closed mine eyes, to helpe (as me seemed) to send it forth, and tooke a kinde of pleasure to linger and languishingly to let myselfe goe from my selfe . . . I knew neither whence I came nor whither I went, nor could I understand or consider what was spoken unto me. They were but light effects, that my senses produced of themselves, as it were of custome. Whatsoever the soule did assist it with, was but a dreame, being lightly touched, and only sprinkled by the softe impression of the senses. In the meane time my state was verily most pleasant and easefull. I felt no manner of care or affliction, neither for my selfe nor others. I saw mine owne house and knew it not; when I was laid in my bed, I felt great ease in my rest . . . To say truth, it had beene a very happy death: For, the weaknesse of my discourse hindered me from judging of it, and the feeblenesse of my body from feeling the same. Me thought I was yeelding up the ghost so gently, and after so easie and indolent a manner, that I feele no other action lesse burthensome than that was . . .

It's a wonderful, and wonderfully comforting, passage, but perhaps the greatest wonder is that in it Montaigne unconsciously —and that's the operative word—achieves what elsewhere in the *Essays* is his avowedly conscious aim: to make, amid a wealth of subject matter, his principal subject *himself*: to offer himself to the world. For suddenly in this passage where, ironically, the concern is death, Montaigne comes palpably, intimately *alive*: this man who on a precise day, in precise circumstances, in the late sixteenth century, fell from his horse, nearly died, yet whose living curiosity was so strong and insatiable that he did not omit to make a study even of this possibly terminal experience.

Why do I dwell on this passage? To illustrate that an interest in death can be an interest in life? In part, yes. If *Last Orders* is about death, then it's about death in order to be about life, or it's about life getting in the way of death, as it does with Montaigne, an intrusion or obstruction which can sometimes be, as I hope it is in *Last Orders*, affirmatively comic. One of the principal tasks of my book is to make a dead man come to life again: to give back life. The same pattern is there in *Ever After*, which begins with a death, with an end, but ends with a beginning. And that making things 'come alive', that simple siding with creation, is a mainspring of fiction.

But I refer to that essay of Montaigne's for another reason. My subject is place. We naturally think of place as a spatial condition but of course we all, just as much, have our place in time. That fall of Montaigne's from his horse is thoroughly placed in time yet, in Montaigne's account of it, it leaps magically free from that dimension. It's the humble glory of us all that while we can share the same physical places with others, our place in time is unique, unrepeatable, irre*place*able; the particular conjunction we embody of an inner world with an outer one is ours and ours only. Our glory, yes, but also our fixity, our isolation. Only death, perhaps, seems to tell us we are part of something beyond personal place and time. Yet we can—and really quite easily—transcend this historical isolation. Montaigne transcends it or transcends it for us as he comes alive at that seeming point of death, and it's in the nature of both the writing and the reading of any work of fiction that we transcend it.

When some readers suppose that fiction is really a version of fact—disguised autobiography—I think that is their sad loss. The whole appeal, the whole challenge and reward of fiction lies in its liberation from personal fact. The very least we should expect of it is that it will, to use the common phrase, 'take us out of ourselves', take us out of the place we normally and sometimes narrowly inhabit. That process is sometimes disparagingly labelled as escapism, a term which can be usefully applied to some *bad* fiction, and perhaps to seaside amusement parks, but surely that initial *escape* is vital, and can be profitable if we are led back in the end, with something more than we started with, to ourselves.

You don't have to have been born in the Fens to set a novel there; you can make the imaginative journey. And that journey applies just as much, indeed more importantly, to the human and psychological content of a novel, since even if you set your story in territory that is geographically close to home, if your characters are to be convincing, then you must still undertake the mental journey to them. As I've said before now, one of the great functions of fiction is to prompt us to try to understand what it's like to be someone else. That attempt is of course vital in life generally, but fiction offers a special stimulus towards it. We all know that the journey from ourselves to another human being, even one who's normally very close to us, can sometimes be immense, yet, in a flash, the imagination can leap the distance. And that imaginative journey to someone simultaneously near yet far is essentially no different from the imaginative journey I might make to someone living in China or Peru, or to someone living in another time, like Montaigne in the sixteenth century, or even to some character in a novel who has never actually existed at all.

There's one place, I'd like to suggest, which belongs peculiarly to fiction, to all good storytelling, while belonging to us all. You don't have to have been born in the Fens, or ever have gone there, in order to *read* a novel that's set there. It's the job of the novel to take you there. I think we all recognize as readers the often rather delicious sensation, as we begin a novel, of entering a previously unfamiliar world and of starting to inhabit it as if it were our own. And we all recognize that much more intense and resonant thrill a novel can give when something in the narrative or in the internal workings of a character makes us stop in our mental tracks and say to ourselves, 'Hold on—I've been here too. I've been in this place too. It's unfamiliar, but it's not.' It's surely this 'I've-been-here-too' territory with its countless possible external approaches but its common centre of identification which is the real heartland of fiction, the real destination of storytelling.

All my books contain, I think, a sense of place, and *Last Orders* could be called my most local book. It's not just set in a particular corner of England, it's even written in a local language. Yet it also goes against locality in being the only one of my novels to make explicit, in its very form, that if we are creatures of place we are also creatures of motion—travellers, wanderers, rovers. Sailors haunt its pages, so do gypsies. There's a good deal of running away and absconding, of leaving or seeking home. One of the chief physical props of the whole story is a camper van: that paradoxical contrivance, a *travelling* home.

If we are all, at least in our minds, travellers, if to write or to read a book is to go on a mental journey, then it is also true that books themselves travel. One proof of this is that books get translated, something which could hardly happen if the experience being purveyed could not be recognized and felt to be true in more than one place. Writers are always trying to touch, to grasp the universal. And the way not to do this, it seems to me, is to write the avowedly universal, global, cosmopolitan book—the sort of book that ought to be written in Esperanto. The key to the universal is always the local, if only because it's a universal truth that all experience is and must be local, all experience is placed. If I read a book set in China or Peru, or indeed Nice, a great many local references may pass me by, but that doesn't matter, it even helps, because through them I nonetheless sense the true, the genuinely local texture of life as it's really lived.

The theme of this somewhat roving talk of mine seems to be that we are all, at one and the same time, inhabitants of place and of placelessness, creatures of tenure, attachment and of no fixed abode. This is nothing new. This almost exhausted twentieth century has taught us, often cruelly, sometimes kindly, that we live in an increasingly *dislocated* world, a world in which cultural as well as geographical boundaries become ever more volatile and confused. Of course, writers should respond to this, but it might be thought that writers, who have to write from some personal fixed point—and particularly writers of an indigenous kind like myself, an Englishman born in England, who's lived most of his life in the same city—would be at a disadvantage. But I don't think so, if only because of the nature of that central imaginative act. I think if you start a story that's going to *go* anywhere, you have to involve yourself, from the outset, in a kind of inner uprooting; you have to become, with all its freedom, risk and excitement, *unattached*. I think all writers, whether they're of the settled, the nomadic or the involuntarily displaced kind, would recognize that mental dislocation is part and parcel of what they do. It's even what initiates and inspires what they do. I've always thought that all narrative starts with the sense of the strange—a strangeness that may be no more, or less, than the sudden appreciation of specialness, of that humble glory of our irreplaceable place in time. As Ray in *Last Orders* observes:

But a few things happen anyway, a few things happen. Like we haven't seen or chosen them, though we would've if we could've, but they happen anyway, like they saw and chose us first, they saw us coming, like we aint been missed or overlooked altogether . . .

Stories begin when strangeness slips into our lives, as it always will and must, because life is, however much we try to domesticate it, constantly, wonderfully, dangerously strange. *Terra incognita* may of course be that remote wilderness at the edge of the map, but it can also be, as we all have occasion to discover, just around the corner.

Margate-Sands

FISHING WITH TED

DEVON, 1998

After I published *Waterland* in 1983, having published the year before a collection of stories called *Learning to Swim*, it began to be supposed that there was something aqueous about me. My lecture in Nice, many years later, acknowledged an attraction to the seaside, but the wateriness had already gained circulation when, back in the early 1980s, I started to say, in answer to the question writers inevitably get asked about what they do when they're not writing: fishing.

That answer was, in truth, a rather complicated mixture of fact, bluff and wish. One Christmas long ago, as this book has already mentioned, I was given a fishing rod. I was certainly of an age by then when I no longer begged Father Christmas for such things. The rod came, along with a set of tackle, from my real father, though it could be said that I'd angled for it. It was anyway a present that added a dimension to my life. I remember, that Christmas Day, repeatedly laying out for inspection the little lead weights and cork floats—far more important to me than any Christmas-tree baubles.

My first outing with my new rod must have been on the day after Boxing Day, in thick snow by almost iced-over water, but I was not to be deterred. I fished as a boy and as a teenager, with moderate success and no great ability, but always with contentment, and when other things gradually began to take over (including the desire to be a writer), I think I knew I was only putting the fishing side of me into abeyance—though I didn't know that it would be fifteen years or so, by which time I'd become a published writer, before it would emerge again, at least in the form of an answer to a question.

The element of bluff in that answer was very effectively called when at a party given by the now long-defunct *Fiction Magazine* I met David Profumo, then its assistant editor. Our conversation quickly turned piscatorial—and a little inquisitorial. Was it all hokum, this thing I claimed, or was it real? I think David sensed that it was a bit of both, but essentially sincere. What I was really saying was: I wouldn't mind going fishing again.

It turned out that I was talking to a fishing prodigy, a demon angler who lived, if not quite exclusively, to fish. Beside David, my dabblings and hankerings were as nothing—as was, I'd soon learn, my skill. David was a fine writer, of fiction and occasional poetry, but there was no doubt that his first calling had been fishing; though he seemed eager to strike some productive balance between the two vocations.

The result of that meeting was that he made two proposals. First, would I like to consider joining him in compiling an anthology of literature related to fishing? It was a rich field and something he'd been keen to do for some time. I might like to think about that for a bit. But, meanwhile, would I like to go fishing?

In the next few weeks, months—years—I went fishing with David many times. In essence, he taught me to fly-fish, something I'd never done before. I couldn't have had a better teacher or companion. For the purposes of my tuition and ongoing practice, I travelled with him to many watery places, and when I was no longer a floundering novice I found my own happy fishing ground in north Devon on the River Torridge, where, by another stroke of piscatorial luck, I met the poet Ted Hughes and occasionally fished with him.

Meanwhile, the anthologizing (to which I'd quickly agreed) had grown into a fat volume called *The Magic Wheel*, which Heinemann published in 1986. It's now out of print, but it represented for its co-editors many busy and beguiling days: fishing of another kind, for books and extracts to include. This mainly occurred in the old British Museum Reading Room, but, given our subject, the scholarly and bibliographical work naturally had to be complemented by a great many of what we called field trips.

The scholarly work also included the co-writing of a lengthy introduction to the anthologized pieces, in which we surveyed the remarkably extensive history of fishing literature ('from Ovid to Orwell') and examined the mystery of why fishing and writing should have any affinity at all. They undoubtedly do. If our anthology wasn't evidence enough, we were living proof.

That introduction remains the only piece of writing on which I've collaborated with another author. I couldn't say for certain now which bits belong to David, which to me, and that wouldn't be in the spirit of the thing. Such joint undertakings are often supposed to lead to quarrels and animosity, but I don't remember any squabbling. It all came together entirely amicably, like our days by or on the water, where there was rather more rivalry and contention, in fact, about the hooking of fish.

All of this, the fishing and the anthologizing, occurred at a good time. By the end of 1983 I'd published a book a year for four years, and though the statistical facts belie my actual rate of production, I think that wishful statement about my non-writing activities was partly a recognition that I needed a change, a rest, some dependable form of refreshing escape from writing. One way or another, in the period following the appearance of *Waterland*, and in keeping with that novel's title, an imaginary sign often went up on my study door: 'Gone Fishing'.

Of many memorable days spent fishing with David one stands out, if only because it began with the normal roles being reversed. I'd fished the Torridge for some years before he and I ever fished it together. I was able to travel down to Devon, when conditions seemed promising, more or less at the drop of a hat; David, with a young family, was less flexible. But one September we made the journey together and I was placed in the untypical and nervous position of introducing him to a new bit of water and one, as I'd learned, that could be testing and unyielding at the best of times. I needn't have worried. The roles were soon re-reversed. Within moments of his first wading in David hooked a salmon, which I netted for him. Moments later, amazingly, I hooked a salmon too, and the roles were reversed once again.

Salmon anglers will know it's really not supposed to happen like that. Or if it does, as David noted when he recounted the episode in a fishing column he then wrote, it only happens to 'the Other Bloke'. Well, there were two happy Other Blokes that day. As there were on many others.

David is the 'good and patient friend' mentioned in the piece that follows, and it was on that same trip to Devon that he and I walked, one afternoon, with Ted Hughes along a stretch of the Torridge as new to me at the time as the whole river was to David. That walk is also mentioned in the piece. Ted's knowledge of the water was seriously impressive, though David and I retain a memory of that day that has always made us laugh. The pools on salmon rivers can have atmospheric names, sometimes with a touch of poetry, known only to fishermen. Ted had stopped by a pool, clearly holding strong associations for him, where, as he pointed out, a deep, salmon-detaining pot had been formed by the remains of a long-ago collapsed and overgrown concrete groyne. We asked him what the pool was called, expecting to hear some suitably evocative words, made all the more evocative by being uttered by Ted Hughes. He continued to stare at the water and, with his slow Yorkshire vowels, said, 'Concrete.'

Ted died, not so very long after that, in October 1998. Soon afterwards I wrote the memory of him, reprinted here, which appeared in *Granta* the following spring. I'd first met him over tea in the house, overlooking the Torridge, of two husband-and-wife fishing friends of his. It was a warm summer's day and he mysteriously wore all the time, without seeming uncomfortable, an old thick maroon-wool cardigan of a very winter-warming kind, though he wasn't a man, as I'd learn when I fished with him in Scotland, who much felt the cold, or minded getting wet. I mostly saw him in old, worn clothes.

Several years before, he'd written a delightful essay, 'Taw and Torridge', about north Devon's two main rivers, for a book called *West Country Fly Fishing* which Batsford brought out in 1983. It had accompanied me when I first started to fish the Torridge myself, and though it's probably one of his least-known productions, it's one of the things by him that most readily evokes for me his now-missing presence. It was lovely to have been in his company now and then in a part of the country to which he was so close and which, by the time I met him, I'd begun to know fairly intimately myself.

When it came to fishing or to his fishing places, he could be quite immovably committed. Once, when I said goodbye to him to come back to London and made that glib and flimsy remark,

'Back to the real world,' he said, without any trace of sentimentality and almost sternly, 'No, this is the real world.' He could also be unbudgingly blunt. When I told him another time, on the phone, that I couldn't get down to Devon (where the fishing was just coming right) because I had to go to a funeral, he asked, with only just sufficient irony, whether they couldn't put the body in the freezer for a while.

As it happens, I learned about Ted's death when I was in Iceland, a country with exceptional fishing opportunities, which Ted had sampled, but also one where his work was loved. Like many people who'd been in touch with him only months before he died, I'd never even known he was ill. It was a sheer shock. I was meeting a journalist in the offices of a Reykjavik paper and her desk was strewn with Ted's books. 'You must be a fan,' I said. She said, 'Haven't you heard?'

I came home from Iceland and wrote the following piece.

Fishing with Ted

I first encountered Ted Hughes as many of my age must have done, when I was a young teenager in the early 1960s, being introduced in English lessons to those electric poems from *Hawk in the Rain* and *Lupercal*. I still remember my English teacher reading out 'Pike'. At that age either you get smitten by the power of words or you don't, though I must admit that the force of that poem had something to do with my dabbling in a small-time way with hooks and floats and lines. But I nursed even then the secret dream of one day being a writer myself. I'd never have dared tell my English teacher about it and scarcely whispered it to myself, so far-fetched and foolish did it seem.

As you get older the phrase 'if only I'd known then' gets ever more called upon. Sometimes it haunts you like a knell, sometimes it's the motto for unimagined privilege. Years later, in the 1980s, when I actually was a writer and had published books, I took up fishing again, after a long gap, or rather I was taught by a good and patient friend to fly-fish, something I'd never done before. So I came to fish for, and sometimes catch, trout, salmon and sea trout.

This in turn took me, two or three times a year, to the beautiful, hidden River Torridge in Devon, where the fishing is now a poor shadow of what it was back in the early Sixties when I was a schoolboy and knew nothing about it, though that in a way is a blessing. It's an unmarauded river and there are places where you can fish all day and never see a soul.

My visits to Devon led to my meeting some fishing friends of Ted, which led to my meeting Ted—an introduction almost entirely non-literary and almost exclusively piscatorial. In subsequent years I got to see him now and then and even fish with him. I'm thinking of just a scattering of days and hours, so I can't pretend to have known him well or closely, but because those days and hours involved being by or near water, if not actually fishing, in places that Ted knew and loved, they went at once beyond the merely social and I quickly learned what good, easy, gentle company he was.

We mostly met in Ted's north Devon, though once I fished with him at the opposite end of the country, on the wind-furrowed lochs of the Isle of Harris. As quite often happens when writers meet writers, especially off the literary tracks, we hardly ever talked about writing of any kind. Once, in a Devon pub, we got tentatively close, though our talk in fact was more about that additional, tricky work writers have to do simply to protect their writing time and space from all that, increasingly in a writer's career, can invade it. Ted was perhaps more besettingly involved in this work than many, but he never appeared to me as anything other than steady and calm, sure of his inner ground. I think he had an admirably unwavering sense of what was properly private and what was properly public.

We mostly talked about fishing and rivers, local things, things before our eyes. I walked with him one afternoon down a stretch of the Torridge new to me while he explained the intricacies and history of almost every pool, run, bend and lie. This was not Ted the poet but a Ted who, for all one knew, might have spent his years being a vigilant, devoted river-keeper. It was almost impossible to imagine him sitting at a desk.

However they stand in his complete work, my favourite poems of his will always be those in the collection *River*, not just because I have, in some cases, waded the very water, seen the very boulders and overhanging branches Ted must have had in mind, but because I have, at least occasionally, experienced the fisherman's state of special attunement to atmosphere—a heightened alertness to particularly charged, expectant conditions of water, weather and light—so I can attest to how hushingly close he gets to the feeling in words. 'Salmon-taking Times' and 'Night Arrival of Seatrout' distil for me not just the essence of fishing for both species of fish but the whole seasonal, riverine harvest of associations each owns. 'After Moonless Midnight', in which the normal fishing premise is turned around and it's the river that whispers of the angler, 'We've got him,' could hardly convey better the breath-holding, almost dreading excitement of wading down a pool alone at night after sea trout.

Ted himself famously wrote about fishing and its similarities to the creative act of poetry. Analogies for how writing gets written can be stretched, but there is some basis in the piscatorial one, in that concentrated dealing with surface and depth, never knowing from one moment to the next what might, if anything, be there, sometimes having a guess, always a hope, sometimes an entirely irrational but palpable anticipation, and sometimes being taken totally by surprise.

With salmon and sea-trout fishing the analogy gets closer, if only because it enters realms of greater mystery. Unlike the permanent residents, the migratory fish which move up a river only at certain times and in certain conditions feed hardly at all, so to fish for them lacks even the fragile logic of presenting the quarry with something imitating its food. No one *really* knows why salmon and sea trout ever take a fly, though they're more likely to be there and do so at certain times and a whole body of fishing lore has tried to reduce this to a precise science—or art—and failed.

It's the enigma of the 'take' rather than the general confrontation of mind and water which most parallels—without in the least explaining—the creative process. And in salmon and sea-trout fishing it's the take, not the capture, which is the essential, heart-stopping thing. Sometimes it comes with a long, powerful, unmistakably connective pull, sometimes there's a boil and a white slash of spray, but when it happens it's always a sheer amazement. And it's not at all unlike how an idea—that limp word we use for want of a better one—bursts, without recognizable correlation to design, effort or receptivity, upon a writer's mind. In both cases exultation can be immediately mixed with high anxiety as to whether fish and angler, idea and writer, will part company.

Thanks to the generosity of a friend of his, I once fished with Ted another Devon river, the Exe, on a stretch where it briefly divides into some deep, narrow streams. I've fished some pools on the Torridge *for years* without success, but under the eye of Ted Hughes—which wasn't an 'eagle eye', it was a soft eye—I hooked, within half an hour and on a strange river, a good-sized salmon, which in that narrow water put up a thrilling up-and-downstream fight. Then, when all was over and the beaten fish was being drawn in, the hook, as sometimes miserably happens, simply lost its hold and there was that awful, absolute separation.

Fishing, if you think about it in a certain way, is a fairly silly, childish activity, absurdly pursued by some till their dying day, a thing of no virtue or importance. This doesn't stop it offering up to fishermen moments of ineffable triumph that imprint every flash of their glory permanently on the brain, or moments of abysmal disaster that will never, ever be forgotten or exorcised. Such dramatic highs and lows life itself doesn't necessarily or so reliably or so intensely provide.

I've known real grief at losing fish—it usually comes mingled with bleak self-reproach, when you know you've done something wrong, lost your head, forgotten to check a knot. Hooking a salmon is, for me at least, such a rare event that any loss is grievous, but with that salmon on the Exe I think I honestly achieved that precarious angler's equanimity of relishing every second of an encounter I might never have had and of not mourning the loss, since, as Walton unanswerably puts it, you cannot lose what was never yours.

Fishing would be a poor thing if it were only about capture and loss, only about fish. While fishing the Torridge I've seen things, known things—you have to use a tired phrase like 'getting close to nature'—which have nothing directly to do with fishing but which I couldn't have seen or known, I think, if I'd sought them deliberately in another way. Standing up to my waist in water, I've watched an otter (a creature which in England most people rarely, if ever, glimpse) occupy a stone barely a yard from me, as untroubled by my presence as a cat. I've watched a weasel do two things weasels are seldom seen to do, let alone in the space of the same minute: dive into water and come up again, then climb a good twenty feet up the nearest tree. I've watched a young deer trot along the bank till abreast of where I stood midstream, then decide to swim cross-river, so close to me that I had to lift my rod and trailing fly-line for it to pass beneath, as a guard of honour arches swords for a bride and groom. Such privileged moments have the magic of making you feel as a human being—it's a paradoxical privilege—secondary, if not superfluous, to the general animal world. Ted's 'animal poems' have the salutary human effect of reminding us that we are just one component in a throng.

The same afternoon I lost that salmon something rather wonderful occurred. First, I hooked another salmon, a much smaller one, which Ted netted. Salmon fishing rarely gives you a consolation prize, even one that makes you churlishly wish fortune had been the other way round, but that wasn't the point. As the fish lay on the bank we both noticed something white and bony among the shingle. Ted picked it up and said I should keep it as a memento. It was the skull of a pike.

I put it in a pocket and then maybe transferred it later to somewhere else. But at some point during that trip to Devon I lost it. Fishermen carry around with them masses of jumble, on their person, in their cars, and they are good at losing things, not just fish. And of course, it was only at the point of realizing I'd lost it that the other realization came fully to me. That I'd lost a pike's skull presented to me by Ted Hughes after the catching of a salmon; by Ted Hughes the poet, whom I could never once have imagined meeting, but whom I'd first known, like many who'd never meet him, through that poem 'Pike'.

There's never a moment in life, perhaps, when we should underestimate the latent repercussions. All this was a few years ago when Ted himself seemed as indestructible as his work, a big, broad, solid man. He died in October, the month after the fishing season ends on the Torridge. No more fishing there before the spring.

What a keepsake that pike's skull would have been, combining a set of chances and associations infinitely more amazing even than the take of a salmon—the loss of that fish that afternoon as nothing really to the loss of that skull. But then the loss of that skull is as nothing to the loss of Ted. He left in a poetic blaze: *Birthday Letters*, the *Tales from Ovid*. The keepsake for us all, of course, is the poetry. Poets, above all mortals, are supposed to offer recompense for their decease by what they leave behind. But not, perhaps, if you've met them, spent time with them, even walked, waded into the very stuff of some of the poems. Then those trade-offs between life and art, nature and art, seem not so simply negotiable after all.

·

FILMING AGAIN, WITH FRED

CANTERBURY CATHEDRAL, 2000

One morning in the late autumn of 2000 I walked through the gateway that leads to Canterbury Cathedral, to be greeted by a terse little notice: 'The Cathedral is closed today.' Several other members of the public who'd unluckily chosen this day to take a look round the cathedral were staring at the notice in puzzlement and disappointment. Weren't churches, let alone cathedrals, always supposed to be open? What calamity or exceptional ecclesiastical event could have caused Canterbury Cathedral to shut its doors?

Looking further along the Cathedral Yard, they would have seen the concentration of trucks, trailers, twisting cables and generators that mark the presence of a film crew. I felt I should apologize to the thwarted tourists. In a sense, it was all my fault. This was roughly halfway through the eight-week shooting of the film of *Last Orders* and one of the more graphic instances of the movie world's powers of physical annexation.

A few years before, I'd walked through that same gateway with the aim of just looking around Canterbury Cathedral myself, though I wasn't, if no one would have known it, an entirely casual visitor. I'd wanted to see if the scenes set in Canterbury Cathedral in the novel I was then writing—I had a clear idea of these scenes in my head—'worked' in actual practice. Whether, for example, some characters standing by the tomb of the Black Prince, east of the choir, would in fact be able to see another character seated in another part of the church.

I'm a reluctant, illogical and rather foolhardy researcher. I rely on guesswork, imagination or sheer wishful thinking in order to write the thing first, then check it up later. Sometimes this can result in some challenging reversals of what I'd envisaged. With my novel almost completed, I'd been spending some time on this checking-up; and Canterbury made a nice day out. It never occurred to me as I confirmed the positions and sight-lines of my characters that I was doing exactly the same thing as a film director might do to construct a scene—or, indeed, that *Last Orders* would ever be filmed. Canterbury Cathedral was the last place you could imagine being turned into a film set.

For a novelist, setting a scene in Canterbury Cathedral is nothing. It requires no special audacity and, of course, affects the material world not one bit. Film-making logistics are quite different. To have your book turned into a film is to undergo a weird process of being taken literally. Your unpresuming mental choices are, sometimes quite disarmingly, flung back at you. So, you wanted Canterbury Cathedral, did you?

It's not just that novels happen inside the skull and films don't. 'Mental choices' is itself an all-too-finite term. In my novel four men transport the ashes of a fifth man from South London to Margate to observe the dead man's mysterious last wish. This is the premise for what I always knew would be a complicated journey, in time and memory as well as space. I felt the book would be rife with detours, but I really didn't know what all the detours would be. The Canterbury chapters occur because, late in the journey, one of the characters suggests, as a joke, that as there have been so many detours already, they may as well take the ashes round Canterbury Cathedral too. Yet the joke gets acted on, with serious as well as comic effect.

As with the character, so with the author. The Canterbury scenes were for me too, once, just a quirk, a whim, a tempting possibility in my head. All novelists know these little flickers that can lead on to something bigger. I followed my whim. But now here I was outside Canterbury Cathedral, which they'd closed, as it were, specially for me. It was the first time, I'd already learnt, that a crew had been allowed inside to shoot scenes for a feature film. The Dean, if not the Archbishop, had had to read my novel and had judged that the scenes in the cathedral were integral to the story. Integral? Well, of course they were *now*.

Films begin more tangibly than novels, if still very tenuously. Some three years before they closed Canterbury Cathedral I'd been approached by a producer working with the Australian director Fred Schepisi, who was apparently eager to film my novel. This was not the only approach to make the film around this time, but eventually I went with Fred.

I was impressed by his distinguished career (*A Cry in the Dark*, *Plenty*, *Six Degrees of Separation*), even more impressed, when I met him, by his genuine respect for writers, not a common trait among film directors. There were also the winning reserves of irreverent Aussie humour. The novelist Tom Keneally, with whom Fred had worked, once described him to me as 'one of the wild men of Australia'. So not only was the first-ever shooting of a feature film taking place inside Canterbury Cathedral, but it was being done by a wild man of Australia.

Waterland had been filmed by an American director and (though the script was by a British writer) large parts of the book had been unfortunately transposed to the States. Approving an Australian director now for *Last Orders* might have seemed an ill-advised and perverse move. But there was no fear that Fred was going to shift my novel to New South Wales. In fact, he kept scrupulously to its topography, in some cases literally to the square yard.

Moreover, Australian humour may have its own distinct tang, but it's not so vastly different from British humour, from the underdog humour of the characters in my book. Between the Australians and the Brits there may be a regular, chafing mutual suspicion—it's part of the humour—but there's also a great deal of mutual recognition. By the time I met Fred I'd been to Australia a number of times. I admit to a warm affection for the place. So my approval was in part a sentimental vote.

The key difference from *Waterland* was that Stephen Gyllenhaal was brought in at the last minute to make that film, while the wish to make *Last Orders* came directly from Fred. But, for the sentimental record, there is an Antipodean touch to the novel itself. One of the characters has a wish, a fantasy, of flying to Australia. We never quite know if it's going to be fulfilled. So a genuine Australian link exists, and it's one that's alluded to slyly and deftly by Fred in the opening sequence of the film.

All other factors apart, I felt when I first met Fred that, if he made the film, some fun and frank sharing of minds might be had along the way. They were. Among my best memories of the filming are the many conversations I had with him in which we both seemed to acknowledge that, different as film directors and novelists are, our abiding obsession was the same: the mysteries of how best to tell a story, of how best to impart information and emotion. These conversations brought back the ones I'd had with Stephen Gyllenhaal at Twickenham Studios years before, but a crucial difference was that Fred had written the script, so I'd got to know him during that process, long before the cameras rolled and indeed before anyone, Fred included, knew whether they ever would.

The scriptwriting was originally offered to me, but I said no, quickly enough. I'm not a screenwriter, and there seemed to me to be benefits in keeping the creative vision all inside one head. That said, Fred was obligingly open to suggestions and I couldn't help being a little possessive. I had a constant look-in on his drafts and was irritatingly free with comments and notes. Fred would thank me for them and usually say: 'Some of them I liked—some of them' (strong Australian cadence) 'I didn't.'

I didn't talk that much with him during actual shooting. Aware of the pressures he was under, I tried to keep out of his way. I wouldn't be a film director for the world—it's colossally stressful. Nonetheless, I'd often feel that I was the only one on set thinking like he was. I shared his anxiety—his baby was also my baby—and I knew that while everyone else had a particular job to do, Fred was the only one who had to keep the whole edifice in his head. It's exactly the same, without the trucks, trailers and scores of attendant people, when you write a novel.

Much more important, in any case, than my rapport with Fred was his with the actors. The film's wonderful cast (on a hardly lavish budget) was largely down to him. It was clear to me at an early stage that actors *wanted* to work with him. I could never have asked Helen Mirren to play a pensioner. On the dream cast-list, there'd simply been no one else for the part of Jack, the butcher, but Michael Caine. Fred's story, here, was that at the first approach Caine had turned down the role on the basis that he wasn't ready to play an old codger. At the second, he'd agreed, saying he'd always known that one day he'd end up playing his father. (Caine's father had been a Billingsgate porter and, like the novel's Jack, had died in St Thomas's Hospital.)

That the cast would all pull together became clear, one morning in Soho, at the first read-through of the script, when the stars met a set of junior actors who would play their younger selves in the film's many flashbacks. One might have thought that, while the juniors could be forgiven for being overawed, the veteran stars would have gathered for a read-through without a hint of trepidation. But I was given a trenchant, whispered insight into the dynamics of such occasions by the drily knowing Bill Nighy, on hand just for the day to read various as yet uncast parts: 'They're *all* nervous as shit. They're all watching each other.' The read-through was a great success.

In the weeks that followed I never saw anyone being a prima donna, never witnessed a tantrum, never heard a lofty put-down. 'Mucking in' would be the appropriate phrase, often suiting the physical conditions (one of the wettest autumns on record turned the sets to farmyard quags) as well as the cheerfully scabrous off-camera repartee. Film-making is a profoundly unglamorous activity—slow, repetitive, uncomfortable—and on a film set even stars forgo glamour and become ordinary people getting on with a job. That said, during the shooting no less than two members of the cast were knighted—or knew they were going to be. Sir Michael and Sir Tom.

And they closed Canterbury Cathedral just for us.

The author's role in it all defies definition—partly because in truth you have no role, *your* work is done. You are vital to the whole enterprise (the megalomaniac inside you can say: all this is happening because of *me*) yet you are also redundant. On set you feel like a visiting ghost, never quite sure if you're there to maintain some regal scrutiny or just to gawp.

The memories you retain also have an uncanny, larger-than-life quality, pitched between the real and the fabricated.

Film-making may be tedious, but at its heart is a dressing-up joy, and while the thrill in the cinema is of seeing something made to look real, the delight during the making is of watching the world turn into fiction. On my first visit to the derelict factory in Peckham used as office and studio (Peckham International Screen Studios, or PISS, as some of the crew called it) they were shooting a scene set in a Cairo brothel and the place was crawling with prostitutes. There was talk of bringing a camel to Peckham. Less colourfully, I went several times to a pub (also derelict) in Clapham that served as the novel's Coach and Horses in Bermondsey, so that it became like popping into some genuine local, except that I had the privilege of seeing the place undergo extraordinary overnight historical changes, from the 1940s right through to the 1980s.

Perhaps most uncanny of all is the memory of standing at the end of a rainswept and freezing Margate Pier for the final ash-throwing scene. Once again, as with Canterbury Cathedral, I was present at a real and precise place (and I'd been here before too, to check out the ash-throwing possibilities) that was at the same time a scene in a film and a place in a book, though it had all been once just a notion in my brain. Not the real place, of course; that existed. Though even here, there was an uncanny twist.

I can confess now, with reference to my lax methods of research, that when I conceived the scene while writing the book I'd never been to Margate. I'd pictured 'Margate Pier' like any other seaside pier—a boardwalked affair on iron struts with white filigree structures on top—not knowing at all that the real Margate Pier, as in finished book and film, is just a rough, grim harbour wall. Margate had never had a 'pier' in the stereotypical sense, though it had had something that looked like it, destroyed by a storm in the 1970s, called the Jetty.

Fortunately, I managed to turn this novel-confounding discovery to eventual advantage. The Jetty–Pier confusion becomes a confusion (or a complication in their memories) that the characters themselves share. It adds, I hope, to the tissue of the novel rather than wrecking it. But as I stood on the very real and very wet Margate Pier I had the fleeting, private thought that the scene I was now 'in' was not, in fact, as I'd once, erroneously, pictured it. I'd arrived here at Margate Pier by my own novel-writing detour.

But there was more than one personal detour involved on that pier. When I'd gone in the 1960s to see David Hemmings in *Blowup*, I could never have imagined he'd one day star in a film of a book of mine, but even less could I have imagined that I'd one day find myself talking to him at the end of a miserably exposed harbour wall. Life and the imagination stage some strange surprises. It was while we chatted at the end of Margate Pier that he told me that his own career had really begun a long time before in Margate, or rather in Cliftonville, just next door. In those days he'd been a boy singer, but then his voice had broken and he'd gone into acting instead.

As we talked, the rain (it was December) sluiced down. I was in full waterproof gear while David was in the ordinary clothes required by his part, and completely soaked. He scorned going into the tent-like structure, with a heater inside, reserved for the actors when they weren't required—claiming that this only made you feel colder when you came out and it took you 'out' of your part. He'd also, I'd noticed, been taking a keen and curious interest, between takes, in the seagulls that were swooping around, sometimes flapping his arms towards them as if offering them something. He had to remind me that in my book when the ashes are thrown, some seagulls momentarily dive towards them, imagining they might be food. He was trying to get the seagulls to perform *their* part.

It was very strange to be talking to the former boy singer and star of *Blowup* at a place on his own personal map that had brought him full circle. It would have been even more eerily, and sadly, strange if I'd known that after the acting renaissance he was enjoying at the time—he'd recently been seen in *Gladiator*—this would effectively be David's last big-screen role.

The seagulls never quite obliged in being faithful to the book, but the actors obliged to the hilt. Another Margate-Pier memory that will stay with me is of seeing, after one of the last takes, all four actors, Hemmings, Courtenay, Hoskins and Winstone, all thoroughly drenched but high on the moment, huddle round the monitor to watch the replay. Without their knowing it, their huddling simply carried on their on-screen grouping. The monitor might have been the jar of ashes. 'It's a blinder!' they yelled through the lashing rain and their chattering teeth. 'It's a blinder!'

To come back to that (dry) day in Canterbury. During breaks in shooting we were put in the remarkable situation of being able to wander freely round the otherwise empty cathedral as no regular visitor can. Film sets hardly come grander and, lit by a low November sun, there was the technicolour glamour of the stained glass. On one of my moochings, I looked across and saw Bob Hoskins, just mooching and gazing too, having a quiet moment. In the film—poignant and funny as Ray, the close friend of Jack who is now ashes—he also has a special, quiet moment in the cathedral. Reality matching fiction again. And it was to check that moment of Ray's, among other things, that I'd made that preliminary novelist's visit to Canterbury.

What they say to you on set is: 'What's it like, seeing your book come alive?' I always wanted to reply, a little indignantly: It already *is* alive, it's already come alive, in readers' heads. That's what fiction is, a coming-alive. It's the film—if you don't mind—that borrows life from the book. But while that is fundamentally and undeniably true and while for me the page will always be bigger and better than any screen, the actual experience of seeing your book filmed, or at least such a fortunate experience as mine with *Last Orders*, can't be nearly so neatly predicated. It's an experience all in itself, quite separate from the experience of the audience watching the finished film, and in itself it can be a lesson in something that every writer of fiction will be familiar with and even trust in: the remarkable and unpredictable way in which fact and fiction, reality and imagination, can collide, collude and conspire.

With Fred in Peckham, 2000.

LOCAL HISTORY AND
AN INTERVIEW

WANDSWORTH, 1851–2005

Until it was hacked apart and turned into something else, my favourite local pub was the County Arms in Trinity Road, on the edge of Wandsworth Common and barely a hundred yards from Wandsworth Prison—a halfway house between one of the nicest open spaces in south-west London and one of its grimmest closed ones.

Those unsettling incongruities and strange openings into the past which the suburbs can be good at affording are rich in this area. Just along Trinity Road from the County Arms is the Royal Victoria Patriotic Asylum, a vast, outlandish building, all pinnacled turrets and steep gables, now converted into apartments and studios. Its original purpose was to house the daughters of servicemen killed in the Crimean War. Its grotesque grandeur, no doubt designed to be edifying, could only have accentuated the misery of being an impoverished orphan, and the girls whose fathers had died so patriotically endured an awful regime. Every morning, heads shaved against lice, they had to muster in the courtyard to be hosed down with cold water.

During the First World War the Asylum became a military hospital, a curious but pressing change of use. In the Second World War it was an internment camp and clearing centre for aliens and refugees, which meant it was also an interrogation centre for suspected spies. One of Wandsworth Prison's wartime functions, meanwhile, was to receive spies for execution, under the Treachery Act of 1940.

The conversion of the Asylum to a large-scale hospital in 1914–18 must have particularly marked local memories. The hospital's dead lie buried in Earlsfield Cemetery, in Magdalen Road off Trinity Road, where, sprinkled among the greyly weathered, ornate civilian memorials, are many simple, pristine-white military gravestones—serial number, rank and name—like those in the great cemeteries in Belgium and France.

I don't have to walk very far from home to feel in close touch with some of the more sombre aspects of my country's history, or of its continuing sociology. Wandsworth Prison remains one of the largest and most forbidding prisons in the land. It kept a working gallows well into the 1990s, capital punishment still being applicable for treason and mutiny. The Pierrepoints, for whom hanging was a family vocation, dispatched in their time over eighty Wandsworth inmates. 'Lord Haw-Haw' (William Joyce) was hanged here, as was Derek Bentley, in 1953, who should never have been hanged at all. Ronnie Kray was once a prisoner; so was Ronnie Biggs, the train robber, who escaped and sent a message on a postcard from Rio: 'Oh to be in Wandsworth.'

So too, briefly in 1895, was Oscar Wilde. In *De Profundis* he wrote that 'while I was in Wandsworth Prison I longed to die. It was my one desire.' During his transfer to Reading Gaol he was made to stand for half an hour in his prisoner's clothes and handcuffs on a central platform at nearby Clapham Junction—'Britain's Busiest Railway Station', as it proclaims itself—while crowds from the stopping trains gathered to mock and jeer. Let no author suppose there isn't a worse fate than their own.

The prison opened in 1851 as the Surrey House of Correction.

It was Surrey, not London, then. The truth is that as the first railways enabled London to spread quickly into the land around it, part of the initial impetus went into finding out-of-the-way sites for its unfortunates: prisons, orphanages, asylums (in the old, bad sense) and infirmaries. The terraces and villas of those seeking leafy respite from the city came soon afterwards, in some areas only to share the space with an immured underclass.

The historical ambiguities live on: homes next to former Homes; former Homes being converted into homes. Parts of Wandsworth—but only parts—have now become intensely moneyfied, which only deepens some of the dichotomies. When does local history ever easily get divided from national history? As a window on a country's soul, the place where I've lived now for over twenty-five years doesn't bear much scrutiny at all.

But I like Wandsworth for at least two reasons. First, it's on a river, by which I don't mean the Thames, though it's on that too. Wandsworth Bridge is one of the least attractive of the London bridges and the views from it (go there to see the ugliness of new 'luxury' riverside developments) don't make you pause. I mean the delightfully named Wandle, which flows north from its beginnings in Surrey to meet the Thames at Wandsworth. One of its original sources was in South Croydon. When I was a boy, representing my South Croydon primary school, I used to play cricket and football in Wandle Park. The river has threaded itself through my life.

When David Profumo and I wrote our introduction to *The Magic Wheel* we gave due place to the Wandle. It's very likely that the poet Donne once fished it. Nelson certainly did, despite having only one arm, when he lived (scandalously, with Lady Hamilton) near its banks at Merton. In the early nineteenth century Sir Humphry Davy, in his *Salmonia: Or Days of Fly Fishing*, sang its praises; and it's ironic that Davy, with his links—as a great chemist and as the inventor of the miner's lamp—to the industrial world, should have extolled a water soon to fall literally foul of industry.

Writing in the 1860s, in *The Crown of Wild Olive*, John Ruskin (who, with a Croydon mother, was something of a Croydon boy too) complained that, 'Twenty years ago, there was no lovelier piece of lowland scenery in South England, nor any more pathetic, in the world, by its expression of sweet human character and life, than that immediately bordering on the sources of the Wandel.' And he was decrying only the start of a process. The picture shown on page 379 was painted also in the 1860s and—with its central dead tree, chimney in the background and ambiguous title—is caught between nostalgia and prophecy.

Until quite recently the Wandle was a filthy and wretched river: polluted first by nineteenth-century mills—making anything from snuff to gunpowder—then by twentieth-century industry and by a general disrespect that it still suffers. In Wandsworth it is obliged to tunnel, like Acheron, under the central shopping mall, under branches of Waitrose, Argos, Superdrug and Boots, before re-emerging beyond the High Street, by the old Young's Brewery, for its final grubby lap to the Thames. It's a general dumping zone. In its never-deep waters I've seen mattresses, fridges and whole rusting motorbikes.

But it remains that marvellous thing, a river that rises through chalk. Though polluted, it runs persistently clear and with a millwheel-driving vigour. Green tresses of weed sway in its current, even just before it slips from sight in Wandsworth; sunlight catches patches of tawny gravel on its bed. It's possible to look at it through half-closed eyes and see again what it once must have been: the quintessential dream of a trout stream.

All the reports are that the Wandle is getting cleaner, that it supports again a few plucky trout. Rivers are supreme survivors, they live vastly longer than we do and, by and large, they can see off a lot of human abuse. But I feel for the Wandle as for some sick, if recovering, child. It still elicits some of Ruskin's lost-paradise sentiment. It's a small river, scarcely ten miles long. For all that it's known and endured, there remains something infant, innocent about its unsuppressed assertion of its right to be there. Its presence, in its sleeve of vegetation, amid so much brick and concrete, is a perpetual, heart-tugging surprise.

I was asked once in an interview what I would like to do if I wasn't a writer: a challenging if entirely theoretical question. I said I'd like to have charge of a stretch of river, maybe just two hundred yards or so: I'd like to be a river-keeper. I recently found this remark worked, with due acknowledgement, into the fabric of a new novel by Michael Ondaatje: a special instance of how things you say in interviews can (not always so pleasantly) come back at you. It had been a rather capricious answer to a fairly capricious question, but such questions sometimes find you out. Rivers get to me, they get in my veins. I don't see why they don't get to everyone.

It's not quite the same primordial thing, but I'm also very fond of Wandsworth Common. I live just a hundred yards from it and I walk across it or by it almost every day. Unlike the exposed and sometimes windswept prairie of Clapham Common, half a mile to the east, it has an intricacy, a sheltering fragmentedness, even bits of sylvan semi-rusticity. When it was still a true common, providing common grazing land, Thomas Hardy, turning forty, lived for a while on its fringes, at 172 Trinity Road. He must have walked now and then over the common, perhaps mulling over some work-in-progress or work-to-be. He may have popped into the County Arms. *The Return of the Native* came out when he'd just moved here. It's a bizarre elision: Wandsworth Common and Egdon Heath.

How do you achieve that tingling sense of palpable contact with a writer you would otherwise know only through their work? You don't associate Hardy at all with the London suburbs, but he wrote two novels, *The Trumpet Major* and *A Laodicean*, while living in the area, and it's not so far-fetched to suppose that it was on the common that he had his first premonitions of the Wessex settings of some of his later books. Those trees that E. M. Forster said *The Woodlanders* 'rustles with', were they really the trees alongside Trinity Road?

If that was at all how Hardy's mind worked, then it chimes with my own experience. It may just be hindsight, but I suspect that the Royal Victoria Patriotic Asylum might have something to do with Kessling Hall, the Norfolk country house turned Great War convalescence home in *Waterland*; or with other 'homes' that feature in my work. Opposite the Asylum, on the other side of a railway line, there still stands, remarkably, a wooden windmill, minus its sails. The road running by is Windmill Road. I'm not sure that this windmill wasn't the origin of the ruined one in *Waterland* where the young Tom Crick and Mary Metcalf have their trysts. At least it enabled me to check out how big the base of a windmill is and to confirm that the hollow stump of a disused windmill might be a handy place for clandestine sex. *Waterland* also features a brewery, with a chimney-cum-clock-tower destined, halfway through the novel, spectacularly to collapse. One day, not trusting to guesswork, I phoned up Young's Brewery to ask the height of its chimney.

I'm not sure, either, that I'd have written *The Light of Day*, a novel centrally featuring a prison, if I didn't so frequently pass by a prison myself. I'm quite often stopped by people asking the way there: new visitors going to see someone inside. I'm sometimes stopped by people with more disoriented questions: 'Which way is King's Cross?' They're prisoners who've just been let out.

Until its recent evisceration, I was also fond of the County Arms, a big barn of a pub divided up into a set of inviting separate enclaves by a wealth of old glinting mahogany and delicately engraved glass panels. All of this was ripped out (perhaps to be sold on as decor for somewhere else) and replaced by ersatz stuff designed, one supposes, to evoke the 'feel' of an old pub. Warders from the prison used to drink regularly in the County, their belts draped with chains. I don't know if they do any more, but the refurbished 'gents' has become a little museum of prison memorabilia: you can read a framed certificate of execution while taking a leak.

Oddly, not long after the County metamorphosed, the high modern brick wall that used to hide the entrance to the prison, and must have had some serious material purpose, was taken down, so that you can now behold the original fortress-like frontage in all its stern glory. It was as if the prison itself—a fully working and full-to-bulging prison—had decided to come out as a piece of heritage.

But this is perhaps the way it's always been. History gets turned, sometimes very quickly, into furniture. The prison, or House of Correction, opened in 1851 (the same year that the Crystal Palace opened for the Great Exhibition). The County Arms (they couldn't quite call it 'The Jailers' Arms') was built in 1852. Then there was a Crimean War. Then the Royal Victoria Patriotic Asylum was built, and the row of tiny, charming, rose-wreathed cottages that still stands between the pub and the prison got named Alma Terrace, after a battle by the Black Sea.

I often chose the County as a handy and congenial spot for interviews: anything from the *South London Press* to the *Guardian*, to meeting emissaries from foreign literary magazines, of whom it was asking a lot that they find their way to Wandsworth. The first interview I gave there was when *Waterland* was published in 1983. Most of that novel was written (incongruously enough) in Balham, but it was finished soon after moving to my present house, which at the time was little better than a ruin. The room in which I wrote the final chapters, which would become the 'study' in which I'm writing now, was stripped back to floorboards and bare bricks and reeked of dry-rot fluid. Rather less pleasant than a prison cell.

The interview that follows has for me the sentimental distinction of being the last one I gave in the old venue. I must have been making only hesitant inroads into the writing of *Tomorrow*, since the novel-in-progress referred to as involving fifty per cent a male narrator and fifty per cent a female narrator was to get eclipsed by one that would be a hundred per cent female.

The author interview is now a routine tool of the publishing process, one of the ways in which writers have emerged from the background in which they mostly existed when I began writing, and one of the ways in which readers may feel they can get to know better the person behind the book. How effective that process is I've no idea. In practice, most interviews occur around a book's publication and are driven by journalistic and promotional pressures. Putting it crudely, they're a system which fills spaces in newspapers and provides publishers with free advertising. The author, who may not have spoken to the press for some time, will suddenly have a series of media encounters and come out of it feeling, at worst, that they've been merely put through a process, or else feeling frustrated that they were only just getting into their stride, that they never said the things they meant to say or they said things they hadn't meant to say. What goes on the record can be highly subject to mood and chance.

I wonder how important these interviews really are. They've become such a currency that they're assumed to fulfil a need. Did Hardy give interviews? Would he have met journalists in the County Arms? No, he lived before the age of interviews—lucky him, perhaps. Would I get from reading an interview with Hardy the same sense of exciting proximity that I get from picturing him walking over Wandsworth Common? I'm not sure I would. And that picture is more than just a pleasing image. The common then would still have been a place of grazing sheep, but also a place starkly overlooked by a new prison. In that dramatic configuring of social change and social difference, that bringing together of the pastoral and the penal, there seems something distinctly Hardyesque.

The most satisfying interviews, perhaps, are the ones authors give between books, when they're not committed to plugging a new title and can feel freer to talk about the business of writing at large. But, whatever the pretext, the best kind of interview is one that forgets it's an interview and becomes just a conversation, public in purpose but candidly private in feeling (though this can have its dangers), even a benign sort of confession in which you can find yourself saying things, you realize later, you couldn't have said in any other way, either directly to some audience or—rather surprisingly, since you're a writer—if you tried formally to write them down.

The interview printed here, for a collection of writers' interviews, *The Way We Write*, took place in the spring of 2005 and has been condensed to take out some material covered elsewhere in this book. It was conducted by Barbara Baker, who has the interviewer's gift of skilful self-effacement, starting out with banally practical questions—Do you use a pen? When do you start your working day? (but I like such questions, they're easy to answer)—then letting the interviewee find their specific course. Her way of presenting the result was also self-effacing, dispensing entirely with the question-and-answer apparatus and shaping the content so that it comes across as a single, meandering declaration: the unattended, unlocated voicing of the author's thoughts. Though it was actually a pleasant chat in the County Arms.

Each author Barbara interviewed was asked to choose a short passage from their work to preface the interview. It's not reproduced here, but I chose the final paragraphs of *The Light of Day*, simply because at the time they were the last words of fiction I'd published. It struck me later that it wasn't a bad passage to have picked for an interview that also took place just round the corner from a prison.

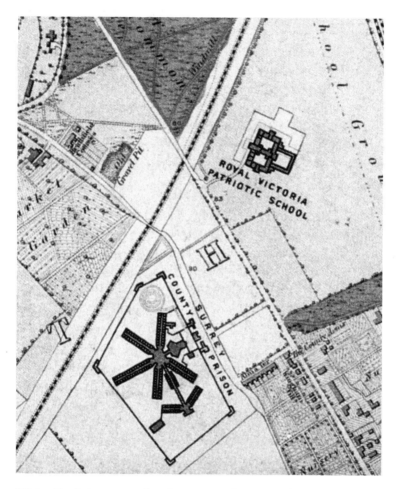

Trinity Road, in a map of 1862, running from top left to bottom right, through Wandsworth Common, past the Patriotic Asylum (or School), the Surrey County Prison (as named here), Alma Terrace, the County Arms and, a little off the map to the south and some years in the future, Thomas Hardy's home.

BIRD'S-EYE VIEW OF THE SURREY HOUSE OF CORRECTION AT WANDSWORTH.

The view of prisoners' dreams, also from 1862.

Hardy at the time he lived in Trinity Road.

The County Arms in the summer of 1912.

Balloon's-eye view: the Royal Victoria Patriotic Asylum converted to a military hospital in the First World War. In addition to the original building, a large part of what is now Wandsworth Common has been occupied by temporary wards and other facilities. Up to 1,800 could be accommodated at any one time. The prominent crosses are perhaps to identify the site against air raids. It is generally held that during the Great War the civilian public lived at a mental distance from the realities of the Front. Anyone living in this vicinity must have grasped some idea of the truth.

Trinity Road runs, lower right, past the main entrance. The wounded would have been delivered by ambulance (see the next illustration) or by hospital trains which stopped in the adjacent railway cutting. It is not an area of happy memory. Just along the railway line, out of picture to the left, is the scene of the Clapham Junction rail disaster of 1988 in which 35 people were killed and over 100 injured.

Soldier's sketch of the Royal Victoria Patriotic Asylum in use as 'The 3rd London General Hospital'.

The same scene, at a quieter time, photographed in the winter of 1918. The snow makes the bulding look particularly eerie. The gateway is still there.

Another gateway that's still there. Prisoners being discharged
from Wandsworth in the 1940s.

An Interview in Wandsworth

I write with a fountain pen and black ink. My fountain pens are very precious to me and I would never take them out of the house. I've written three novels with my current pen and all the others were written with another fountain pen, which died, but I still have it. I'm very much a hand-writer. I have a computer and in the last stages of a novel I use it and, indeed, find it very valuable for doing all those editing things which used to be incredibly time-consuming on a typewriter. But I would only go to it at that late stage. The actual creative work of composition is always with pen and ink. I just don't think, for me, it could be otherwise. I believe a pen gets whatever is in your head onto the page more quickly and efficiently than anything that's been invented. Computer people would dispute that, and my hand-writing is virtually illegible, even for me, but when I write I do any number of squiggles and little signs which are messages to me about things, and I could only do them with a pen.

I have a room at the back of the house where I write. I'm not a systematic note-taker or planner, but I do jot things down if a thought comes to me, before I forget it, on anything available, like the back of a bus ticket. I don't have a neat notebook, but masses of bits of paper with odd scraps of information, which may or may not go into the final mix. I scarcely think about it all now, in that it's so routine that I pick up a pen and scrawl, if I can, on a page. But even routines start with their rituals and have a sort of spell. I would probably get quite upset to have the routine taken away. If I didn't have my room with its corners, my pen, the ordinary lined notepad that I use, I would feel a bit lost, for a while at least. I know there are plenty of writers who can do it anyhow, anywhere, travelling, using a laptop—I don't understand that, but we are all different.

I would like to be as honest as I can about how I start a book, but the more honest I am, the more it will seem that I'm not really telling you anything. I've written seven novels and am writing another now. How they begin really is a mystery to me. Usually, when I'm asked, what I would say, which is half true, is that it's always something small. A novel is a very big undertaking, but I don't have a big idea. Even the phrase 'having an idea for a novel' is a rather bogus one for me. It grows somehow mysteriously from some small beginning, which even I can't necessarily remember.

What happens is that you are glad that it's beginning, even if it proves to be the wrong thing. You are so glad that it's started that you don't really care how it began or how it will continue. I will get to a point where I feel inside it is brewing. Then you feel two things in conflict: you just want to get on and write, but you can't afford to do that because you must have some sort of shape. So you look for the framework so you can continue to write, while another part of you knows that you are only going to discover some things by the writing anyway. You're in a weird double bind where neither thing guarantees the other. It's a crazy situation, but I accept the illogicality of it. I'm sure there are many writers who just sense there's a novel there, and make a plan and then write it, but I can't do that.

My biggest fear all the time is to lose the real inspiration.

If you sit and think carefully and systematically about something, your fear is that such thinking will cancel out the real emotion. I'm guided very strongly by instinct, intuition and feeling, which don't fit into rational schemes. I've found this to be the case the more I have written. On the other hand, I don't think you can separate form and content, and both things are as important as each other to me, and together they make the thing itself. I do care about shape and form and have that real artistic ambition and instinct that I want to make something well-shaped. But I also care about content very much. Novels don't happen to me very often, I don't write them easily or quickly, and that's really because strong content doesn't come along very often. So it matters that if I'm going to write something which may take me years, I've found the strong content that will propel it.

My working day is very early. I can be at work as early as five thirty in the morning. That's how it's been for a long time. I need, I relish, I've got into the habit of this early part of the day, when I have the feeling that the rest of the world is asleep, but I am alert and am not going to be interrupted. If you get going in those early hours you are launched and safe. The theory is that I work up till midday, and will have done a real day's work, and the rest of the day is open. It seldom goes according to this plan, but that's the idea and the early morning thing is peculiarly important. It's almost like getting up early to go hunting: the feeling that it *will* happen in these special hours. Often it doesn't, but that's in the nature of writing. Of course if you have a late night, you are tired, but at best there's a real excitement. I make myself a pot of coffee and take it up to the room where I work. It's dark outside, everything is quiet and I feel a nice, intense, concentrated feeling and I get on—I don't think I could do that if I started work at nine or ten in the morning.

I do a hell of a lot of rewriting, both as I write and at later stages, so a book tends to take about three years or longer—more, if you count it from when you have the first notion to when you have the final manuscript. And sometimes I don't just rewrite: I reject completely and start again. My finished books are not in straight chronological sequence—anyone reading any of my novels would see straight away that I move around in time—but I do the moving around even as I write. I make some decisions afterwards about rearranging the order here or there, but I would more or less write it in the order in which the reader reads it, embracing all the leaps in time as I go along. For example, *Last Orders* jumps around not just in time but from one character's narrative to another's, and conceivably someone could take it all apart and wonder if I might have had a completely different structure at first where I followed one character all the way through. But no, I somehow knew when it should be Ray or Vince, and when it should be in the present or the past. I had an intuition about it and that's very much how I write.

This condition of shifting time is a natural habitat for me and one I think we all exist in, because it's the habitat of memory. Memory is not sequential. We're all formed by our past, and even as we walk about in the present we are the creatures of time. I've almost always written in the first person, and one thing that gives you is immediate access to a character's memory as it exercises itself. That would be a much more laborious thing to do in the third person, where you would constantly have to flag it, saying something like, 'As X walked along the street he was remembering that time . . .', which is all rather tedious and stagey, whereas I can just go directly to it.

Men tend to predominate in my books, and in one way you could say that's not so surprising, since I am a man—I would feel comfortable writing from a man's point of view. On the other hand, I don't really see it as such a big divide. The big challenge in writing is to write a character, to get from yourself to this other being, and whether they're male or female is, in a way, secondary. I'm writing something now which could work out as about fifty per cent male and fifty per cent female. I've found that the way I do it is not to think male or female. When they are delivering their inner thoughts, are they actually so different? I think it would be a great mistake for a male writer writing a female character, or the other way round, to be constantly tapping themselves on the shoulder and saying, 'Remember you are writing a woman here. Now what would a woman think?' That would be artificial and needlessly self-conscious.

In a sense, there's no point in writing a novel unless you are communicating and someone is going to read it, but I don't think about that at the time. I just have immense faith and trust that a reader will be there. But the reader isn't this person who's inspecting what I do as I write and saying, 'No, you should do it a different way or it won't satisfy me.' I just go by intuition, and I don't think I'm very different from the reader. I happen to be the writer and I happen to have some talent, but I am just another human being.

When I've talked about writing in the past I've stressed the fact that my own life, my biography, is not the stuff of my fiction. I have said things like, 'One writes fiction because one doesn't want to write fact,' and I do feel that you need to keep your subject matter at a distance from you, so that your imagination can take flight to it. That's what's exciting, getting from what you know into what you don't know. I really do have a tremendous faith in writing as a leap into the unknown. But it's a leap you take with the rope of the imagination to hang onto.

Some novelists, particularly in their early work, write fairly autobiographically and are taught to write what they know, and there is a logic to that. But my first novel, apart from its south London location, was not autobiographical. I frequently write about parents and children—being responsible for another generation—but I don't have children, though I obviously had parents. I'd say that my early family life was quite happy and secure, which wouldn't be true of the many families I've written about. Also, people tend to assume that because I've written about the Fens, where I've never lived, or eels, or the French Revolution, I do a great deal of research. In fact I don't; I find that all rather tedious and try to get away with the minimum.

A thing that really does interest me and is a real area of my work is the question: should this thing be told or not? Maybe this is partly because, as a novelist, I'm a teller in a quite practical sense—always making decisions about what should be told at this point or later. But that's all fairly technical. I'm more fascinated with how, in life, we all come up against knowledge which may or may not be shared or imparted; with how knowledge can be both an enlightening thing, but also sometimes dangerous and destructive. Secrets fascinate me. We're all embedded in secrets, in that none of us knows the whole story about where we are in relation to other people. I think I'll always write about that.

Sometimes I've taken it to a sort of intellectual pitch. For instance, I wrote a novel called *Ever After*, where there's quite a lot about the Darwinian moment in the nineteenth century when this enormous piece of knowledge, virtually held by one man, was released. That was a case of a scientific truth, needing to be told, which upset a great many people's understanding of the world they lived in. But this sort of thing happens in much more intimate ways in personal life. It's something which is curiously important to me and that, despite myself, I keep coming back to.

My instinct goes against the advice that writers are often given: 'show, don't tell'. In many cases you *should* show rather than tell, if that effectively means show rather than *explain*. But the word 'tell' is a great word. It means more than just the simple 'I am now telling you this thing.' We use it in so many ways. 'I can tell,' means something quite different from the business of relating something; it suggests knowing and understanding, a seeing into the situation. There are times when what you have to do is not show, which would be almost the easy, even the evasive thing, but find a way of telling.

There are moments in writing that are not unlike those occasions in life when you say to someone, who may be very close and it may be a very painful thing, 'I've got to tell you something.' Once you've said those words you know there's no going round or going back. It's not a question of showing, but of finding a way inside you of how best to impart what you have to impart. Finding the way to tell things goes with being human. Any serious act of telling brings out in you your ability to shape something so that it will communicate without its being a mere matter of informing or explaining, it will give something more than that. And of course that can sometimes depend on what you choose not to say; and that is the same with writing. It may sound a contradiction, but you can often better tell something by not telling it completely. I'm very aware that you must leave spaces for the reader's mind to operate in, just as in some intimate disclosure you might leave a gap, a silence for your listener to make some vital connection.

Storytelling is a primitive thing going back long before books. People have a need to tell and hear stories: it's human nature. But we live more and more in a world where we pretend we don't need that—where it may be considered a bit naive and sentimental, compared to the culture of information and to the easy communicativeness technology seems to offer. So I think the novel needs more and more to hold its own against that sea of stuff around it. But I think it will always survive, because although it's a sophisticated literary form it is, at bottom, just storytelling and people will always turn to it. I'm a storyteller working in the form of the novel—this wonderful, all-embracing, elastic form—but even as I work in it I often have a primitive, pre-verbal sense of how it should be employed, a kind of musical sense of storytelling. I will feel a story needs to move in a certain way or to have a certain rhythm and echo before I've necessarily found the right words or even the precise narrative situation.

I taught myself to write—I didn't have any mentor or teacher. I began in earnest in my early twenties, but I had wanted for some time before then to be a writer. I grew up in the 1950s when the book, or the word, was what you did for entertainment. I read a lot and I listened to the radio, so I was very word-conscious. There was a time when I thought how nice it would be to be one of these people who made books and created these wonderful worlds which opened up as you opened the page. My thoughts were very crude and naive, but enthralled. I wanted to do this magic stuff that writers did. I would find it absolutely charming now to be presented with those books that I read when I was eight or nine. I've forgotten what they were. I would have got them from the library, and to pick them up again would take me back to the germ of it all.

At that time it was not literary ambition, it was just wanting to write books. I do remember reading, as I got older, people like Rosemary Sutcliffe, who wrote historical novels I would get lost in. But I was able to stop and look at a paragraph and say to myself, 'Gosh, that bit of description is wonderful. How do you do that? If only I could do that!' I can remember having feelings like that which evolved into a desire to be a writer—a bit like wanting to be an engine driver. It never went away and started to move towards a serious intention. All the way through my teens I nursed this without really owning up to it. Then I went to university at Cambridge and other things got in the way, but when I left I sort of grabbed myself by the lapel and said, 'Well, are you serious about it? Are you really going to be a writer? Because if you are, you must start to write properly.'

I am unquestionably proud of every book I've written. If I wasn't, I wouldn't want them to be seen by anyone else. With *Last Orders* something happened which made the language different. I think it was to do with trusting, more than I ever had done, so-called ordinary language—the language of people who you could say, wrongly, aren't so articulate. I was using a sort of language of the street; not directly, in that it was not like a tape-recording, but I was using it and found it very liberating. I found all the apparent limitations of it not to be limitations at all. This language could be very eloquent, just as more articulate language can be a barrier. So I got interested in simpler words, simpler phrases, shorter and more economic sentences which might be more transparent and might get you more quickly to the things that matter.

That seemed to continue with *The Light of Day*, but I don't know if it will be a continuing trend or not. I chose the passage at the end of *The Light of Day* for you to quote before this interview because it is, at this point, the last thing I wrote that's published. There's something nice about that. I always intended that the final words of the book should be its title. Another thing

I did with this book, as with *Last Orders*, was to structure it around a single day. I don't see myself doing that constantly as a formula either, but it was certainly very helpful as a discipline. In *Last Orders* there is a one-day journey and whatever else is going to happen, and a lot else does, I had to get the characters from London to Margate, so I had to think, 'Well, they should be getting to Chatham about now,' or whatever.

In *The Light of Day* George has shorter journeys to make through a certain geography on a certain day. Both novels had that discipline, although in both I was also dealing with other levels of time. However, I like the focus of a fairly short, defined period more than I used to. But I wouldn't like to predict how my writing will go. I'm writing a novel at the moment which is first-person and more than one narrator. Who knows if one day I might produce a third-person novel? It's a thing which I have always felt isn't me, but it might be a good thing if it happened. You have to surprise yourself.

The thing I *can* say is that I am a novelist. It's a long while since I have written any short stories, though I began with them and once thought I would never write anything else. Just occasionally I've produced something short, and I would always be happy to spend some time just doing stories again, but it doesn't happen. One of the pleasures of writing a story is that you start and very soon it will be finished—it might even be finished today. That's tremendously morale-boosting. But I think I have a mindset now that belongs to the novel. You know you are there for a long haul, which is quite daunting, but I like the feeling that once you have begun a novel, you have your job. You know that you will get up in the morning, in my case quite early, and you will continue this task which is all there for you to do. And it will be like that for a long while and then it will be finished. I like the feeling of being in something big and continuing.

I haven't lost the sense of the magic of storytelling that I had when I read those books, now forgotten, as a child. Writing is my life. It is not all of my life by any means, but it is my life and my work in a way that not so many people can say. People do their jobs, but they wouldn't necessarily say, 'This is my life. This is me!' And they wouldn't say either, sadly, in most cases, 'This is also what I love. It is the love of my life.' By doing anything that you fundamentally love to do, you are going to suffer for it too, it's going to be painful at times. Love is like that —it's not just a wonderful thing, it's demanding. But I do what I've always wanted to do. Often, on the bad days, I can think, 'Am I really loving this?' But I do love it and I hope that I write with love. And on the wonderful days, when it goes like it should go, when you know that what you've just written you will never have to change, it's more than that. It makes you feel that everything is worthwhile. The possibility on any one day of having that feeling is by itself a perfect reason for doing it. It makes you feel in touch with life and the world; it makes you know why you are here.

Sunset on the Wandle: John England Nicholls, 1860–61.

MICHEL DE MONTAIGNE

PÉRIGORD, 1533–92

In 2004 the Folio Society, preparing for its sixtieth anniversary, asked a number of people to choose one book they couldn't be without. I chose Montaigne's *Essays*. A little later the Society asked me if I'd like to write a short introduction to a special edition of the *Essays* they'd be bringing out. I'm no Montaigne scholar or expert, but it wasn't difficult to accept such a flattering invitation about a writer I love. The clincher was that the Society would be using John Florio's original English translation, one of the great works of Elizabethan prose. I spent a very happy part of 2005 rereading (the verb is properly used) Montaigne.

On my ideal desert island, as my introduction suggests, there would be both Shakespeare and Montaigne. In some ways it's impossible to separate the two authors—though it would be a case of extracting Montaigne from Shakespeare rather than the other way round—while in other respects they are opposites. What do we know about Shakespeare? Virtually nothing. What do we know about Montaigne? Virtually everything. To read him is to feel you've known him all your life.

Montaigne couldn't have been a more 'writerly' writer, deliberately retiring to his tower to 'consecrate his life to the Muses', but no writer seems as unwithdrawingly close to us as we read him. This book began with the position that fiction isn't, in my case, an autobiographical exercise. Montaigne is the shining example of an opposite or, rather, complementary position: a writer of non-fiction who was, in effect, a great and irrepressible autobiographer, a universal writer who embraces almost every subject, yet infuses almost every page he wrote with his personal touch.

An Introduction to Florio's Montaigne

In 1571 Michel Eyquem de Montaigne took a self-effacing decision that would make him known for ever. He retired to his family estate in Périgord, recently inherited on the death of his father, with the aim of devoting himself to study. He was thirty-eight. Until then he had led the more or less active life of a well-educated gentleman with some scholarly leanings. He was a member of the *parlement* of Bordeaux, where his father had been mayor; he had visited Paris and the royal court and had military experience. But, plainly, a life of public ambition was not for him.

Nor was there anything secretly ambitious about his retirement. The *Essays* might never have happened had not Montaigne in his new seclusion fallen into the state of 'melancholy' to which the essays themselves allude. They were begun in an ad hoc way as an antidote to his troubled mood. Gradually, they became the story of his life, they became *him*. By accident, Montaigne had found his theme: to present 'my selfe unto my selfe for a subject to write, and argument to descant upon' (II.8). Yet the *Essays* are far from being the work of a melancholy or withdrawn man. They address some of the most serious aspects of the human condition, but they are one of the happiest journeys of introspection ever undertaken.

They have no apparent design. Montaigne writes about what seizes his interest—now it will be 'Of Fear', now 'Of Thumbs' —and part of the *Essays'* huge charm is the sense of a man constantly saying, 'Let's take this subject and see where it leads us . . .'. Often it leads us far from the matter at hand. But for all the multiplying haphazardness, the unifying feature becomes more pronounced. By the eighteenth essay of the second Book, Montaigne can say: 'I have no more made my booke then my booke hath made me. A booke consubstantiall to his Author.' In the final essay of all he can write: 'I study my selfe more than any other subject. It is my supernaturall Metaphisike, it is my naturall Philosophy' (III.13).

In Montaigne's time, this dedication to depicting the self was almost unprecedented. On the face of it, it may also seem self-regarding in the worst sense. But Montaigne could hardly be more candidly, unassumingly honest about himself, or more exacting about the nature of the self in general. Though the candour can seem modern, he was fostered on the Aristotelian notion that any individual man embodies the characteristics of Man at large ('my supernaturall Metaphisike' is both an impertinence and a bow), which saves him from self-indulgence, as it can give even his most private revelations a universal context.

In any case, the word 'essay' is significant. For Montaigne it retained its fundamental, experimental meaning: 'assay', 'attempt', 'test'. My mind, he wrote, is 'a Prentise and a probationer' (III.2). Whatever the subject, Montaigne tests it against himself, himself against it. He sifts all received wisdoms through the filter of intimate experience. All the time he is saying, 'But how does this square with what I'm actually made of?'

In well over a thousand pages Montaigne never foists himself wearyingly upon us, because he typically looks even at himself with bemusement, confusion and, often, undeluded disappointment, and he presents the spectacle with apologetic frankness. He does not see himself as special, and so, spontaneously, he achieves the common touch. His famous motto, *Que sais-je?*, is extended to, 'Do I even know what *I* am?' 'Where I seeke my selfe,' he writes, 'I finde not my selfe: and I find my selfe more by chance, than by the search of mine owne judgement' (I.10). 'I am most ignorant in my owne matters' (II.17). And the ignorance is matched by a vivid sense of his own changeability. In by far the longest and in some ways most abstruse essay, 'An Apologie of Raymond Sebond', he pauses to offer a whole catalogue of personal inconsistencies:

> I dare very hardly report the vanity and weaknesse I feele in my selfe . . . If my health applaud me, or but the calmenesse of one fair day smile upon me, then am I a lusty gallant; but if a corne wring my toe, then am I pouting, unpleasant and hard to be pleased. One same pace of a horse is sometimes hard, and sometimes easie unto me; and one same way, one time short, another time long and wearisome; and one same forme, now more, now less agreeable and pleasing to me: Sometimes I am apt to doe any thing; and other times fit to doe nothing: What now is pleasing to me, within a while after will be paineful. There are a thousand indiscreet and casuall agitations in me. Either a melancholy humour posses-seth me, or a cholericke passion swaieth me, which having shaken off, sometimes frowardnesse and peevishnesse hath predominancy, and other times gladnes and blithnesse over-rule me. If I chance to take a booke in hand, I shall in some passages perceive some excellent graces, and which ever wound me to the soule with delight; but let me lay it by, and read him another time, let me turne and tosse him as I list,

let me apply and manage him as I will, I shall find it an unknowne and shapeless masse.

There is surely no one for whom this self-portrait cannot, in some respects, strike home—how delightfully he lets his reader know of his own lapses as a reader. This is Montaigne, but it is us: the very fickle stuff of everyday consciousness.

The *Essays* are full of such recognizable immediacy. Montaigne may have literally retired to a tower, over the gateway at his house, where he kept his library and had the walls inscribed with favourite Latin and Greek sayings, but the *Essays* do not smack of the ivory tower. So much of what they contain comes not from a 'life of the mind', but just from life. They never pretend to be, or are simply unable to be, rarefied.

They are certainly erudite. A list of Montaigne's quotations from classical authors would itself make a book, and it is not encouraging for the modern reader to learn that Montaigne was brought up to hear and speak only Latin—French was his second language. But we are not in the hands of some advanced swot. Montaigne gleefully admits that he repeatedly works into his own text, without flagging them, the words of classical authors, so that, should his readers disagree with them: 'I will have them to give *Plutarch* a bob upon mine owne lips, and vex themselves, in wronging *Seneca* in mee' (II.10).

He is often called a 'philosopher', but the term is somehow inadequate, like calling him an 'essayist'. The long *Apologie of Raymond Sebond* is his most philosophically rigorous piece, attempting nothing less than to place in proper relationship a theology of faith and revelation with a 'natural theology' drawn from rational examination of the world. It reminds us that, for all his modernity, Montaigne was a staunchly conservative Catholic, which makes those other labels—'humanist', 'sceptic'—not quite right either. But it contains some of Montaigne's best observations on how we live in, with and by our bodies—on body-language, in fact. Where it dwells for several pages on the instinctive abilities of animals, the aim may be to chide the human presumption of superiority over the beasts, but what most comes across is Montaigne's pleasure in creaturely life. Any philosopher who can write, 'When I am playing with my Cat, who knowes whether she have more sport in dallying with me, than I have in gaming with her?' is surely not a philosopher in an austere sense, but is expressing the common conjecture of us all. An intellectual point is made, but the real joy is in the little gift of personality: we see Montaigne playing with his cat.

Time and again, we get such glimpses. Without appearing to mean to, Montaigne offers us almost every unadorned facet of himself: his weaknesses and impracticalities, his illnesses (he suffered painfully from gallstones), his sexual failings, the way the smell of food stays on his moustache. We know he is forgetful, indecisive and ham-handed. He becomes real for us by listing what he can't do: 'I cannot very wel close up a letter; nor could I ever make a pen. I was never good carver at table. I could never make readie nor arme a Horse: Nor handsomely carry a Hawk upon my fist' (II.17). His actual knowledge becomes more trustworthy when he tells us what he doesn't know: 'Since I must make ful shew of my shame and ignorance, it is not yet a moneth since, that I was found to be ignorant, wherto Leven [yeast] served to make bread' (II.17). He redeems his shortcomings in the vividness of describing them: his mind, he says, has to go at things in fits and starts, 'even as to judge well of the lustre of scarlet we are taught to cast our eyes over it, in running it over by divers glances, sodaine glimpses, and reiterated reprisings' (II.10). And if he likes his cat, he does not forget his dog: 'I am not ashamed nor afraid to declare the tendernesse of my childish Nature, which is such, that I cannot well reject my Dog, if he chance to fawne upon me, or beg of me to play with him' (II.11).

Montaigne, in short, needs no label, he is simply *there*. Few writers feel so present, so in the same room with you as you read them. Few offer themselves so persuasively as a mirror. Montaigne hardly believes he is peculiar. He reasonably suspects that we are all a little like him inside or, rather, that we all find it oddly hard to *be* inside ourselves. The very thing that we are, he repeatedly tells us, is the most elusive or the most evaded. 'We are never in ourselves, but beyond' (I. 3). 'Every man runneth out and unto what is to come, because no man has yet come into him selfe' (III.12).

Those first experimental pieces, written as private therapy, grew over some fifteen years into three Books of more than a hundred essays whose range and profusion is evident from a glance at their titles. Though they never lose their idiosyncrasy and spontaneity—their capacity to let us just dip into them if we wish—they can be read as a single progress, a single, over-arching 'assay' of authority against actuality. It is no accident that the last essay of Book III is called 'Of Experience', or that it is preceded by 'Of Phisiognomy', a culmination of Montaigne's observations on what our physical constitution has to teach us.

If Montaigne is 'there', it can also be said of his work, as it is of Shakespeare's, that all human life is there. Shakespeare's and Montaigne's attitudes are not dissimilar: the desire to apprehend the larger world through what Shakespeare called our 'little world of man'; the urge, apparent in Shakespeare's soliloquies, to link the biggest themes to an unsparing gazing-in. Shakespeare's comedy constantly trips us up over the concrete, as does

Montaigne's. Shakespeare's tragedy strips us bare, as do Montaigne's most intense passages.

Both men lived in the same violent times. The first complete edition of the *Essays* was published as the Spanish Armada sailed towards England. Montaigne is influenced, as much as by his reading of classical authors, by his direct experience of the French religious civil wars, which raged throughout his lifetime. He was also keenly aware, perhaps even more than Shakespeare, of the opening up of the New World of the Americas, an explosion of preconceptions hard for us, now, to imagine. The link between the New World and Montaigne's old, war-torn one was cruelty, the title of one of the *Essays* and a recurring incidental theme. In 'Of the Cannibals', without elevating the New World natives into 'noble savages', he pleads that they should have their fair 'assay'. What is their supposed barbarity against our own? The history of colonization, he well knew, was one of appalling slaughter; the mildly titled essay 'On Coaches' contains a vehement indictment of it. But he could look closer to home to see the same savagery. In 1572, on St Bartholomew's Day, even as his first essays were germinating, two thousand Huguenots were massacred in Paris.

The direct link between Montaigne and Shakespeare is the magnificent translation by John Florio. It is one of the great bridges of literature. Shakespeare would have read it in the later part of his career. He certainly raided it. The first full edition appeared in 1603, but it is probable that individual essays circulated before this, so Shakespeare may have ingested Montaigne even earlier. *The Tempest* is clearly influenced by 'Of the Cannibals', and while Shakespeare went to Holinshed or Plutarch for narrative material, Montaigne provided more meditative fuel. *Hamlet* seems imbued with Montaigne, and Montaigne lies behind the last great tragedies, behind *Measure for Measure* and behind the whole Shakespearean questioning of 'man, proud man, / Drest in a little brief authority, / Most ignorant of what he's most assured'.

With North's Plutarch, Florio's Montaigne is one of the pillars of Elizabethan translation, and a great piece of English prose in its own right. Even without Shakespeare's use of it, it has the Shakespearean physicality, energy and tang; which is only to say that Florio responded directly, as Shakespeare did at one remove, to the concreteness, the mingling of the mental and the bodily, in Montaigne. Montaigne's preference in language was for the tactile: 'upon the paper, as it is in the mouth, a pithie, sinnowie, full strong, compendious and materiall speech' (I.25). Though Florio was of Italian stock, one might say he drew something Anglo-Saxon from his source.

But the difference between Shakespeare and Montaigne is striking. Shakespeare is a standard 'desert-island' book—he would bring the world to you; but Montaigne would be my second choice, if not possibly my first. Montaigne too would bring the world to you. He would not bring the great Shake-spearean glories, but he would give you something Shakespeare never gives: his presence, his implicit conversation. 'What good company he is,' wrote Madame de Sévigné, several decades after Montaigne's death, and company would surely be what you would crave on a lonely island.

One personal gift Montaigne never disclaimed was a talent for friendship. It is possible that his 'melancholy' on retirement rose from having leisure to reflect on the two great griefs of his life. His father, to whom he was close, had died in 1568. His good friend Étienne de la Boëtie, a fellow member of the *parlement* of Bordeaux, who had the leanings of a scholar too, had died in 1563. His friendship with La Boëtie seems to have been exceptional, a rare marriage of minds and hearts, and when it was truncated Montaigne might have thought he would never know such friendship again. Except with his reader. In all Montaigne's gradual revelation of himself to us, something very simple is perhaps at work: the wish not to be alone; to share, to make mental friends. We read, too, it has been said, not to be alone. Few writers meet that need better.

If Montaigne had his griefs, one of his inevitable subjects is the final solitariness of death. He was, in fact, fairly obsessed by it or, rather, by the act of dying, which he regarded as the last 'assay' of a life. He certainly observed it several times, and in 'Of Exercise or Practice' even rather wonderfully describes the experience of nearly observing it—'practising' it—in himself. But he is never morbid on the subject; he is often remarkably level-headed and reassuring. One reason for reading him is the solace he offers on this universal prospect. If one had to die alone on a desert island, it would be a comfort to have Montaigne to hand.

Several of the essays concern themselves with death and at least one (I.19) takes up the traditional notion 'That to Philosophize is to Learne How to Dye'. But in 'Of Phisiognomy', the penultimate essay, Montaigne gives us in effect his last word on the matter. What is striking now is how the prop of philosophy has fallen away. No, Montaigne says, as he nears the end of his great, assaying journey, philosophy won't help you in this case. What he offers us is something better; plain, sane, sympathetic and emphatically on the side of life—humanity speaking directly to humanity on how to be mortal:

If you know not how to die, take no care for it, Nature her selfe will fully and sufficiently teach you in the nicke, she will exactly discharge that worke for you; trouble not your selfe with it. We trouble death with the care of life, and life with the care of death. The one annoyeth, the other affrights us. It is not against death, we prepare ourselves, it is a thing too momentary. A quarter of an hour of passion without consequence and without annoyance, deserves not particular precepts. To say truth, we prepare ourselves against the preparations of death. Philosophy teacheth us, ever to have death before our eyes, to fore-see and consider it before it come: Then giveth us rules and precautions so to provide, that such foresight and thought hurt us not. So doe Phisitions, who cast us into diseases, that they may employ their drugges and skill about them. If we have not known how to live, it is injustice to teach us how to die, and deforme the end from all the rest. Have wee knowne how to live constantly and quietly, wee shall know how to die resolutely and reposedly. They may bragge as much as they please: *Tota Philosophorum vita commentatio mortis est. The whole life of a Philosopher is the meditation of his death.* But me thinkes, it is indeed the end, yet not the scope of life. It is her last, it is her extremity, yet not her object. Hir selfe must be unto hir selfe, hir aime, hir drift and her designe. Hir direct studie is, to order, to direct and to suffer hir selfe. In the number of many other offices, which the generall and principall Chapter, to know how to live containeth, is this speciall Article, *To know how to die.* And of the easiest, did not our owne feare weigh it downe.

Voicy du grand Montaigne vne entiere figure
Le Peinctre a peinct le corps, et luy son bel esprit:
Le premier par son art égale la Nature,
Mais l'aultre la surpasse en tout ce qu'il escrit.

                    Thomas de Leu fecit.

Acknowledgements

The author gratefully acknowledges the following publications from which the pieces in this book have been reprinted or, where they have been revised or expanded, on which they are based:

Fiction Magazine for 'Santa's Clinic'; the *Independent Magazine* for 'Isaac Babel'; *Time Out* for 'Guildhall Farce'; *Bomb* magazine (New York) for the interview of the author by Patrick McGrath and for the interviews by the author of Kazuo Ishiguro and Caryl Phillips; *Granta* for 'Looking for Jiří Wolf', 'Making an Elephant' and 'Fishing with Ted'; the *Daily Telegraph* for 'Reading Aloud'; the *Bulletin de la Société des Anglicistes de L'Enseignement Supérieur* for 'I Do Like to Be Beside the Seaside'; the *Observer* for 'Filming Again, with Fred'.

Grateful acknowledgement is also made to Picador Books for 'Greece Again', which appeared in an earlier form in the anthology *21* (1993); to Continuum publishers for the interview of the author by Barbara Baker which appeared in *The Way We Write* (2006); and to the Folio Society for the Introduction to Florio's Montaigne (2006).

Special thanks are due to Barbara Baker, Kazuo Ishiguro, Patrick McGrath and Caryl Phillips for permitting the interviews in which they participated to reappear here. Warm appreciation is extended to them and to other friends who kindly assisted and co-operated with this book.

Kazuo Ishiguro: Interview first published in *BOMB Magazine*, Issue #29, Fall 1989, pp. 22–23. © Bomb Magazine, New Art Publications, and its Contributors. All rights reserved. The BOMB Archive can be viewed at www.bombsite.com.

Patrick McGrath: Interview first published in *BOMB Magazine*, Issue #26, Winter 1989, p. 20. © Bomb Magazine, New Art Publications, and its Contributors. All rights reserved. The BOMB Archive can be viewed at www.bombsite.com.

Caryl Phillips: Interview first published in *BOMB Magazine*, Issue #38, Winter 1992, pp. 32–35. © Bomb Magazine, New Art Publications, and its Contributors. All rights reserved. The BOMB Archive can be viewed at www.bombsite.com.

Illustrations

Illustrations

A Note About the Author

Graham Swift was born in 1949 in London, where he still lives and works. He is the author of eight novels: *The Sweet-Shop Owner; Shuttlecock,* which received the Geoffrey Faber Memorial Prize; *Waterland,* which was short-listed for the Booker Prize and won the Guardian Fiction Award, the Winifred Holtby Memorial Prize, and the Italian Premio Grinzane Cavour; *Out of This World; Ever After,* which won the French Prix du Meilleur Livre Étranger; *Last Orders,* which was awarded the Booker Prize; *The Light of Day;* and, most recently, *Tomorrow.* He is also the author of *Learning to Swim,* a collection of short stories. His work has been translated into more than thirty languages.

A Note on the Type

This book was set in Adobe Garamond. Designed for the Adobe Corporation by Robert Slimbach, the fonts are based on types first cut by Claude Garamond (c. 1480–1561). Garamond was a pupil of Geoffroy Tory and is believed to have followed the Venetian models, although he introduced a number of important differences, and it is to him that we owe the letter we now know as "old style." He gave to his letters a certain elegance and feeling of movement that won their creator an immediate reputation and the patronage of Francis I of France.

Printed and bound by R. R. Donnelley
Harrisonburg, Virginia

"Thunder & Lightnings
by GS – 1994